Reviewers Praise *When We Get to Surf City*...

"There is something absolutely magical about Bob Greene's voice. No, not his voice onstage, singing backup with Jan and Dean. But his voice in this book, well, it just soars. It's a voice that is all at once lyrical and heartfelt and full of great humor. After a thousand summer choruses, Bob Greene's voice has never been better."
— Jeffrey Zaslow, co-author, *The Last Lecture*

"I love this book . . . It takes me back to an age that, for all who lived through it, never ends: a time of sun and surf and fun before the cynicism and war and rebellion. . . . Reading it, I am there again without a care and with friends I have never met, but whose music is as much a part of me as my closest relative . . . Wonderful, wonderful."
— Cal Thomas, syndicated columnist

"Greene has distinguished himself as America's poet laureate of summer."
— *Baton Rouge Advocate*

"Joyous, loving, funny, and touching, like a salty breeze blowing memories across the page. And it puts that music—that wonderful music— right back in your head where it belongs."
— *Huntington Beach Independent* (California)

"The perfect summer vacation book . . . It takes you back to the feeling of those hot summer nights when you were younger, and every day was about fast cars, fast food, your favorite friends, and favorite records."
— Bob Sirott, *One More Thing*, NBC-TV

"A dream come true."
— *New York Post*

"Four stars . . . revealing . . . hilarious . . . about the still-redemptive powers of rock and roll at any age, and, ultimately, of friendship."
— *Mojo* magazine (UK)

"A great read . . . pack the suntan lotion and head to the beach with this book."
— *Entertainment Today*

"Through the endless road trips, the triumphs and struggles and disappointments, Greene learns that the destination is not as important as the ride."
— *Columbus Messenger* (Ohio)

"Bob Greene rode this perfect wave .... back to cloudless blue skies and 'two girls for every boy.' Back to burgers and shakes at the Dairy Queen and the thrill of the perfect song on the radio. Like the *New Yorker's* John McPhee, Greene has a writer's gift of breathing unexpected life into the seemingly mundane . . . real affection and poignancy."
—*The Christian Science Monitor*

"Wonderful . . . masterful."   —*Hutchinson Leader* (Minnesota)

"I didn't want this book to end. . . . The ribbon of highway with its pleasures and perils is worth it all when you roll up to the next stage and unload your gear. The band, the audience, and the music will soon become one again, and is there anything better than that? . . . Absolutely essential reading."   —Bob Stroud, WDRV radio, Chicago

"Bob Greene is speaking your language. . . . The transforming power of music, how it can bring you right back to the first time you heard it, how it can make you feel sunny on a gray day, how it can be enough to make your life work . . . It gets right into your heart and soul."
—Bob Lefsetz, *The Lefsetz Letter*

"For Bob Greene, touring the country and singing backup in a rock group was the equivalent of running away and joining the circus. Wasn't that everyone's dream at some time? . . . This guy is amazingly versatile. He can write about anything and somehow make it relate to almost any reader."   —*North Platte Telegraph* (Nebraska)

"A home run."   —David Galassie, *Associated Content*

"One of the best books on music of the year . . . A sentimental journey through the heart of America . . . the true story of a rock-and-roll band that has been to the top of the charts and seen it all, only to have it quickly and brutally fall apart."   —*Crawdaddy!* magazine

"It's all golden . . . It's about being on tour with a band that brings summer everywhere they go, but more than that, it's a story of love and loyalty, and the freedom of the open road."   —Ken Shane, *Popdose*

...And Readers Love It

"It's a 98-degree day here, and, sitting on my screened porch with the fan whirling and a cool drink a reach away, I just finished *When We Get to Surf City*. I've run across few writers who can put the human experience into words better than you. Thanks for giving me the chance to ride along with you and the boys in the band."
—Gary McCann, Rock Hill, South Carolina

"You have stirred me, moved me, ignited me. I was transported back to the summers on the Iowa farm, listening to the Top 10 on the radio while enyoying the quiet breeze coming in the window. I am grateful."
—Rhea Sprecher, Oak Creek, Wisconsin

"Someone once said that F. Scott Fitzgerald wrote of the Jazz Age both as a participant and as someone looking in through a window. You have that ability: to participate fully, and to step away and watch everything that is happening. Your books just weave their way through my life, both in good times and in bad."   —Don Peri, Davis, California

"I sang lead on 'My Boyfriend's Back' with our group the Angels. Last night I finished reading *When We Get to Surf City*, and I cannot really express how it reached me. I laughed, sometimes felt like crying—your words truly sang to me. I'm telling everyone about this book."
—Peggy Santiglia Davison, Westminister, Maryland

"Thank you for taking me along for the ride, from Waffle Houses to canoes full of shrimp, from small clubs to Three Rivers Stadium, from Chuck Berry to Frank Sinatra. Your writing voice is so clear and vivid that I felt like a roadie traveling right alongside you and the band. You brought tears to my eyes, out-loud chuckles, and countless smiles page after page."   —Charles J. Garcia, Erie, Colorado

"Boys at the ballpark, walking in the surf, hitting the neighborhood bar for a cold one after work—once again, you have shared a story that touches my heart. Thank you for taking me back, making me yearn for 'one more summer.'"   —Diane Zenchuk, Omaha, Nebraska

"Your book is bringing back so many memories. It's like someone else was there when I was growing up. Here I thought it was a secret, and you go blurting it out over all the pages."
—Jerry Horvath, Fort Collins, Colorado

"'Oh, the book was so good, I just couldn't put it down.' I bet you've heard that a million times. But here's what I bet you haven't heard: the flight attendant had to remind me that everyone else had gotten off the plane, and that I had to get off, too. We had landed, and I had missed that everyone had deplaned—I was so engrossed in *When We Get to Surf City*."
                                              —Dorothy Ramsey, West Des Moines, Iowa

"*When We Get to Surf City* is, in my humble opinion, your best book of all. You see and hear things that most of us never even knew took place, even though we were right in the middle of it. When I finished the book, I realized how you and the band felt when the summers came to an end. As you looked for more days, I looked for more pages. I hope you have already started another."
                                              Jim Permantell, Jamestown, Rhode Island

"You never disappoint. You've taken me along back and forth across the country—county fairs, new sights, sounds, and experiences in small-town America. Please keep writing—at the end of each of your books, I feel the way I feel at the end of summer."
                                              —Carol J. Barker, Morehead, Kentucky

"Your book brings memories and feelings I have not had for quite some time. That really is the magic of your writing. You take me to the places where I retreat when things 'in the now' are perhaps less than smooth, places I recount from time to time to my growing children to let them in a bit on who Dad really is."   —George J. Szary, Albany, New York

"You did it again. Thank you for your honesty in sharing the hard times, the struggles, the little moments of exasperation—the happy times, the hours onstage, the moments of caring and concern. I feel like we're old friends. Keep those stories coming. I'm hooked."
                                              —Sue Bellman, Fishers, Indiana

"Once again, you have brought home a winner. As you so gracefully stated, we're all looking for that beacon on a hill, that place where we will find everlasting peace for our souls. You have helped to create that place for so many of us. Thank you for allowing me to view through your eyes such a beautiful and meaningful piece of my America."
                                              —Gary Brown, Birmingham, Alabama

WHEN
WE GET TO
SURF CITY

BOOKS BY BOB GREENE

When We Get to Surf City

And You Know You Should Be Glad: A True Story of Lifelong Friendship

Fraternity: A Journey in Search of Five Presidents

Once Upon a Town: The Miracle of the North Platte Canteen

Duty: A Father, His Son, and the Man Who Won the War

Chevrolet Summers, Dairy Queen Nights

The 50-Year Dash

Rebound: The Odyssey of Michael Jordan

All Summer Long

Hang Time

He Was a Midwestern Boy on His Own

Homecoming: When the Soldiers Returned from Vietnam

Be True to Your School

Cheeseburgers

Good Morning, Merry Sunshine

American Beat

Bagtime (with Paul Galloway)

Johnny Deadline, Reporter

Billion Dollar Baby

Running: A Nixon-McGovern Campaign Journal

*We Didn't Have None of Them Fat Funky Angels on the Wall
of Heartbreak Hotel, and Other Reports from America*

BOOKS BY BOB GREENE AND D. G. FULFORD

To Our Children's Children: Journal of Family Memories

*Notes on the Kitchen Table: Families Offer Messages
of Hope for Generations to Come*

*To Our Children's Children: Preserving Family Histories
for Generations to Come*

WHEN
WE GET TO
SURF CITY

A JOURNEY THROUGH

AMERICA IN PURSUIT OF

ROCK AND ROLL, FRIENDSHIP,

AND DREAMS

Bob Greene

St. Martin's Griffin ☚ New York

www.stmartins.com

Library of Congress data available upon request.

ISBN-13: 978-0-312-37691-8
ISBN-10: 0-312-37691-X

First St. Martin's Griffin Edition: May 2009

10 9 8 7 6 5 4 3 2 1

For Kenny Stone
1947-2005

ONE

The rental car, for the moment, was just a speck in the distance, and things this wonderful are not supposed to happen in a man's life.

I caught sight of the car when it was maybe a hundred yards away, its tires kicking up big clouds of brown dust on the rutted and narrow dirt road by the side of the crowd of forty thousand people.

From where I stood on the stage, the car, and the dirt access road, were to my left. The sun was just starting to dip; the people in the crowd, in their shorts and T-shirts and bikini tops at the end of a broiling June day near the banks of the swollen-almost-to-overflowing Ohio River, were on their feet and dancing to our music. We were singing "Barbara Ann"— . . . *Ba-ba-ba, Ba-Barbara Ann, Ba-ba-ba, Ba-Barbara Ann* . . . —and the people out in the audience were singing right along with us, forty thousand voices joining ours, and that's when I first saw the car.

There was a chance that Chuck Berry was inside.

And I found myself hoping against hope that he wasn't.

That's why I'm telling you this—to give you some idea of the extent of the joy.

I was hoping that Chuck Berry wasn't in the car because if he was, it would mean that we would have to leave the stage.

The others onstage hadn't noticed the car yet. Maybe they weren't looking for it; maybe I'm the only one who for whatever reason always seems to have one eye constitutionally searching for trouble. But the others—Jan, Dean, the four guys who in addition to me were backing up Jan and Dean—were unaware of the car, drawing closer with each passing second.

1

We had been told that Chuck was an apparent no-show. That's why we were up here and singing for the second time today. Not that we minded. It had been an afternoon so bright, so warm, so awash in beginning-of-summer sun that no amount of time on the stage was going to feel like enough, no number of songs were going to feel sufficient. An early-June afternoon bursting with the promise of summer days and summer nights to come, one of those afternoons that fills you with the illusion that against all odds you can be a kid again—that you can get back summer as summer had existed when the music you were singing right now had been brand-new, when you had been brand-new yourself.

But when you had been brand-new yourself, in a world that had felt constantly new, you could not have conceived of ever standing on the same patch of land as Chuck Berry, of ever breathing the same air, never mind hoping that a car just entering your line of sight did not carry him inside.

After we had first played earlier in the afternoon and had finished our set, we had been in the backstage area having ribs and sandwiches and beer while some of the other acts on the bill—Sam the Sham, Little Eva, the Marcels—had performed. As we had been getting ready to go back to our hotel we could see that the promoters were getting jittery. They had been whispering among themselves; clearly something was wrong.

What had been wrong was Chuck Berry—the absence of Chuck Berry. He had been signed to be the headliner—he was supposed to close the show. But he hadn't appeared, and no one had been able to find out where he might be. The promoters had made some calls and had been told that Berry had apparently missed all of that day's flights out of St. Louis; he had not been in contact with them, and it was nearing his time to be onstage.

So the promoters had hurriedly called Dean Torrence aside and conferred with him. They had asked if Jan and Dean would do a second set to close the show, and Dean had said yes, and thus here we were.

And there, to the left of the sea of bare, sunburned arms that were waving in the southern Ohio air as we sang, was the car, moving toward us, and I could see through its windshield that it contained only one person: the driver.

He hit the brakes and brought it to a halt directly to the side of the stage, throwing one last billow of thick dirt toward the sky. He opened his door and stepped out.

Chuck Berry.

Dean Torrence was in the midst of his falsetto—he always loved singing this song, he was in his fifties now and sometimes there were songs, I could tell, that he sang just because the audience expected him to sing them, songs he just as well could have done without, but this wasn't one of them, he never seemed to tire of it—and he was singing *Oh, Barbara Ann, take my hand,* and I thought I should let him know.

Why I had to be the bearer of these particular bad tidings, I'm not certain. He was going to find out anyway, soon enough. No one was making me do it. But then, no one was making me be here in the first place.

I let my right elbow nudge Dean's left arm, careful not to hit his lime-green Stratocaster as I did it, and he looked over at me, not breaking his vocals— . . . *you got me rockin' and a-rollin'*—and I motioned with my head to the area below the stage.

Chuck Berry had walked around to the rear of his rental car, and now he popped open the trunk and pulled out his battered guitar case.

There wasn't a cloud in the sky, but invisible clouds covered Dean's eyes as soon as he saw what I was seeing.

The others in the band weren't aware of it yet, weren't aware that our day—the glory part of it—was about to abruptly end. They were still singing— . . . *tried Peggy Sue but I knew she wouldn't do* . . . —some of them making eye contact with women in the first few rows of the crowd, and they didn't know.

Chuck Berry climbed a short flight of metal stairs until he was on the stage, to the side of the drum kit and behind the equipment crates so he was hidden from the audience. Singing, I wheeled in his direction, just wanting to take in the moment. There was that skinny, sharply angled face of his, a mirror reflecting all the aspects of the lifetime he had led: rough-edged, angry, incarcerated, uncompromising, suspicious, solitary, profane, stubborn. . . .

Went to a dance, lookin' for romance. . . .

I sang the words, and he caught my gaze, and I couldn't help it, I burst out laughing, this was too much, this was too great. What are the chances that this could ever happen? What are the chances that the day will ever come when even though you're not much of a singer at all, you're singing in front of forty thousand people, you're singing the songs you grew up loving with a band you grew up loving, guys who, deep into your life and theirs, have against all probability become some of your best friends in the world, guys with whom you perpetually travel America in the hopes of finding the best parts of summer again. . . .

What are the chances that you'll be singing a song in the June heat, and that even as your voice booms out of the speaker towers and sails into tens of thousands of ears, your eyes will be looking into the eyes of Chuck Berry, and he'll be watching and listening? How can such a moment ever come to pass?

I knew this would be it for the day; I put as much as I could into the vocals, because I understood, with Chuck on the skirt of the stage now, it would be ending for us.

At least for today, it would. But there would be others: day after day after summer day. That was the gift.

The seven of us at the front of the big wooden stage sang it one last time: *Ba-ba-ba, Ba-Barbara Ann.* . . .

I was still half turned so I could see the wings, and Chuck Berry shot me one of those cold and wary Chuck Berry squints that meant: What are you looking at?

And I thought: Don't you know? I'm looking at you, Chuck. I'm looking at you.

. . . saw Barbara Ann and I thought I'd take a chance. . . .

I decided to take my own chance. So as I sang the words I smiled in his direction and nodded my head in time to the music.

And Chuck Berry, after a flicker of hesitation, returned my grin, and nodded back, and, with his eyes locked on mine, for a few brief seconds he sang along.

There were moments, moments like that, when it seemed the gifts would never stop.

TWO

There must have been a time in American life when people really did run away to join the circus.

That was always the phrase—the shorthand slogan to describe the ultimate fantasy. Slip out the window and sprint away from home in the middle of the night, follow the Big Top as it is torn down and moves from city to city, jump on the circus train and ride it wherever the voyage may lead.

It was always spoken about as the kind of dream a child would have—it didn't sound like something for grownups to long for. The dreams of adults were supposed to be more responsible, considerably more staid. Weren't they?

To chase that circus when you are no longer a kid, when notions like this aren't supposed to even occur to you anymore—to follow the sounds of the calliope just when life, by all measures, is scheduled to be turning gray and grim and stolid—is an option that is presumed to be lost to you.

But in the middle of a person's life, or so it turns out, it is possible to find that feeling. Because just when we think we have given up on ever capturing again the freedom and the exhilaration and the blithesome mornings of our world when it was first forming; just when we have begun to settle in for the long, slow slide; just when the sun begins to feel not quite so high in the sky. . . .

Sometimes something happens to keep the sun up there a while longer. Sometimes we find something we weren't even aware we were looking for.

If we're very lucky, we run to catch up with it before it has the chance to leave us behind.

THREE

It started simply enough.

Someone picked up a paperback book in an airport.

I found this out when, in the middle of a stack of letters in the Chicago newspaper office where I was working, I came upon one addressed to me with a Panorama City, California, postmark.

I didn't think I knew anyone from there. I opened the envelope; the letter was from a guy who said his name was Gary Griffin.

He'd bought a book of mine called *Be True to Your School*, he wrote; just something to read on the plane.

Be True to Your School, a nonfiction book based on a diary I had kept in 1964, when I had been a teenager in central Ohio, had been written in the form of the diary itself: a journal divided into 366 days (1964 had been a leap year).

Gary Griffin said that he had been especially interested in the entry from April 11—the first paragraph of that day's entry:

> Saturday. Dan and Jack and I went downtown; at Lazarus I bought two records—"The New Girl in School" by Jan and Dean, and "I Am The Greatest" by Cassius Clay. We cruised most of the afternoon.

In his letter, Griffin wrote that although he enjoyed the book, that wasn't the reason he was getting in touch. He was a musician by trade—a rock-and-roll keyboard player. Specifically, he made his living as part of Jan and Dean's touring band.

7

It was 1992 when I received that letter; I was forty-five years old.

That's just how quickly your life can change. You distractedly rip open one envelope from a pile of many, and even though you have no idea at the time, nothing will ever be the same.

They had been California idols—about as far from our landlocked and humdrum existence in the middle of Ohio as anyone ever could have been.

Jan and Dean—their blended voices coming out of our car radios day and night—sang of high surf and competition hot rods, of beautiful girls and endless West Coast summers. They were golden—literally. They had the look, the million-selling records, the flashy swagger; their lives, we knew without ever having to think about it for even a second, were everything that our lives weren't. We'd struggle to wakefulness on a subzero Ohio morning, our alarm radios clicking to life before the sun had come up, reminding us that another dreary day of school awaited . . . and before we could open our eyes, their voices were already coming at us, with the effect of a friendly taunt:

Oh she's my Honolulu Lulu, she's my Honolulu Lulu,
Queen of the surfer girls. . . .

Jan and Dean and their buddies, the Beach Boys, would sing their songs, and it never had to be said out loud: what they had was what we wanted. Not that we resented them; far from it. Listening to their music, we could feel, at least for three minutes, that we were them. It wasn't a matter of pretending—there was no delusion involved. It was more like they were inviting us along for the ride. A Jan and Dean record would come on the radio, and with its high harmonies, its whining, urgent beat—like an exquisitely calibrated top-horsepower car engine—it would allow us into that world. There wasn't an ocean within five hundred miles of us. It didn't matter.

Jan and Dean's signature song—their first Number One hit—was "Surf City," and I can tell you exactly where I was the first time I heard it:

In my father's Thunderbird, backing out of Dave Frasch's driveway on Roosevelt Avenue in our hometown of Bexley, Ohio. We were on our way to a late-spring junior tennis tournament at Ohio State University, where, as high school sophomores, we were competing. I'd just gotten my driver's license; my dad, on a Saturday, had let me borrow his car.

The radio was tuned to WCOL, the local rock station, and Jan and Dean's voices—mingled falsettos in the leadoff phrase—blared out of the dashboard:

Two girls for every boy. . . .

Before they could sing another word, it was already obvious: this was going to be the song of the summer ahead. Some records sound so good, so right, that they announce themselves as anthems the first second you hear them. They speed up everything inside of you, they thrill you, they— although you would be embarrassed to admit it—make you glad. You don't comment—you merely reach for the knob and turn up the volume.

I got a thirty-four wagon and we call it a woodie. . . .

Surf City, here we come. That was the promise of the song. They were going to Surf City, where it was "two to one"—where every boy could count on two willing girls, could count on mountainous blue-and-white towering waves, could count on parties every night. Not only were there "two swingin' honeys for every guy," but "all you gotta do is just wink your eye."

The song—the pure, soaring sound of it, the electric insistence of the beat, the cocksure voices airlifted from the hot sand near the Pacific Ocean directly to where we were sitting in Franklin County, Ohio— was inebriating. Every season or so, back then, a song like that would come along: a song you knew would dominate the soundtrack of your life for months. It was the song you would wish for, every moment be- hind the wheel—the one song you hoped the disc jockey would decide to play.

In the summer of 1963, "Surf City" was that song, all across America. By going to Number One with "Surf City," Jan and Dean won their southern California competition with the Beach Boys; the Beach Boys, at that point, had never had a Number One hit. A top-of-the-charts single, in those years, had a bigger audience than the best-selling book of a given year, than the biggest movie of that year—by the nature of a Number One song's distribution, floating for free out of all those radios, it became part of the very atmosphere, as constant as the air itself. So it was for "Surf City" that summer.

. . . and when we get to Surf City we'll be shootin' the curl,
and checkin' out the parties for a surfer girl. . . .

Jan and Dean had hit after hit—"The New Girl in School," "The Little Old Lady from Pasadena," "Dead Man's Curve," "Honolulu Lulu," "Ride the Wild Surf," "Sidewalk Surfin'," "Drag City"—and then the Beach Boys eventually caught up with them and soon enough surpassed them; the Beatles came along, and then the Rolling Stones, and meanwhile those of us who merely listened went on with our own lives, even as the everlasting car-radio symphony shifted seamlessly between different voices, different sounds.

It was big news for a day or two in 1966 when Jan Berry had the very car accident that, two years before, he had sung about in "Dead Man's Curve":

. . . Well, the last thing I remember, Doc, I started to swerve. . . .

He hadn't literally swerved—he smashed straight into the back of a truck parked on a California street. In his Corvette, Jan Berry had been driving at a foolhardy and frightening rate of speed. The police officers who first got to the scene believed that he was dead.

He wasn't, but for weeks he was in a coma, and when he awakened he found that his body was broken, his speech was slurred, his memory was muddled. He would have to learn to walk again; he would have to learn to talk.

So much for the golden dream. Other stories came into the news; other singers came onto our radios.

And now, all these years later, this letter from Gary Griffin had arrived. He had read about that day in 1964 when I had bought the Jan and Dean record.

He had enclosed a phone number; I called him in California. Jan and Dean were still out on the road, performing their hits, he said; he'd been touring as their keyboard player for more than a decade.

"Why don't you come out and join us to see a show?" he said.

I told him that I had a recollection of hearing, from time to time, about what Jan had been through: how he had struggled to come back from the accident, how Jan and Dean had disappeared from public view for awhile.

"We're playing all the time," Gary said.

I asked him if what Jan had contended with would be evident to me.

"You'll see," he said.

In the American Airlines concourse at Chicago's O'Hare International Airport, I sat at the gate where a late-morning flight to Kansas City would be boarding.

Jan and Dean and their band would be arriving at O'Hare at another gate; that's what Gary had told me. The night before, they had played at the Marion, Ohio, Popcorn Festival. Today—a Sunday—they were booked to do an afternoon show in Kansas City. Gary had said they would meet me at the departure gate.

Twenty minutes before flight time, I saw them coming down the corridor, some of them with their instrument cases slung over their shoulders. Dean Torrence, I recognized immediately; he was fifty-two now, with more of a country-club-grill-room look to him than when I'd last seen him on album covers, or watched him on Dick Clark's *Where the Action Is* television series almost thirty summers before. There was a hint of the dissolute in his features—this was a man who over the decades had had his share of long nights that turned into raw mornings, you could tell—but his face was still a rock star's face, the hair was surfer-long, everything in his bearing said that this was not a fellow who made his living in an office building.

Gary Griffin spotted me, and came over. He was a red-haired guy in his early forties, with something about him that could have come out of a 1958 comic book: Archie Andrews grown older, but Archie, you suspected, with a private and off-kilter twist of some sort, maybe more than a few purposely hidden secrets. He made the introductions to the others, and I couldn't even attempt to keep the names and faces straight, at least for now. One of the oldest and uneasiest feelings known to humankind, one we all first encounter at some point as children: here's a group of people who all know each other, who have a common history and shared jokes, people who can finish each others' sentences, and you're the stranger. So I shook hands with bass guitarist Chris Farmer, lead guitarist Philip Bardowell, rhythm guitarist Randell Kirsch, drummer David Logeman, and if you had told me at that moment that fifteen years down the line I would still be keeping company with these men, that they and I would be sharing the laughter and the long nights, in good times and sorrowful, as we traveled the country together—if you had told me that the time would come when, on more occasions than not, we could finish each others' sentences—it would not have seemed believable. Now, on the first day, we made our ritual hellos, and I was half-wondering why I was wasting a weekend on this trip that seemed to have no goal. If I hadn't kept that diary in 1964, if Gary Griffin hadn't read the book that I had turned it into . . . if, on that long-gone April day in the diary, I had bought some record other than a Jan and Dean record . . .

"Where's Jan?" Dean said to his band members now, in O'Hare.

One of the musicians pointed down the concourse.

Jan Berry, carrying a sack of fast-food burgers, walked slowly, unevenly. He was considerably heavier than in the old publicity photos; as a young singer he had been staggeringly handsome, with a face made for the silver screen. Teen magazines would constantly splash him all over their pages—they knew that the girls who bought each issue salivated over him. Now, limping—this wasn't some new injury, it was the nature of his gait every day, a sustaining aftereffect, a quarter-century later, of the 1966 accident—he hustled as best he could to make the flight.

I had used some frequent-flier stickers to upgrade. I'd figured that a big-name band would ride first-class to their concerts, and because as long as I was making the trip I thought I should talk with them en route, I had cashed in some of my miles for a first-class seat.

So when the agent announced that it was time to board, I walked onto the plane and took my place in an all-but-empty first-class cabin.

And watched as Dean Torrence, Jan Berry and the band strode past me and back to coach.

"Living high, huh?" Dean said to me as he passed. There didn't even seem to be an edge to his voice.

My assumptions were going to need some adjusting.

In the Kansas City airport, as we waited at baggage claim, I asked Philip Bardowell what he knew about this day's concert.

At twenty-seven by far the youngest man in the band, he had a dark-without-needing-to-bask-in-the-sun complexion, a day or two's growth of beard, long and undiffidently unkempt black hair, and the sleepiest of sleepy eyes.

He reached into his guitar bag and pulled out his tour itinerary. He skimmed it for a few seconds.

"Outdoor show," he said. "At the Worlds of Fun amusement park."

I nodded.

"Rule of thumb," he said to me. "If a gig has the word 'fun' in the title, it won't be."

At the clamorous amusement park we grabbed a quick meal catered behind the stage, and then the band went out, in high humidity, before a crowd of about four thousand.

I watched the first few songs from the side of the stage. The musicians had changed into surf shirts; Jan, by smiling entreatingly at the audience as he and Dean walked to their positions at the stage's front, did, with the somehow shy grin, what he could to deflect all the eyes from his awkward limp. It appeared to work, mostly; I looked into the first few rows, and the people seemed not taken unawares at the sight of him. Probably they knew the story.

He began the lead-in to "The New Girl in School":

Papa-do-ron-day-ron-day, do-ron-day-ron-day . . .

Dean joined in for the initial full sentence of the song:

I got it bad for the new girl in school. . . .

When they had first sung those words, so many years before, the words may have sounded plausible; what was surprising was that the audience was buying it now, completely. All the way back to the last row, people were up out of their seats and singing along phrase for phrase.

I tried to see if the people in the crowd were doing it with an implied wink—whether they were making a little fun. Not a bit; they were entranced, they plainly loved this, loved being in the presence of the men whose music had once served as a daily definition of good times. A significant part of the band's set list was composed of Beach Boys songs—"Shut Down," "Little Deuce Coupe," "409"—because Jan and Dean, as many gold records as they had made, didn't have quite enough of their own hits to completely fill a one-hour show. From what I could see, the audience didn't make a distinction—the songs of Jan and Dean and the songs of the Beach Boys had doubtless melded long ago in their memories, the songs were all the official motifs of summer, and the people standing and singing seemed more than pleased that Jan and Dean had come all the way to Missouri on this day to personally deliver those songs.

With the amusement park's pivoting-and-twirling rides visible off to the side of the audience, the people singing along hit full stride as Jan chanted the opening to "I Get Around":

Round, round, get around, I get around . . .

And when the guitarists bore down and the drummer assaulted his kit and the first verse kicked in, you could barely hear the men onstage, because the voices in the audience all but drowned them out:

I'm gettin' bored driving up and down this same old strip,
I gotta find a new place where the kids are hip. . . .

I left the stage, cut around a low fence, and walked into the audience. I stood about halfway back, in an aisle; what struck me was that the people surrounding me were not what you would necessarily expect: were not just men and women Jan and Dean's own age, who had grown up with these songs.

Instead, I saw teenagers and people in their twenties and thirties, almost all of whom had been born after the songs had first been hits. I saw families in which children of six and seven appeared to know every word of every song, the children clapping hands with their parents to the tempo of the drumbeats David Logeman was pounding out onstage. One such family was standing directly next to me; as Jan and Dean sang "Help Me, Rhonda," a brother and sister, each of them younger than ten, danced in front of their parents and literally screamed the words, without any prompting:

Well, Rhonda you look so fine,
And I know it wouldn't take much time. . . .

Everyone on this amusement park afternoon just seemed so . . . *happy.* I was accustomed to regarding the world around me pretty much as it was presented on newspaper front pages: astringent, violent, full of conflict and discord. The headlines taught their constant lesson: if the world hasn't let you down today, don't worry; it will tomorrow.

So to stand among the people in this audience, to listen as they hollered the words to "Fun, Fun, Fun" toward the men on the stage:

> *Well, she got her daddy's car and she cruised through the hamburger stand now,*
> *Seems she forgot all about the library like she told her old man now. . . .*

To see that as the amped-up guitar lines ascended made me curious not so much about the people who had paid for tickets and had come here this afternoon: I could see very well what the appeal was for them.

What I was thinking about was the men who were rendering the music. This life of theirs, seeing this every day and every night . . . like the milkmen of the era from when these songs were new, these men were expected to make their deliveries, to be faithful to their route—they were entrusted to deliver the enchantment. The audience was seeing the musicians; I found myself wondering what it was that the musicians saw every night, as they looked at the eyes looking at them. What was it that they were looking for out here?

Toward the end of the show I circled back around to the stage. As Jan and Dean began to sing "Surf City," Gary Griffin motioned for me to join him at his microphone. I pointed at myself—*you want me to come out there?*—and he nodded and waved me over, and I haltingly walked out and self-consciously stood with him—hands in pockets, probably, at least this is how I remember it—and sang backup the best I could. It was so disorienting and I felt so nervous and uncomposed that I couldn't even look directly at the people in the seats. I stared over the tops of their heads and sang the words I had first heard in Dave Frasch's driveway:

> *Surf City, here we come. . . .*

When it was over Dean, mopping the sweat from his face with a towel he found on a picnic table in the unroofed backstage area, said that we should all get together for beers and sandwiches once we'd showered back at the Holiday Inn.

"Yeah, we used to have a touch football league on the weekends," Dean was saying. "Elvis would come by and play all the time."

The bar/restaurant in the open lobby area of the hotel smelled like chlorine—that redolence mid-level chains off the interstates often have, at least the ones that feature indoor pools to attract families who want to give their children, cranky from miles and miles of being cooped up in the back seat, something to do.

"He wasn't living at Graceland?" I said.

"He had Graceland back in Memphis," Dean said. "But when he was making movies, he also kept a house in California."

We had the place pretty much to ourselves; the Holiday Inn wasn't doing a lot of business on this Sunday night. Dean had changed from his stage clothes to baggy sweatpants and a T-shirt. His speaking voice was animated and lively, with an unanticipated trace of a twang to it; he seemed to be in no hurry at all.

And I didn't surmise that he was trying to brag by talking about Elvis Presley—the conversation up to this point had been about football, not music, and he was describing the games between teams made up of young actors and young rock stars back when his fame was new.

"Presley was a pretty good receiver," Dean said.

Made sense, I supposed. In 1963 and 1964—the era of the touch football league he was recounting—Jan and Dean were about as celebrated as singers could be. Elvis was back from the Army and had begun his descent into mediocre movies, and had given up performing in concert—the Las Vegas portion of his life had not yet commenced. So of course, if Elvis Presley wanted to play in pickup games of football in those years, Dean Torrence would be a logical teammate or competitor. They were members of the same club.

Now Elvis was long dead, and Dean was in the Holiday Inn with the pool smell so pungent that it could make your eyes sting. Some of the band members were at the tables we had pulled together—Gary Griffin and Randell Kirsch and Chris Farmer and Phil Bardowell were eating with us, but Jan had gone straight to his room after the show and had not emerged, and David Logeman was yet to be seen. There was something very settled-in and relaxed about this; whatever the stereotype of touring bands used to be—wreckers of hotel rooms, pursuers of drugs and loud times—that's not what this felt like.

Dean seemed, at least from these preliminary observations, quite un-full of himself for a man with a famous name; I didn't know what he had been like as a teenage star, but at fifty-two here he was. He had sung this afternoon and been paid for it; he would sing again tomorrow and be paid for it. People today had screamed their approval at what he was doing. There are worse ways to end up, I silently figured. Elvis may have been bigger than Jan and Dean could ever hope to be, but Elvis never made it to fifty-two.

"You play at all?" Randell asked me. He was a tall, Ichabod-Crane-ish-looking man with a kind voice and eyes that seemed ever on full alert.

"Football?" I asked.

"Guitar," he said.

"Same four chords I could play in high school," I said.

"You coming to Indianapolis?" Dean asked.

"What's Indianapolis?" I asked.

"Tomorrow's show," he said. "We're playing for a convention of Kroger grocery store managers tomorrow night."

I was surprised that he was bringing it up. "I hadn't thought about it," I said. "I'm supposed to have lunch with a federal judge in Chicago tomorrow."

The lunch appointment had been set up for several weeks; it was to do research for something I was planning to write about.

"Have lunch with him some other time," Gary Griffin said, Archie goading Jughead.

We ordered another round of beers. "Did Elvis have an attitude around you guys?" I asked Dean.

"Not really," Dean said. "He knew he was Elvis, obviously. But in the football games he was just another player."

"That's sort of hard to believe," I said.

"Well, there were times when new guys would show up to play," Dean said. "And I'd tell one of them to play linebacker, and I'd tell the guy, 'All right, on this next play, you guard Presley.'"

With that, Dean said, the new linebacker would look across the line of scrimmage and notice for the first time who the wide receiver on the other team was.

"And he would just stare as Elvis ran past him for a pass," Dean said.

But that kind of rattled reaction was the exception, he said. In that football league, it was no big deal to be young and in the money and internationally famous. So many of the players were.

There have been times, in the more than fifteen years that have followed that night, when I have felt like I am living on some sort of Island of the Lost Boys—but an island without an anchor, an island that never stops moving.

Most of the time, it has also felt like living inside a jukebox—the best jukebox I have ever found, a jukebox programmed with songs I never tire of hearing. It's as if the names on the little labels beneath the unseen jukebox's glass cover—the names of the men and women who once sang the 45 rpm rock-and-roll singles that roused a drowsy nation, that lit it up and brought it to its feet—have come to walking, talking life. The men and women were fuzzy black-and-white images on a living-room television set when I was very young; they were distant and daring and more than a few of them seemed vaguely dangerous:

Dion. Martha and the Vandellas. The Everly Brothers. Jerry Lee Lewis. James Brown. Lesley Gore. Freddy "Boom Boom" Cannon. The Kingsmen. Brian Hyland. The Drifters. Jay and the Americans. Chubby Checker. Lou Christie. The Ventures. The Coasters. Gary U.S. Bonds. The Monkees. Ronnie Spector. The Grass Roots. Fabian. . . .

For these fifteen-plus years those are the kind of people with whom I have been spending my weekends and summer nights. Indelible names and elaborately posed ballyhoo pictures from long ago and far away, names and pictures I first encountered on rough cardboard posters nailed to wooden telephone poles, promoting long-lost caravan-of-stars tours that would pass through big towns and small during the years when color television was a rumor and hi-fi had yet to be supplanted by stereo. The posters would fade and curl up in the rain after the caravans had moved on.

But it turns out that the caravans never quite shut down.

So it has been, for me, a time of living inside that invisible jukebox, with my favorite songs ceaselessly playing full blast—except that somehow, against all odds, one of the voices coming from the jukebox, singing ragged harmony, is mine.

Once this had begun—once the destinationless journey with the Lost Boys was on its way, and the unmoored island carrying us was afloat, adrift—I tried to explain it all to my younger brother. (Are you still allowed to think of someone as your little brother when he is in his forties?) He had asked me why I was doing this.

He's a football fan. I asked him what he would do if he were invited to play free safety for the Denver Broncos. He said he would drop everything, of course, to do that. I told him that then he knew the answer to his own question.

Dean was telling his own football stories and I excused myself from the table and said I would be back in a few minutes.

I went to my hotel room, sat on the bed and picked up the phone, and called a number inside the Everett M. Dirksen Federal Building in Chicago. On a Sunday night, I knew the call would go straight onto an answering machine.

The voice on the machine was that of a judge's clerk. I said that I was very sorry, but that I was going to have to reschedule tomorrow's lunch.

Something important had come up.

FOUR

"Where were you last night?"

In the lobby, early the next morning, Dean was directing the question at David Logeman. The drummer had never shown up in the bar the night before; we had stayed fairly late, but he never arrived.

Logeman—a muscular man in his forties with blond beach-wanderer hair over a tanned face that could have passed for that of a Golden Gloves boxer who had fought to more than a few fifteen-round split decisions— flashed a bright-white grin.

"Didn't you see the signs on the doors to the rooms?" he said. He was the only man in the band who could readily have passed for a surfer. He looked like he had probably been a heartbreaker since the age of five.

"The 'Do Not Disturb' signs?" Dean said.

"You should have looked more closely," David said. When pleased about something, he tended to talk in an overly loud and exultant voice, as if doing an imitation of a World Wrestling Federation announcer.

The signs on the doors, he pointed out, had not been of the standard "Do Not Disturb" variety. They had said, in big letters: SERVE ME! The signs had advised guests:

Cookie Cart is on a roll. If you are interested in hot fresh cookies with a glass of cold milk before bed, place this card on the outside doorknob. We deliver from 8 P.M. to 9 P.M., Sunday through Thursday, and it's FREE.

That, he said, is why he had not joined us: "I had to wait for my cookies."

"You mean you put that sign out?" Phil Bardowell asked him.

"Of course," David said.

"And the cookies actually came?" Phil asked.

"Right on time," David said, triumph in his tone. "A lady came with a cart."

"How many did you get?" Dean asked.

"Well, they had chocolate chip and oatmeal raisin," David said. "The lady asked me how many people were staying in the room. I said just me, so she gave me one bag with three cookies in it. I could have lied and said there were two people in my room, and she would have given me two bags. I sort of wish I would have."

"And the milk?" Randell Kirsch asked.

"Very cold and delicious," David said, earnest. "Two percent."

A white stretch limousine, provided by the promoter of yesterday's concert, waited outside to take us to the airport. All over America, men and women were reporting for another day in the office cubicle. The Lost Boys—at least one of them full of praise for last night's cookies—prepared to commute to their own job, which on this day would be in Indianapolis.

Jan was the last man out of the hotel. The driver of the limo helped him into the back seat; Jan appeared to be in some discomfort, if not downright pain, as he bent to get in.

If the luxuriousness of this lift to the airport gratified him, or even registered with him, you could not see it. He had been riding in limousines since he was a very young man. This particular car had bench seats running along the sides of the rear passenger compartment. I was sitting on one of those seats, perpendicular to and directly next to his seat, and I told him I was glad to be coming along on this next leg of the trip.

It took him a fraction of a second to process what I was saying—this tiniest of cognitive lags seemed to be an abiding part of what he dealt with every day. He had a sweet and trusting smile; when he spoke, it was in a deep, mildly slurred voice.

"You sang yesterday," he said, apparently remembering having seen me on his stage.

The car filled with chatter from the others as we pulled away from the hotel, and Jan mostly looked straight forward. At one point, wanting to make conversation, I asked him what he thought he would be doing with his life if he weren't doing this.

That little pause, and then:

"Well, I would have been a doctor."

Of course. I'd half-forgotten. Jan Berry, at the time of his accident, had already started medical school. He was said to be brilliant. On that day he had climbed into the Corvette, not only was he the singer of million-selling records, not only was his voice coming out of car radios across the country, not only was he a whiz at arranging and producing music in sound studios—a man handsome in the way name-above-the-title movie stars are handsome, as wealthy as an industrialist, a steady presence on network television variety shows where he and Dean would sing in front of audiences of trembling, crying girls. . . .

Not only had he achieved all of that before he was old enough to vote, but he had decided to give it up. Medical school challenged him—made him stretch. He had concluded that the next act in his life was going to be a career as a physician. He knew that a man could not—or at least should not—spend his life singing "The Little Old Lady from Pasadena."

Then, the accident.

"Had you decided what kind of doctor you were planning to be?" I asked him.

The involuntary hesitation, then: "A surgeon, maybe?" He said it as if asking a question.

He looked at me and said:

"But . . ."

Then he shrugged, as if to indicate: Who can ever know.

Randell Kirsch, riding in front, asked the driver to stop on a city street called Broadway.

"What are you doing, Randell?" Dean asked with some annoyance.

"I'll just be a second," he said. "I saw this store yesterday."

He ran into a place with a sign that said it was Big Dude's Music City. When he ran back out, he had something in his hand.

He got into the front seat and flipped what he had bought toward me. It was an inexpensive black cloth guitar strap.

"You may need this tonight," he said.

On the airplane I heard singing from in front of me.

It was a voice singing "Drag City"—the late-1963 Jan and Dean hit about car racing.

The voice was loud enough that it was carrying for several rows. I could make out every word:

. . . Drag City races are the fastest in the nation. . . .

I stood up to take a look. It was Jan singing. He was holding a tape cassette player, and he had a set of foam earphones connected to the machine. His eyes were closed.

. . . I'll get my honey, grab some money, split for Drag City. . . .

He was in an aisle seat; the middle seat was empty, but a woman who appeared to be in her seventies was by the window, and she was looking over at Jan, out of the side of her eyes, with evident concern. She was leaning so hard into the wall of the plane that I thought, if she could, she would ride the rest of the flight on the wing.

Gary Griffin was reading a magazine a few rows behind mine. I walked back to where he was sitting.

"Do you know that Jan is singing?" I said to him.

He barely looked up. "He does it every day," Gary said.

"Why?" I said.

He closed his magazine, moved to the empty seat beside where he had been, and beckoned me to sit down.

"He has to relearn his songs before every show," Gary said to me. "He puts on the tape and listens to the songs and learns the lyrics again."

"But they're his songs," I said. "He wrote them, didn't he?"

"Doesn't matter," Gary said. "I guess it's the effect of the brain injury from the accident. Part of it is rehearsal, but mainly he just has to learn the words again every day. We're so used to it we don't even notice."

I could still hear Jan, quite clearly. These songs he'd written, these songs he'd sung—songs whose words were still remembered by millions of people, songs whose lyrics those millions could effortlessly sing along with as they listened to oldies stations on their car radios—Jan didn't know them when he woke up every morning. He had to teach them to himself before going out onto a stage and hearing the applause.

"Bob!"

The voice called my name as I was standing at the front desk of a high-rise Marriott in Indianapolis. I had phoned the night before to make a reservation at the hotel, where the band would be staying; I was handing the clerk my credit card.

"Don't," the person calling my name said.

It was Chris Farmer, the band's bass guitarist. He tossed me a little envelope with a keycard inside.

"Save yourself some money," he said. "They gave us one too many rooms. You can use the extra one."

Chris had the smooth, soothing voice—both onstage and in the wider world—of a corporate-training speaker. Dark-haired and a little stocky, he favored a gleaming and seemingly permanent smile that could be deceiving—it was not the smile of a person filled with constant mirth, but rather another permutation of a corporate archetype: if his voice was that of the reassuring company-orientation leader, the smile was that of a human resources vice president who could, without a moment's hesitation or apparent remorse, inform any number of employees that they had been downsized and would be leaving the firm, and do it in such a convincingly genial manner that they wouldn't fully realize they had been fired until they were three steps out the door. Alec Baldwin with a Fender bass.

In addition to singing and playing, Chris picked up a little extra money as Jan and Dean's musical director and as Dean's de facto business assistant on the road; the band did not travel with a road manager, so Chris, I was to find out, was the person who usually dealt with the airlines, the hotels, the promoters. "Soundcheck in the ballroom in an hour," he said to me, smiling all the while.

I hadn't played since early in the Lyndon Johnson administration.

But the same three "Louie Louie" chords I'd known then—the basic guitar chords of rock and roll—were waiting somewhere in the recesses of my mind, and in the tendons of my hands, just where I'd left them.

"This is amazing," I said to Gary Griffin, who was standing next to me on the stage in a ballroom uninhabited except for us and waiters arranging white tablecloths and silverware.

He made a quizzical face as he looked at me and fooled with his keyboard, his expression meaning: What's amazing about it?

Maybe nothing for him—he did this every day. But for me . . .

The chords themselves may have been long-absent friends—my fingers found them without any conscious thought on my part, the chords were as instantly familiar to my fingertips as holes in a once-favorite bowling ball stored in a back-hall closet and rediscovered decades later—but I had never played them on an electric guitar. As a high school kid, when I had learned the chords from a sheet music songbook purchased at the F & R Lazarus department store on High Street in downtown Columbus, I had played them on a nineteen-dollar acoustic guitar: an instrument fit for the Kingston Trio, not the Beatles or the Who. Some friends and I would gather in various basements, strumming the nylon strings on our wooden guitars, shaking marbles in a glass jar in lieu of a drum . . . we may have thought that we were a band, but we never made it out of those basements, and we never touched an electric guitar.

Now I was hitting the "Louie Louie" chords, and they were banging off the back wall of the ballroom.

"Yeah," Gary said, his voice flat for maximum effect. "Amazing."

Phil Bardowell had lent me one of his guitars—he always traveled with two—and I had fastened to it the Big Dude's guitar strap Randell had given me. Phil handed me a few guitar picks, and showed me how to plug the power cord into the right amplifier, and . . .

"'Louie Louie'?" David Logeman called to me from behind his drum kit.

"Yeah!" I said. "You can tell?"

"It's not the first time we've heard the tune," Chris Farmer said.

Still, I liked the fact that it was not so off-pitch as to be unrecognizable. I twisted the knob on the face of the guitar so the volume leaped a notch or two, and I kept hitting the chords, and on the left side of the ballroom I could see a waiter and a waitress dancing a little as they put water glasses on the tables. I could hear them sing as I played:

Ah-Louie Louie, oh yeah. . . .

In Chicago, I figured, a federal judge was just about finishing his lunch right now, and I wasn't with him.

The waiter and waitress sang:

Every night, at ten . . .

There is something about hanging around a hotel room when you know that, in a few hours, there will be music. . . .

Something about doing the same things you've always done in a hotel room as daylight turns to dusk: watching the local television news, making some phone calls, reading the city-guide magazines left on the dresser top for guests. . . .

There is something about knowing that what lies ahead is not a business meeting, not a dinner appointment, not an event to which you are expected to wear a name tag and a resolute expression—knowing that your reason for being in this place this dusk is music and music alone . . . there is something about that that makes the hours of waiting more vivid, more pace-the-floor giddy, something that makes those hours feel Technicolor.

I obsessively checked the clock on the nightstand, and at the appointed minute went to a conference room where dinner, Gary had told me on the phone from his room, would be served to us before the show.

"*Damn* him," Dean was saying as I walked into the room.

He raised his hand to his mouth and bit the heel of his palm. I would learn, soon enough, that this was his usual reaction to frustration about Jan.

"Jan's up in his room throwing up," Gary said to me.

It had been the backstage food in Kansas City, apparently; something Jan had eaten there had not agreed with him. He'd been violently ill—or so he had told Dean—ever since we had checked in here.

"Is he going to sing?" I asked Chris.

"We don't know," Chris said.

"Can you do the show without him?" I asked.

"They didn't hire Jan *or* Dean," Chris said. "They hired Jan *and* Dean."

Which meant: Dean was fearful that if Jan couldn't perform, the organizers of the grocery convention might ask for a good portion of their money back.

So we ate with scant conversation at a long table where hotel waiters had laid out catered meals, and a little after eight P.M. we rode an elevator to the main ballroom, where the grocers were just finishing their own meals.

We climbed up the stairs to the stage, and the head of the grocers' organization said into the microphone: "Ladies and gentlemen, here's what you've been waiting for . . . all the way from southern California . . . *Jan and Dean!*"

The guitar players began hitting the first bars of "Ride the Wild Surf," and Dean, in his Hawaiian-print shirt, walked purposefully to the front edge, and before singing a word said to the grocers: "It's just me."

Then: "Jan's a little under the weather. He's upstairs in his room."

Then: "He *hurled*."

The grocers, who had been drinking with their dinner, laughed—I think they assumed this was part of the act—and Dean and the band began their opening songs. The men and women in the ballroom were standing and dancing from the first verse of the first tune, and after a few minutes Dean motioned for me to come onstage.

He and Chris had told me earlier that they'd bring me on toward the end of the show—at the start of the dance-music set ("Let's Dance," "Do You Wanna Dance," "Dance, Dance, Dance") that would lead into the surf-song set ("Sidewalk Surfin'," "Surf City," "Surfin' U.S.A."). But without Jan on the stage there was a vacant space, so I walked on to fill it.

I didn't know the chords to the songs—"Honolulu Lulu," "California Girls," "The Little Old Lady from Pasadena"—so I kept my guitar and amplifier turned all the way down, and sang backup vocals, softly in case I was off-key, into a microphone I shared with Gary. The whole set had turned into a dance party—in Jan's absence the regular running order of the song list had been all but tossed out, and in between the usual numbers the band was playing songs whose titles were being yelled toward the stage by the audience. A man near the front bellowed "Twist and Shout," and Dean nodded his head in assent, and the guitarists, and David Logeman on his drums, began the song.

Now, *that* one, I knew. Same chords as in "Louie Louie," but even simpler. "Twist and Shout" had been one of the first songs I'd learned on that nineteen-dollar acoustic guitar, so I walked back to the amplifier, turned it up all the way, and played.

Well shake it up baby, now. . . .

What a feeling. Hit the strings, hear the chords thunder from the speakers, watch the people dancing and singing along. . . .

. . . come on and work it on out. . . .

From the other side of the stage Chris Farmer flashed me that glistening smile, which I made the mistake of assuming to be a smile of approval, a notion of which I would be disabused later. About twenty minutes into the show Jan appeared—looking pale and disheveled, but present nonetheless, and with no small effort he climbed the stairs and joined Dean.

"How ya doin', Indianapolis!" he called out, as if the show was just beginning. Which, in a way, it was—now it was Jan and Dean. I saw Dean shake his head briskly, more a signal to himself than to anyone else. Like a man trying to knock away cobwebs, or exasperation.

"Hey, Surfer Man."

The bartender/manager at a dimly lit pool hall called Mr. Lucky's in Tulsa, Oklahoma, was addressing David Logeman.

We had all agreed to meet for lunch at Mr. Lucky's, which was across the highway from the motel where we had just checked in. We were in town for the Tulsa State Fair—smaller and less ambitious in its aspirations than the Oklahoma State Fair—and Mr. Lucky's seemed to be the closest dining opportunity for us. We did not have a car.

As we had left Indianapolis weeks before—the band en route to California, me en route to Chicago—Dean had given me a schedule for upcoming shows, and had said I was welcome to come along on as many dates as I wanted. I'd asked him if he was sure I wasn't getting in the way; he waved away the question and said, "I've been going to these grandstands and arenas for more than thirty years. I don't know why you like this so much, but you can come, if you want. It's good to have someone new to talk to."

And now we were at Mr. Lucky's on a blusterly October day. The Tulsa State Fair is held each year after summer has taken its leave; we wouldn't be going over to the fairgrounds until after dark, and the air by the busy highway was already laced with chill by midday.

Mr. Lucky's was an establishment of the sort that features darkened windows so that people outside the building cannot look in and observe what is going on inside the building. At lunchtime today, what was going on inside the building was a lingerie show.

It was a lingerie show of a variety you will not find on the high-fashion runways of Paris or Milan. None of us had entered the premises desiring anything racier than a cheeseburger and maybe a Coors. Now a couple of young women paraded the floor, in front of mostly unoccupied tables, wearing filmy little garments you could see straight through.

"So you're going to play at soundcheck?" Chris Farmer, wearing that only-too-happy-to-evict-the-destitute-widow-on-Christmas-Eve smile, said to me.

For a second I didn't understand.

"Feel free to play as loud as you want at soundcheck," he said.

Translating to: Don't turn your guitar up during the show itself.

"Don't get your feelings hurt," Dean said, looking at his menu through reading glasses. "I'm not turned up during the shows, either. That's why I pay these guys."

Evidently I hadn't been quite as good on "Twist and Shout" in Indianapolis as I'd thought I'd been.

The jukebox over in the corner at Mr. Lucky's was stocked with oldies, and a succession of them played in the shadowy room—"House of the Rising Sun" by the Animals, "Marie's the Name (His Latest Flame)" by Elvis, "Time Is On My Side" by the Rolling Stones—and then, as if on cue, "Surf City" came on.

I got a thirty-four wagon. . . .

I thought this was astonishing, I thought this was a sign from above—no one in the band had put any money in the machine, this wasn't a setup, it had just happened: Jan and Dean's record coming out of the jukebox as the band sat in the booth—but Dean continued to study the menu as if moments like this had been occurring all his life, which they in all probability had.

One of the lingerie models—she looked to be about twenty-two, dead-tired in the daytime—was half-sleepwalking past our table, and because I was still entranced by the serendipity of the song that was playing I pointed to the jukebox, and then to the guys in the booth, and said to her: "That's them."

"Who's them?" she said.

"The song," I said. "It's theirs."

"Right," she said, as if I had told her that the men in the booth at Mr. Lucky's had just come in from painting the Sistine Chapel.

But she walked over and said something to the bartender/manager, and he looked at the booth and said something back to her—Jan and Dean's appearance at the fair had been promoted on the radio in town, so maybe he had heard about it—and when she reapproached us, it was with renewed interest.

She stood very close to David Logeman, the one person at our table who, with his blond hair and weightlifter's body, looked as if he might conceivably live within view of the Pacific Ocean. In a lineup, he would most likely be the one who strangers picked out as Dean.

From this range, she might as well not have been wearing her lingerie. It was transparent, and she was giving David an inviting look, equally transparent. He was a guy who had probably been getting these kinds of looks from women since he was old enough to notice, and perhaps even before that.

"Hey, Surfer Man," the bartender said to David. "Jackie here's got something she wants to talk to you about."

Dean Torrence's voice was still coming out of the jukebox, singing the hit that had first made him famous in 1963. *Two girls for every boy. . . .*

Dean lowered his menu and peered over the tops of the lenses of his glasses. "Do the fries come with the burgers?" he asked Jackie.

"I'm not your waitress," she said.

In the grain-warehouse-like main pavilion on the Tulsa State Fairgrounds, with the aroma of rodeo clinging to the walls and floor, Jan made his entrance to enthusiastic hollers from the crowd.

His face lit up. He had learned the words to his songs again; that part of his day, the audience did not know about. He seemed genuinely elated to see all the faces—the pavilion was almost full, these were city people and ranch people, farmers and white-collar workers, and Jan and Dean were, to them, on this night, living representation of the word that had been used to describe them in the onstage introduction: legendary.

That word did not seem to surprise either Jan or Dean—Dean showed no more reaction to it than he had to the all-but-naked lingerie model who stood between him and his cheeseburger—and maybe that was because in their line of work, Jan and Dean had been encountering nearly-naked women, and strangers calling them "legendary," since they were little more than boys. Like photocopy toner and embossed business cards for people in other occupations, those two things were apparently simply a part of the atmospherics of their particular trade.

So the word had not seemed to faze Jan or Dean, but I could see in Jan's eyes that he was happy—or was it merely relieved?—to see the seats filled to the farthest reaches of the pavilion, and to hear the strangers calling his name. He started to sing those first words:

I got it bad for the new girl in school. . . .

And as discrepant as those words were with the sight of the man singing them, the people as far back as I could see were joining him by shouting out every syllable, locking their eyes on his and Dean's, jumping up and down to the beat being provided by Phil and Gary and David and Chris. Randell hadn't come on this trip; budgetary concerns, Dean had told me at Mr. Lucky's, determined whether he would use three guitarists or only two on a given leg of the tour. But they sounded great; they were in fourth gear right from the start, they were solid and tight, driving the show like NASCAR pacesetters—that's what they were being paid for and that's what they were proud of, and I could understand why they wouldn't want the likes of me, or even of Dean, to mar their musicianship with work that couldn't come close to measuring up to theirs.

I watched in the wings until the dance-song set was ready to begin; Dean was obviously in a good mood—he looked over toward me with a mischievous expression as he was ready to bring me on, and he said into the microphone:

"We have a special guest with us tonight. Do any of you remember Roy Orbison?"

The audience erupted in cheers. I didn't know where Dean was going with this.

"Well," he said, as his amplified words filled the pavilion, "this is Roy Orbison's . . .

"cousin's . . .

"gardener."

Phil Bardowell was just about doubled over. I ran out, with Phil's backup guitar strapped around my neck, made certain that my amplifier was set low, and joined with Gary at his microphone for the next six songs, plus the encores of "Barbara Ann" and "Fun, Fun, Fun." My ears were ringing as the show ended—it was the first of two we were scheduled to do tonight—and I descended from the stage once the house lights came up, and a man from the audience, who said he lived on an Oklahoma ranch, approached me.

"You guys put on a real good show," he said. "And I loved your cousin's records."

I didn't quite understand that second part.

"Anyway," he said, extending his hand, "it's really good to meet you, Gardner."

He had misheard.

Dean had said I was Roy Orbison's cousin's gardener.

The rancher thought he'd said I was Roy Orbison's cousin, Gardner.

"Glad you enjoyed it," I said, shaking the man's hand. "Come back for the second show."

The Oklahoma Cattlemen's Association would be serving us dinner between shows, and in the pavilion one of their members handed Dean a map of the fairgrounds, with a yellow highlighter already having been applied to show us the proper path to the building where we'd eat.

An official from the fair had driven a golf cart to the stage, so that Jan could have a ride to dinner. The rest of us left the performance pavilion and went out into the now-frosty October night.

The midway of the fairgrounds was ablaze with lights—green, blue, red and white bulbs twinkling on the ferris wheel, the tilt-a-whirl, the smaller and less daunting rides designed for children. It all had a Christmas look: all that candescent color in the darkness.

"If you're going to keep doing this, you're going to have to get some stage clothes," Dean said. I'd just been untucking my button-down shirt and wearing it, sleeves rolled up, with the tail hanging loose over a pair of jeans. The rest of them wore crazy-hued surf shirts.

The sounds of the midway were packed with their own woozy frothiness: reedy music piped from cheap speakers clamped to the iron skeletons of the rides, oversized baseballs toppling bottom-heavy bowling pins at win-a-stuffed-animal booths, the occasional whir of machines churning out cotton candy. We found the building we were looking for on the edge of all that lightness, and volunteers from the women's auxiliary of the cattlemen's association were waiting for us inside with platters of steaks and baked potatoes, and bowls of freshly mixed salads.

"Sit down and eat, boys," one of the women said. "The food's nice and hot."

And so we boys—boys so far along in our lives—ate quickly and energetically, because we were due soon enough at the second show. We'd be doing it the next night, too: two nights, four shows at this fair, before packing up.

Returning through the midway to the music pavilion after dinner, Gary Griffin said to the rest of us, "Hold on. How much time do we have?"

"About ten minutes," Dean said.

"I want to get some dessert," Gary said, and stopped at a booth, fished into his pocket for some money, and bought a cherry Sno-Cone.

"Excellent idea," Chris said, stepping up to buy his own.

"I'd better get one for Jan," Dean said. "He'll go nuts if he sees everybody else eating them."

Sno-Cones in hand, Dean lugging two—lime for him, orange for Jan—we moved toward the building where, we could see, there was a jam-up at the door as the audience funneled in.

"Pretty nice night, huh?" said David Logeman, his face washed in a blue-green-red blend of reflected midway lights.

I nodded in agreement, thinking: It sure is. It's a night as lovely as can be. Or my name's not Gardner Orbison.

On a snow-dusted December dusk, my mother, my father and I sat in a white-tablecloth restaurant on an upper floor of the Vernal G. Riffe Center in downtown Columbus.

"This whole evening is against my better judgment," my father, who was seventy-seven years old, said.

The Riffe Center—a government building named in honor of a former speaker of the Ohio House of Representatives—was located across High Street from the Ohio Statehouse; from where we were sitting waiting for our dinner, we could see the statehouse lawn, with its statue of longtime Ohio Governor James A. Rhodes, the only statue I have ever beheld that features the sculptee carrying a briefcase.

"I think the evening will be interesting," my mother said.

One of our longest-standing family stories—it has needed no embellishing at all over the years—concerns what happened during a particular meal at our dining table at home in 1957.

Elvis Presley had only recently come upon the scene. To me, at age ten, he, and the first wave of rock and roll, represented everything stirring and illicit and full of promise that life could possibly offer. To my father, Elvis and rock and roll signified the certain downfall of everything good the United States had ever stood for.

I would talk about Elvis incessantly. My life had become consumed by thoughts of him and his music.

And at that Eisenhower-era meal, I must have been talking about Elvis even more than usual, because my father had erupted.

"All right!" he had said. "Get off this Presley!"

"What's wrong with Elvis?" I had said.

"*What's wrong with Elvis?*" my father had said.

I was wearing, at the table, a shirt with a little decorative patch of some sort on the chest—probably, knowing my mother's shopping habits for her children, a cute animal.

"I'll tell you what's wrong with Elvis," my father had said. "If you were walking down an alley, and Elvis was coming the other way, and he didn't like that patch on your shirt—he'd come up to you and rip it right off!"

And with that my father had reached across the table and tried to rip the patch from my ten-year-old chest.

Now, thirty-five years later, here he and my mother and I were, in the restaurant of the Riffe Center, because in an hour or so I would be onstage with Jan and Dean. The band had flown to Columbus, having been hired by a central Ohio architectural firm to perform a concert at the firm's annual Christmas party for employees and clients; I had arranged for my parents to be guests. It would be my father's first rock concert.

And it would be Jan and Dean's last show of the year. They were chiefly a warm-weather band; 90 percent of their bookings were during the summer, when the songs of surfers and fast cars and girls on the beach had context. But the paycheck from the architecture firm had been sufficient to inspire the band to fly cross-country in the weeks before Christmas.

Thus, my mother and father and I had dinner, and we rode the elevator downstairs just before showtime and they took their seats in the Riffe Center's theater. When I came out with Phil's standby guitar around my neck just before "Let's Dance" I could see my father, in a dark suit, sitting about ten rows back, his arms folded across his chest. He had told my brother and sister and me, all through our lives, that the most arduous time of his own life was during World War II, in the bitter winter of the Italian campaign. At this moment, he looked as if he would rather be there than here.

Gary Griffin and I sang "Let's Dance" and "Do You Wanna Dance" together at his microphone, as we'd been doing, and then, just as "Dance, Dance, Dance" was about to begin, Gary grabbed my shirt and pulled me, by myself, in front of the mike, and he backed away . . . and stayed away.

By myself, I sang:

After six hours of school I've had enough of the day,
I hit the radio dial and turn it up all the way. . . .

I sang lead for the entirety of the song, hearing my voice sound throughout the theater, and then Gary rejoined me at the mike for the surf songs and the encore, and at one point, during a Phil Bardowell guitar solo, I said to Gary:

"What was *that*?"

"It's your Christmas present," he called back to me, loud enough so that I could hear him as Phil played.

"Dance, Dance, Dance" was mine—they were giving it to me, from that night forward.

When the concert ended and the theater started to empty out, I left the stage to say goodnight to my parents. Dean, Gary, Phil and Chris followed me down, to introduce themselves.

My father didn't seem to know what to make of it.

This was the kind of music that had once provoked him, in a rage, to grab for that patch on his son's shirt.

But in 1957, when he had lunged for the patch, when rock and roll was new, my father had been forty-two years old.

Tonight Dean was older than that. Jan was older than that.

I was older than that.

"Nice show," my father said to Dean, "except for *him*"—gesturing with his thumb at me.

"I know what you mean," Dean said.

Nothing could make me feel bad tonight.

I'd been given my own song.

No matter how cold or how long the winter, spring already beckoned, somewhere down the road.

FIVE

Thick drops of grimy water dripped slowly from the roof of the San Diego Padres' dugout.

Jan Berry and I sat on the Padres' bench, the remnants of a brief midgame rainshower forming puddles at our feet. Crumpled-up green-paper Gatorade cups—tossed to the ground by the ballplayers who had, minutes before, completed a 9–7 loss to the Houston Astros, in which the Padres had gone scoreless in the final three innings—littered the hard, damp floor of the dugout.

"I just live for this," Jan said to me. "Sometimes, at home, I think that summer will never come."

"What do you do in the off months?" I asked him.

"Not a whole lot," Jan said. "I try to stay in shape, so I'll look good when the new season starts."

Out just past the pitcher's mound, sound technicians were getting the stage ready. The announced crowd for the Padres-Astros game, on this Sunday afternoon in May, had been 13,895; Jack Murphy Stadium could hold well over 50,000. The "California Beach Party"—the promotion scheduled to begin after the completion of the baseball game—would be held in a big-league ballpark with far more unused seats than ones that were occupied.

"I guess you could have asked for better weather," I said to Jan.

"Oh, it doesn't matter," he said. "It's so good that this is beginning again. I go crazy sitting at home."

This was my second time at the ballpark within twenty-four hours.

I had arrived in San Diego the afternoon before, on a flight from Chicago. I dropped my bags at my hotel, then, with nothing to do until morning, took a cab to Jack Murphy Stadium, bought a ticket along the first-base line, and watched the Padres and the Astros play an evening game. Intermittently during the contest the scoreboard would flash an invitation to the crowd: "Tomorrow—The Coors Light Summer Beach Party Featuring the Legendary Jan and Dean." Two seats away from me, a little girl was gulping at her Coke. Her father said to her, gently: "We're not going to hurry so much. We're going to take our time."

Sounded good to me. Even in an age in which you can eat lunch near Lake Michigan and be watching a ballgame on the California coast the same day before the sun is all the way down, the idea of taking your time had an indisputable appeal. With a new summer ahead and the slap of the baseball against the leather of the infielders' gloves easily audible from where I was sitting, I munched peanuts from a paper sack and observed the occasional action on the diamond.

In the morning Gary Griffin picked me up in front of my hotel—he and the others had driven down from Los Angeles; San Diego was a quasi-local show for them, they didn't have to spend a night away from their own beds—and we did a soundcheck outside the stadium on the back of a flatbed truck that was going to be driven onto the field and serve as a stage. The other acts on the bill—Dick Dale, King of the Surf Guitar; the Chantays; the Surfaris; all names from the circular paper labels of black-vinyl 45 rpm records I once had been the eager owner of, records that I had kept in a box in the bedroom of the house of my growing up—were in the parking lot, too, early in the day, looking cross and bleary-eyed and anything but in a convivial mood as they waited to rehearse.

Our show was intended as a bonus to ticketholders, an extra lure to get them to the ballgame. We were assigned to the visiting football locker room used, in the fall and winter, by opponents of the San Diego Chargers.

Dean Torrence leaned back against one of the football lockers; he seemed wholly unimpressed to be here—this may have been a big-league sports stadium, but he had known since he was barely out of his teens what it felt like to be big-league; he and Jan were a brand name just as lasting as that of the San Diego Padres or the San Diego Chargers. The football players, each October and November, changed into their pads and game uniforms in this room; Dean already had on his uniform—the surf shirt—and he looked at his watch and said: "I just hope this doesn't go into extra innings."

We wouldn't be starting until the baseball game ended; the overcast skies had opened up once or twice already. The guitarists—Chris, Phil, Randell, each of whom I had talked to on the phone several times, but hadn't seen, in the off months since Ohio—strummed away absentmindedly, their instruments not plugged in to anything, their picks against the strings making a sound like a playing card being run against the tongs of a metal comb.

Jan, the headphones from his tape recorder covering his ears, sat in front of another football locker, singing:

Go, Granny, go. . . .

We couldn't hear what he was hearing, but it was evident that, pumping into his ears, was "The Little Old Lady from Pasadena." His voice, unaccompanied, was almost a cry:

Go, Granny, go!

Dean, listening to this, said to me:
"And how was *your* winter?"

Meaning that it was probably better than Jan's had been. But now it was May.

And now we were sitting in the Padres' dugout and Jan was saying how contented he was to be here.

"Do you like baseball?" he asked me, and I could see that his foot was tapping nervously; he was just making conversation, wanting the minutes to pass so he could be out there singing.

The stage was eventually readied; the Chantays, whose big hit had been the instrumental "Pipeline," opened the show ("Surf music is alive and well in San Diego!" the lead guitarist called out, with an absence of unalloyed conviction), and then came Dick Dale, and I sat with Jan on the baseball bench as the Surfaris sang their hits "Wipeout" and "Surfer Joe," and finally it was time for the headliners.

We sang on the back of the truck between the pitcher's mound and the outfield, and at one point Gary grabbed my arm and had me look at one of the overlarge stadium scoreboards.

It was the kind that can show live video. There we were. We were on the field, and our electronic image was high above the field, and just to make certain I was seeing it right, I jerked the neck of my guitar sharply. Sure enough, up on the scoreboard screen, the bigger version of the guitar jerked at the same time.

The Jan standing next to me, and the giant Jan on the scoreboard, sang:

He passed me at Doheny, then I started to swerve,
When I pulled her out there we were, at Dead Man's Curve. . . .

I asked myself briefly how I had ever ended up here. A major-league baseball diamond. It may not have been a big deal to Dean. But it sure was to me.

Hagerstown, Maryland; Jackson, New Jersey; Klamath Falls, Oregon; Ashland, Kentucky. . . .

The band moved from town to town as the summer began. I joined them on weekends when I could get away from Chicago, and the next time I met up with them was in Madison, Wisconsin, where a show at the Dane County Coliseum had been booked.

"Five hundred dollars is five hundred dollars, as many times as you can multiply it," David Logeman, in a pair of shorts and a muscle T-shirt, said to me as we crossed John Nolen Drive on foot to take a look at the arena.

That was how much each man in the Jan and Dean band was paid: five hundred dollars each performance. I tried not to show how surprised I was by the paucity of the payday. At least it seemed low to me: to play drums for a name band, as David did, to play guitar, as Phil and Chris and Randell did, and to earn only five hundred dollars for a night's work . . . and that didn't even take into consideration the fact that sometimes it was three complete days out of their lives for that five hundred dollars: one day to fly to the Midwest or the South or the East Coast from California, one day to do the show, one day to fly back.

"It adds up, during summers when we have a lot of gigs," David said. "Dean actually pays pretty well—a lot of bands pay their musicians less than that." Dean and Jan, David said, divided, in some manner, everything that was left over from the main fee after paying the musicians and the travel expenses; the backup guys weren't exactly sure just how much money the two principals were able to net, and knew instinctively not to ask. But no one was getting rich. Of that, David said, he was sure.

"Jan and Dean are out here because they have to be," he said. "This isn't some pleasure trip for them, recapturing old times. It's their living."

Inside the cavernous coliseum, Dean was already on the bare stage, looking around. "I have to go do a radio interview," he said to us. "Please—don't tell Jan."

"He doesn't know?" I asked.

"Radio is what really works in getting people to the shows," Dean said. "I'm more effective doing the interviews by myself. If Jan knows I'm going, he wants to come along. So don't say anything to him."

A couple of old friends of the band—Ray Underwood and Steve Moris were their names—had come to Madison with their girlfriends.

"You ladies want to do us a favor?" Dean said to the girlfriends.

"Sure," one of them said.

"Take Bob shopping and get him some stage shirts," Dean said.

Then, to me:

"I told you last year—I don't want to see your button-down shirts onstage anymore. It's supposed to look like a beach party, not an accountants' convention."

They drove me to a mall about five miles away, and after some false starts we found a store that had a rack full of shirts that might have been designed for men aspiring to be the jovial toast of the neighborhood Sunday barbecue, circa 1953. They would have to do, at least for now; I bought two.

In the car on the way back to the hotel we tuned the radio to WOLX, Oldies 94.9. Sam Cooke's smoother-than-goosefeathers voice was crooning: *Another Saturday night, and I ain't got nobody. . . .* When the song ended, the disc jockey said:

"Continuing with our *special* guest in the studio now—Dean Torrence, half of the *great* Jan and Dean, is with us today . . . Dean, we were asking you before that last song, Jan's here in Madison with you for the *big* concert at the coliseum, isn't he?"

"Oh, of course, Jan's very excited about the show," Dean said. "He said to say hello to you guys—he has some fan mail he's working on answering back at the hotel, and he said he was sorry he couldn't come over to the studio today, but he looks forward to seeing all your listeners at the concert."

You've got to work the territory. Willy Loman understood it, and Dean understood it: a salesman on the road must nurture his accounts.

"Why don't *you* introduce this next song for us, Dean?" the disc jockey said.

Dean's voice said: "We got the idea to record 'Surf City' when we were talking to our friend Brian Wilson. . . ."

The song commenced: *Two girls for every boy. . . .*

In the car, two girls, one boy and two new and garish shirts sped toward the Sheraton, while Jan and Dean, their voices youthful and untroubled, serenaded us from the dashboard.

I knocked on Gary Griffin's door a few hours before showtime.

He had a pair of glasses on, and a book in his hand—a hardcover biography of George Gershwin.

"Come on in," he said. "I've just been lying around with this all afternoon."

One of his favorite songs to sing solo onstage was an old Fats Domino hit, "I'm Ready," a roisterous, up-tempo tune. Midsong there was a hard-driving couplet, sung almost as a swaggering boast:

Talking on the phone is not my speed,
Don't send me no letter, 'cause I can't read. . . .

It was a longstanding and cardinal conceit of much of rock and roll: a determined posture that the niceties of the cultured world—intellectual discourse, the value of the written word, the linear exchange of ideas— have meager value. From the earliest days of the music, the singers seemed to understand that there wasn't much to be gained by admitting there may have been a loftier element to their inner lives.

Don't send me no letter, 'cause I can't read. . . .

"This is really a pretty good book," Gary said. "I've always wanted to know more about Gershwin."

Fellow keyboardists, I supposed. Fats Domino was in the brotherhood, too.

"Did you listen to Dean on the radio?" I asked.

"Nah, I've heard it a million times before," Gary said. "He pretends not to care about it. But he really works at it. I don't know why he doesn't want any of us to know how much it matters to him that people come to the shows."

My phone rang just after three A.M.

The concert had been a success: more than five thousand people in the coliseum, two encores. I'd leaned into "Dance, Dance, Dance"; Chris Farmer, with seeming approval—but with him there was no way of really knowing—said, "Man, you bounced your vocals off the back walls."

Now, in the hours between midnight and dawn, the phone on the night table was ringing, and I grasped for it, managed a weak "Hello" . . . and heard Jan's voice.

"Where are you?" he said.

"Jan?" I said. "What time is it?"

"Did you leave?" he said.

"What are you talking about?" I said.

"You're on my TV," he said.

"I'm not on your TV, Jan," I said. "I'm right here."

"Turn to Channel 32," he said. "I thought you left."

I fumbled for the channel zapper, clicked the television set on, found Channel 32 . . . and indeed, saw myself, in a coat and tie.

Earlier in the week, I had done an interview with one of the national cable channels about a book I had written concerning Michael Jordan. Apparently the channel was rerunning its weeknight programming at odd hours over the weekend.

"I didn't leave, Jan," I said. "That's an old show. What are you doing up so late?"

"I don't sleep so well," he said.

"You've got to learn to take your phone off the hook when you go to bed," Chris said.

We were on our way to Dane County Regional Airport in two cabs. Jan, Dean and David Logeman were in the one following us.

"What if there's an important call?" I said.

"I'm telling you," Chris said, "if you don't take your phone off the hook, then you can't complain if Jan calls."

"I think he may be taking too much of his pain medicine," Gary said. "He seems really confused these last few days."

"The poor guy," Chris said. "I took one of his bags to his room last night after the show. And he tried to tip me five dollars."

"No," Phil said.

"Yes," Chris said. "I stand beside him on the stage every night playing guitar, and I come to his room and he thinks I'm a bellman."

We passed a body of water. The cabdriver said:

"That's Lake Monona. Where Otis Redding died."

On December 10, 1967, Redding, on tour with a show booked into Madison, was aboard a twin-engine Beechcraft that went into the lake in bad weather, killing him and members of his touring band. He was twenty-six years old. For all his galvanizing talent, he had never had a record in the Top Forty. But three days before his death, he had recorded a new single: "(Sittin' On) The Dock of the Bay." In the wake of the publicity about the fatal accident, the record was rushed out and went almost immediately to Number One.

"What do you think would have happened to his career if he hadn't been on that plane?" I asked.

"If he'd lived?" Chris said. "He'd probably be out here with us, eating the free breakfast buffets at the Hampton Inns."

We looked at the surface of the water. I don't know if the others were thinking about Jan, and the vagaries of happenstance. By their silence, I guessed that they were.

Not the kind of thought you want to linger on on a sublime summer morning.

"Hey, Gary," Phil said. "Where was that cheerleaders' convention you played at?"

"Before you joined the band?" Gary said. "South Bend. Notre Dame."

Lake Monona was already in the rearview mirror.

"Did they wear their uniforms to the show?" Phil asked.

"Oh, yeah," Gary said.

Dean was in his underwear in a trailer behind the stage at the Elkhart, Indiana, County Fair.

We were in Goshen, a town of twenty-three thousand in Amish country; earlier in the day we had checked in at the Carlton Lodge, a cozy place on Route 33 with the feel of a chalet, all rough cedar and fieldstone. We had been getting very settled-in there, but now it was nighttime and we were at the fairgrounds.

A cooler filled with Budweiser and soda pop was in the corner of the trailer; this would be our dressing room.

Chris walked in and said to Dean, "Someone wants to take some pictures of you and Jan." So Dean stood up, pulled on his pants, and walked out into the darkness of the summer night.

The grandstand was packed; Jan and Dean coming to Goshen was a major event. Onstage at this moment was the opening act, Brian Hyland. Every time we played with one of these singers or bands, I was seeing the invisible parentheses after their names—the parentheses that contained their hit songs. To me, he was Brian Hyland ("Itsy Bitsy Teenie Weenie Yellow Polka Dot Bikini," "Sealed With a Kiss"). He was about a minute into that first one as Dean looked in the backstage area for Jan.

. . . that she wore for the first time today. . . .

Jan was standing with some local photographers. About a hundred fans behind a thick rope were straining to see him, pushing for position. Dean draped his arm across Jan's shoulders, the photographers clicked away—the ones with us inside the rope, the fans with cameras on the other side of the rope—and for that moment the two men were, for all purposes, one person: Jananddean, an entity, three words said as one word. They were both smiling as if they didn't have an apprehension in the world. As if nothing in their lives was at all complicated.

I could hear, from the far side of the rope, some voices saying:

"That's the new one."

I turned to look. They were pointing at me.

As soon as I made eye contact, they waved.

The new one.

What a nice thing to be, at a point in your life when you had sort of given up on ever being such a thing again. The new one. What a gift.

They kept waving, so I waved back. The last of the flashes from the cameras flared, and Dean took his arm from Jan's shoulder. The two men separated; Jan sat on a metal folding chair by the stage, Dean returned to the trailer. The moment was gone.

The reigning queen of the Elkhart County Fair, wearing a sash and a tiara, had a seat of honor in the front row.

I could see her from a little wooden pagoda next to the stage, where I waited until it was time for Dean to call me on. That's how we were doing it; halfway or two-thirds of the way through each concert, he would beckon to me, and I would come onstage for the rest of the show.

Phil was singing the lead on "Summertime Blues," the vintage Eddie Cochran rocker, and the queen of the fair knew every word, even though the Cochran hit had already turned into an oldie many years before she was born. I could see her mouth moving beneath the tiara:

. . . like to help you, son, but you're too young to vote. . . .

Behind me was a second trailer—smaller than ours—and in the blackness beyond the stage I could make out through its windows an illuminated interior, with Brian Hyland ("Sealed with a Kiss") standing at a table and settling up with the promoter. Dean motioned for me, and then I was singing "Dance, Dance, Dance," trying to see individual faces out in the darkness, wondering if this night would end up, many years from now, being a summer memory for any of the people. The night someone fell in love, the night someone broke up . . . and the way they would recall it was that it was the night Jan and Dean came to town.

Later, back at the hotel, hungry, I walked across Route 33 and went into a McDonald's.

"You guys were great," a woman with her three daughters said.

I realized I was still wearing my stage shirt.

She had a camera with her, and told me she had taken pictures of the concert. I asked her to send me some, just so I could know for sure that all of this was really happening.

In the morning the countywide daily newspaper—the *Elkhart Truth*—said in its review that I "didn't do badly at all."

I cut it out, of course, and purchased additional copies. The story said that fifty-five hundred people had been in attendance. Being told that I didn't do badly—like being defined as the new guy—was something that, for whatever reason, felt quite welcome. And no one could ever say it wasn't true. It was in the *Truth*.

In a roadside Iowa restaurant called the Country Kitchen, in Des Moines, Dean was scrutinizing the laminated menu and talking about litigation.

"I heard that Mike Love is suing Brian Wilson," he said.

We were having an early dinner—he, Gary, Phil and I—before going over to the Iowa State Fair. Dean, as he decided what to eat, was saying that the lead singer of the Beach Boys was suing the former leader of the group. Brian Wilson—brilliant, haunted, often referred to, almost by rote, as a genius—had stopped regularly performing with the band decades before. Now, according to Dean, Love—Wilson's cousin—was going to court claiming that he had written or helped to write some of the songs that Wilson had received credit, and payment, for.

Gary Griffin, choosing to pretend not to hear, and thus eschew mealtime discussion of courthouse conflict, said that he was considering ordering a country-fried steak.

"I've thought about doing that," Dean said.

"Eating a country-fried steak?" Gary said.

"No," Dean said. "Suing to get credit."

"For what?" I said.

" 'Surf City,' " he said. "The writing credit went to Jan and to Brian Wilson. I found the original handwritten lyrics. The way they were written, someone wrote 'I got a thirty-four panel truck and they call it a woodie.' Then 'panel truck' is crossed out and my handwriting replaces it with 'wagon.' The original lyric says 'two swingin' girls for every guy.' My handwriting changes 'girls' to 'honeys.'

" 'Not very cherry,' I don't know about," he said. "But that looks like Brian's handwriting. It sounds like him."

I wasn't sure I needed to be knowing this, in the Country Kitchen on a Midwestern sundown. I thought of that first time I heard "Surf City," as Dave Frasch and I backed out of his driveway on the way to the tennis tournament. Such a perfect song, such a harkening of summer and all its pleasures. If the disc jockey that day had somehow interrupted, and started talking about cross-outs of lyrics, of future legal disputes over snippets of words about cars and beautiful young women . . .

We ate our supper. Halfway through peanut-butter-and-chocolate pie dessert, Dean said, "I've got to iron some stage shirts." We walked the two blocks back to our motel on a gravel shoulder next to the traffic on Northeast Fourteenth Street.

It was the summer of the terrible floods in Iowa—of sandbags and fear and homes destroyed. For nineteen full days, the people of Des Moines had no drinking water.

There had been rumors that the unthinkable would happen—that the Iowa State Fair would be canceled.

But it wasn't. "Iowans did not have a summer this year," Kathie Swift, an executive with the fair's organizing committee, said. "This is our chance to have a summer."

We pulled onto the fairgrounds in a white van. The opening acts had already begun; Gary and David and I climbed some stairs at the rear of the stage, and . . .

What we saw was close to breathtaking. The biggest grandstand I have ever encountered—towering, and wide, more like a trick photograph of a regular grandstand blown up to two- or three-times standard grandstand size—was teeming, with not a seat to be had. It was swaying—the people were standing and clapping and moving, and the grandstand moved with them.

Little Eva, in a cocktail dress, was singing her romping hit "The Loco-Motion." There was a horn section behind her, and a portly master of ceremonies in a neon-hued tuxedo—this felt like an old Alan Freed rock-and-roll stage show, or, more accurately, like an old CinemaScope movie about an Alan Freed stage show. I think it was the horns, and the guy in the tux—there was a frenzied sense of scale to this, of willful bigness.

Little Eva wasn't so little anymore, but she was magnificent, with a throbbing, throaty voice:

Everybody's doin' a brand-new dance now,
Come on, baby, do the Loco-Motion. . . .

She was perspiring and winded and a bit unsteady on her feet as, to the roars from the lurching grandstand, she finished her set and walked past us to the stairs. A man passed her going the other way—to the front of the stage—and the M.C. yowled into his microphone, "Ladies and gentlemen, Bobby Lewis!"

I leaned toward Gary and said loudly into his ear, so he could hear me above the crowd:

"Does this mean that we can't do 'Do You Wanna Dance'?"

He shouted to my ear: "'Do You Wanna Dance' was Bobby Freeman. This is Bobby Lewis. He's 'Tossin' and Turnin'."

Indeed he was. He sang:

I couldn't sleep at alllll last night,
Just a-thinkin' of you. . . .

What affected me the most that show was something that happened when the singer right before us on the bill was on the stage. He was Lou Christie ("Two Faces Have I," "Lightin' Strikes," Rhapsody in the Rain"). For his encore he borrowed a ballad originally sung by the Association.

It was the sweet, slow "Never My Love." The thousands in the giant grandstand were still on their feet. But it was what I saw in front of the grandstand, below the stage and off to the side, that was so splendorous.

Twenty or thirty couples—people in their thirties and forties and fifties—had come down to dance. They were waltzing, really—there was no word to describe it better. The husbands and wives held each other, and for all the awfulness of this Iowa summer, at least for these few minutes the awfulness was over, pushed aside.

From where we were standing on the stage, waiting to go on next, we could see the nighttime panorama of the fairgrounds: the lighted rides on the ten-acre midway cranking high in the air, then swooping down toward ground level; the people heading toward the twenty acres of agricultural machinery on display; the farm families who had come to take part in the array of livestock exhibits, having brought their sheep and cattle and swine and horses to Des Moines, almost fourteen thousand animals in all.

"The fair is always a reunion for the people of Iowa," Kathie Swift had said. "This year, though, it means more than usual."

Lou Christie was finishing up his song:

Never my love,
Never my love. . . .

And in front of him the couples waltzed. Full of summer, dancing in the starlight.

In the van on the way back to where we were staying, Dean was upset. You could read it in his silence.

We'd had a fine time during our show—the sound system was clean and cranked up, the sight of the ever-undulating grandstand hypnotic, the air crisp and warm—but something had gone wrong.

David Logeman had predicted it, even as we had been listening to Lou Christie sing that end-of-set song of his.

Christie had allowed his final phrase to echo:

Never my love. . . .

And, on the darkened stage, he had knelt. I'd assumed that was it.

"Watch," Logeman had said to me, standing with the rest of us with his drumsticks in his hand, waiting to go on. "He'll come back three or four times. He does it every time."

And—Logeman had seen it before—Christie did just that. He milked the encore, pretending to depart, then returning again and again to reprise the end of the song.

So, when we eventually took the stage, things were running late. Jan and Dean were the headliners. But when, after the last song of our main set, "Surfin' U.S.A.," we departed the stage to a standing ovation, the

M.C., instead of calling us back out, thanked the crowd for coming and sent them home. Apparently there was a curfew.

Dean, pacing behind the stage, his guitar still around his neck, pretended not to care. The M.C. himself left the stage; Dean said to him, feigning casualness: "I thought you wanted us to do an encore." The M.C. shrugged and pointed at his watch.

Now, in the van, Dean just stared out the window. Chris, deducing his mood, said to him:

"It was the time situation. I asked the promoter straight out. 'Lou Christie gets to stretch "Never My Fucking Love," and Jan and Dean don't get an encore?' They let the time get away from them."

The van dropped us at the hotel—a low-slung, German-themed place called the Bavarian Inn, with flower boxes mounted outside the windows—and, out of nowhere, something salvaged the night.

As we walked through the cramped lobby, Chris asked the desk clerk if there was a room in which to lock our equipment until morning. She came around the desk, led him down a short storage hallway, and unlocked a door for him.

For some reason, in the little hallway there was a battered wooden upright piano.

Chris said to the rest of us, "What do you want to hear?"

I said, "How about 'Don't Worry, Baby'?"

"Gary can play that," Chris said.

So Gary sat on the piano bench, and began the first notes of that lovely, plaintive Beach Boys song. The chords, reverberating against the walls of the skinny hallway, were rich and full.

All of us stood around the piano, still in our stage clothes.

Dean was the first to sing:

Well, it's been building up inside of me for oh, I don't know how long. . . .

One by one, the rest of us joined in.

The men in the band all had graceful, pitch-perfect voices; onstage I took this as a given, but here in the corridor of the hotel, with no guitars, no drums, just the piano, the clarity and range of those voices as they interlaced was even more conspicuous because the setting was not supposed to be a place for such a sound. It was a setting where you would more likely expect to hear a vacuum cleaner, or a maintenance man's hammer.

Don't worry, baby, everything will turn out all right. . . .

Gary kept playing and we all kept singing—no one was fooling around, each man was putting his all into it—and the desk clerk who had unlocked the storage room stood tentatively to the side, and then, as if she couldn't help herself, joined in:

Don't worry, baby. . . .

Gary nodded his approval at her as he played, not wanting her to feel embarrassed. She continued to sing the song with us; a security guard in uniform—he seemed to be assigned to the hotel during the late-night hours—heard us, and came into the hallway, and soon he was singing too:

Everything will turn out all right . . . .

There we stood, as midnight approached, knowing that when morning came we would be on our way to sing in yet another town.

Don't worry, baby. . . .

The journey was so full of music. It was the reason, and the context; the music was why we were here. Right now it was the only sound in the first-floor corridor of the Bavarian Inn, and though the hour was late and we all were tired, Gary made the song go on and on, and no one wanted to go to bed just yet, no one wanted the music to stop.

SIX

The man and woman sitting at the picnic table were by far the oldest people backstage.

This was in Eaton, Ohio, just before an outdoor show that was supposed to begin after dusk.

The members of the band seldom talked much about the lives they led away from the tour. Some had families. Some lived with girlfriends. Some were temporarily unattached. Dean, I knew, had a wife and a daughter; Jan, I was surprised to find out, was married: he had met a woman on a concert tour in Canada in 1990, they had hit it off, and were wed the next year. I had yet to meet Gertie Berry; she had not come to any of the concerts where I'd sung. Neither had the families or girlfriends of any of the other musicians. This was a boys club—Lost Boys, perhaps, but a boys club nonetheless.

It wasn't some permutation of what-happens-in-Vegas-stays-in-Vegas; it was almost the converse. This road world in which the band lived—the planes, the hotels, the shared meals—was like an alternative universe they had become accustomed to, a traveling cocoon they automatically entered whenever they left Los Angeles. They seemed to prefer to keep the two worlds separate.

So when Gary Griffin introduced me to the couple at the picnic table— his parents, Tom and Esther Griffin—it was an unusual moment on tour.

He had told me about his father. And when I had looked up the history . . .

Well, there are moments in life that humble you and leave you silent.

Tonight Mr. and Mrs. Griffin, who had driven over from their home in Cincinnati, were polite and friendly, and a little shy, as if they didn't want to intrude on their son's evening.

"Gary's told me all about you," Mrs. Griffin said to me as we arrived at the show. "We're so glad to meet you."

Mr. Griffin—he was seventy-seven—rose to shake my hand.

In 1942, in the months after the attack on Pearl Harbor, when all the war news from the Pacific seemed to be bad news for the United States, a decision was made: the one way to turn things around would be if American planes could somehow conduct a surprise bombing attack on the Japanese mainland.

But how? There were no U.S.-controlled airfields close enough to Japan.

The answer was the Doolittle Raiders. Sixteen specially modified B-25s under the command of Colonel James Doolittle, each bomber carrying a five-man crew, were assigned to take off for Japan from the deck of the USS *Hornet*. Returning to the carrier was an impossibility— no bomber had ever taken off from an aircraft carrier before, and there was no way the heavy B-25s could land on the deck. The Raiders were ordered to hit Tokyo and then try to make it to safety in China.

On the day of the raid—it came to be known as the Thirty Seconds Over Tokyo mission—there was a report that the U.S. task force had been spotted by the Japanese military. Originally the Raiders had thought they would have a four-hundred-mile flight to the Japanese mainland, with just enough fuel and virtually no margin of error; now they were ordered to take off from six hundred and forty miles away.

And—knowing they didn't have sufficient fuel—the Doolittle Raiders took off. As soon as they left the deck, the *Hornet* and its task force reversed course.

The Raiders bombed Tokyo, giving the American people their first ray of hope in the Pacific war—finally the United States was striking back. Eleven of the five-man crews had to bail out. Four more crews crash-landed. One plane landed in Russia, and its crew was taken prisoner and held for more than a year.

Two of the Raiders died as they bailed out. Eight others were captured by the Japanese; three were executed and five were sentenced to life in prison. One of the five died of starvation in a Japanese prison camp; the others endured forty months of mistreatment.

And here was Gary Griffin's dad, Tom Griffin. A Doolittle Raider. He had parachuted into China during a thunderstorm, had survived, and had then been sent back into the war.

"It looks like you boys should have a nice crowd tonight," Mr. Griffin said to me. "Everyone seems real excited to hear you."

I didn't even know what to say.

"That pumpkin pie fainted."

I had walked over to the Household Arts Building of the Preble County Fairgrounds. There were still a few minutes until our concert was to begin—the Eaton show was in conjunction with the Preble County Fair—so I decided to look around.

The woman pointing out that the pumpkin pie had fainted—she was saying this to her husband—was referring to one of the winning pieces of pastry in the fair's baking competition; the slice of pie did, in fact, appear to have collapsed in the heat, its blue ribbon attached to the plate beneath it.

The white-frame building was mostly empty of people, but it was full of winners. There was the winning bale of alfalfa, entered by Bill Rushbush of West Alexandria. The winning bale of clover, entered by Christine Howard of Somerville. The best chocolate pie—actually the "best chocolate pie baked from scratch"—entered by Shirley Fisher, also of West Alexandria, and the best tendersweet carrots, grown by Roger Gebhart of Lewisburg.

A woman representing the office of Ohio Auditor Thomas E. Ferguson sat at a table, ready to take entries in a free lottery that would award one flag (your choice of Ohio or United States) to the person whose name was drawn at the end of the fair.

I noticed one name that appeared on quite a few ribbons: Gib Harris, who, according to the tags, lived in the town of Eldorado. He had taken second in the alfalfa, had won an award for his shelled corn (displayed in a large jar), had done well in the wheat competition.

I was due onstage, but I was curious about Gib Harris and all his entries, and I made a vow to find him later. When I did, he told me he had been submitting entries to the Preble County Fair for more than twenty-five years. This year he had won eleven prizes.

"It's a lot of work, but it makes me feel proud when I win," Mr. Harris told me. "It makes me feel I've accomplished something in my life." He said that farming was hard and getting harder, and that the fair contests were a way to make him and his family feel that what they were doing was worthwhile. This year, he said, "My son got a first and second in corn and soybeans. My wife, Anna, baked the grand champion coffee cake. My daughter-in-law got a first in noodles."

There were no ceremonies to announce the winners, Mr. Harris said: "You just go look at your entries after the judging, and the ribbons tell you whether you've won." He said he kept his quarter-century of ribbons in a box, because he didn't know what else to do with them. "But my wife tells me she may make a quilt of them."

We all find our victories where we can. An hour or so later, onstage, Jan was into the part of "Dead Man's Curve" where he stops singing and delivers the spoken words:

Well, the last thing I remember, Doc, I started to swerve,
And then I saw the Jag slide into the curve.
I know I'll never forget that horrible sight,
I guess I found out for myself that everyone was right.

From the crowd, a voice of encouragement yelled out:
"We're glad you made it, Jan!"

With that, a wave of applause steadily built, and soon everyone was standing and cheering for Jan. He was beaming; for a moment, I thought he might cry, so appreciative did he appear to be.

Within seconds we were into the next songs. As Gary sang the lead on "Let's Dance," I saw someone doing exactly that: the woman from the Ohio auditor's flag-giveaway table. She had left the Household Arts Building, had come to the show, and now she was up on her feet and frolicking in the aisles to Gary's voice.

I looked to the side of the stage.

There was Gary's dad.

When I had read up on the history of the Doolittle raid, I had been especially stirred by the wording of the attack order, sent by Admiral William F. "Bull" Halsey from his command post on another ship, the USS *Enterprise*. Halsey had to have known that some of the raiders would not be coming back.

Launch planes. To Col. Doolittle and Gallant Command
Good Luck and God Bless You.

Tom Griffin stood by the side of the stage and basked in the applause that was directed at his son. Mr. Griffin had made it home from the war; he and his wife had had a boy. Our victories in this life come in any number of ways.

"They're going to have canoes full of shrimp," I said.

"What are you talking about?" Chris Farmer said.

We were in the first-floor bar of the Marriott in Greenville, South Carolina, with a waitress approaching. The band had played in Sacramento the night before, had left their hotel in California at four A.M., had taken three Delta Airlines flights across the country to get here, and, having just arrived in eighty-five-degree Carolina summer heat, looked like candidates for an intensive care ward.

"There was something in the paper about the event," I said. "There are these canoes set up around the property every year, and the canoes are filled with shrimp."

In an hour we would be going over to the Lawn and Lake Gala, an annual charity benefit that was a mainstay of Greenville society. I was telling them that there was no need to order food here at the hotel.

Gary, eyes red from lack of sleep, said, "Rule: Always eat now, even if you think there's going to be food later."

"I'll have a full rack of ribs," Chris said to the waitress.

"The newspaper said there will be ribs at the event," I said.

"Then we'll have more ribs," Chris said.

Phil Bardowell hadn't come on the trip; he was at his high school reunion—his tenth, which made the rest of us think about how less far along life's path he was than us. Randell Kirsch was subbing for him on guitar. He, too, ordered the ribs, and plopped something onto the table.

"What is that, Randell?" Chris, irritable from the day's travel, said.

"Sea salt," Randell said.

"You carry your own?" Chris said.

Randell nodded.

Chris shook his head in disgust.

"According to the paper, this party is on a two-thousand-acre estate," I said. "The year John Denver played, they built a forty-foot-high replica of the Grand Tetons. The stage is next to a lake."

"Sounds great," Randell said.

"Sounds like mosquitoes," Gary said.

Mosquitoes it was.

And, as advertised, canoes brimming with shrimp.

I had never before seen a canoe used as a serving platter, but these canoes—full-sized, big enough for two adult canoeists—were propped on wooden sawhorses and were absolutely overflowing with the pinkest, plumpest shrimp a person could ever desire. The gala was being held on the estate of Pat Hartness, one of Greenville's wealthiest and most prominent industrialists; we must have driven through thirty or forty acres of the property—I think we saw a private airfield on it—before we even caught sight of the house.

Jan and Dean might be legendary—the publicity for the gala had used that word again—but here, there was no question about it: if they were legendary, they were legendary hired help.

"Look," Gary said. "We aren't even the main act."

He was pointing across the way, to a dizzyingly tall series of light towers that had been erected next to a full-sized Las Vegas–style stage. This was for country singer Barbara Mandrell, who would be the evening's headline entertainer. The advance publicity had said she would bring twenty-eight dancers and backup singers, and her own sound system. When her show was finished, we would play on a smaller stage, on the other side of a lake; the two thousand partygoers would dance to our music on the Hartness's tennis courts.

As the sun set and then disappeared we mingled with the guests as we ate chicken and cole slaw and baked beans and our second consignments of ribs of the day. In the newly arrived darkness we stood with the audience as Barbara Mandrell, in a sparkly red dress, belted out:

I was country when country wasn't cool. . . .

"Where's Jan and Dean?" I asked Randell.

"At the hotel," he said. "We don't play until ten-thirty."

There were booths with waiters handing out cans of cold beer, so we took some. A line of porta-potties seemed to stretch beyond the horizon.

"Any time you think you have a bad night and ask yourself why you're doing this," I said to Chris, "think of the guys who'll come here in the morning to clean up the toilets."

"Don't say that," Chris said. "That may be us, in three years."

We soundchecked our instruments on the tennis-court stage while Barbara Mandrell was winding up her show.

The air was still broiling and humid, late into the night. The technicians assigned to us were adjusting the stage lights; one light, turned up to full intensity and heat, was right above Gary's head as he tested his keyboard.

"Could you turn that lamp down?" he yelled to the light booth. "I feel like I'm an Arby's."

We could see and hear the Mandrell concert—her colossal stage on the other side of the private lake was like a mansion on a hill, and we were like poor kids living down in the bottoms, looking up longingly at it.

She was into her big finish, designed to score with this crowd. First came "God Bless America." Then, as if that were not enough, "The Battle Hymn of the Republic."

We stared across the water, and listened to her:

Mine eyes have seen the glory . . .

"Oh, this is going to be just great," Chris said. "We get to follow this with 'The New Girl in School.'"

There are certain less than readily discernible advantages to being the hired help.

We got started tardily because of the Mandrell show; it was almost eleven by the time we sang our first song. As we took to the stage—Jan and Dean had been dropped off by a van from the Marriott just before showtime—we could see that most of the people from the Mandrell concert had come over, and that many of them had been served more than generously at the various bar stations.

We were merely a diversion, as, I supposed, we were every night. That's what Jan and Dean were paid to be, whether in big arenas or at private parties. Although, as we finished "Dance, Dance, Dance" after having invited people up on the stage to do just that, a woman hugged me and thanked me and—seeming to mean it—said: "This is such a terrific night." And perhaps it was, in which case being a diversion wasn't such a bad thing.

But it was what happened a little later that made me understand some truths anew.

Contractually, Jan and Dean had agreed to do two sets. Because it was so late, though, and because most of the partygoers left after our first show, the organizers said that Jan and Dean themselves could go back to the hotel if they wished—only a hundred or so people remained, and the organizers said that the backup guys could do the last set on our own.

Which we did. More than a few of the guests still present had that end-of-the-night look, a little glassy-eyed and noticeably tottery on their feet; Chris told me to go ahead and turn my guitar up—I sensed that it was only when Jan and Dean were onstage that he felt protective and prideful about keeping each note flawless—and he signaled for me to sing lead on "Pretty Woman."

After that we slowed it down and sang the sad old Ritchie Valens ballad "Donna," and on the tennis-court dance floor some men and women were embracing; some, without partners, wandered aimlessly; some kissed; some turned their faces away from proffered kisses. . . .

And it was as if we were shielded. Whatever matters of the heart might have been on display down below us, whatever twinges of melancholy, or stabs at happiness, whatever slivers of rejection, pangs of hurt or hopefulness might have been unfolding, there was an essential buffer between that and us. The stage—the invisible wall at the front of it—provided the barrier.

It might not have been true; the supposed distance the stage afforded might have been a lie—as we looked at those men and women, the joyous ones and the dispirited, we might in our own lives have been feeling close approximations of what they were feeling. But there was no way for them to know that. Up on the stage, behind the barrier, we were presumed to be immune.

I knew the syndrome well. A lifetime of taking notes for stories— using a notepad to pretend, at places of great emotion, that I was at that place but not of that place—had made me more than familiar with the phenomenon. It was a useful illusion, as long as the people on the other side didn't see through it.

We sang:

I had a girl, Donna was her name. . . .

The couples danced, and hugged. One man stormed away from the woman he had been holding. One woman, being held, stifled sobs.

. . . since she left me, I've never been the same . . .

We could see it all. But I don't think they understood we were seeing it. We were, after all, just the hired help.

On old Route 22, the William Penn Highway, America as it must have looked before the interstates batted its eyes at us along every mile.

We were on our way from the airport in Pittsburgh to a Pennsylvania town called Ebensburg. We passed the Rock Springs Roller Rink; Allegheny Records Storage and Destruction Service; Dea's Diner; Willow Terrace Garden and Groceries.

The outlet roads were lined with pebbles. Deb-Tone Printing offered its services to those in the vicinity who might need them; Long's Taxidermy operated out of a trailer. DO NOT PASS signs periodically came into view on the narrow highway, to be followed by other signs offering LIVE BAIT — NIGHT CRAWLERS, and BEAGLES FOR SALE, and JUMBO NECTARINES.

It made me wonder: How do some of these places stay in business? But, then, perhaps there were people who wondered the same thing about the very enterprise that was the reason we were heading across this highway: the Jan and Dean business. Two young men had recorded "Surf City" more than thirty years before, a song that lasted only two minutes and forty-one seconds, but it had endured far longer than that. It had lingered in the air, and had gotten us to here, on this road on this day.

We passed Russ's Pit Barbecue, and the Pink Cow Restaurant, and a sign with a single word — SEWING — and a local telephone number. The town of New Alexander promoted itself with the slogan "The Choice for Me — Drug Free!", as if a boast, and we saw The Sheepskin Shop ("Vests, Mittens, Slippers") and a placard declaring Indiana County to be "the Christmas Tree Capital of the World," followed in quick succession by one announcing the immediate availability of "40 Acres, 11 Dwellings."

A carpet shop offered "Delivery to Your Door," and so did we. The door we pulled up to this time was at a Howard Johnson's Motor Inn, the kind with, in actuality, two doors on each guest room, one door opening into the parking lot, one into the interior hallway. I hadn't seen a HoJo Inn in quite a few years, but apparently the affiliation was considered an upgrade for this property; the old wooden sign, discarded on the ground out back but not yet hauled away, indicated this was formerly the Ebensburg Motel.

When we checked in the clerk gave us not only our keys, but zappers for the television sets. He said they tended to be stolen if he left them in the rooms. Above the front desk, arranged festively, were old Jan and Dean album covers. "This will be exciting for the town," the clerk said.

"Oh, we're just one big happy family," Dean said.

The weathercaster from WTAJ television in Altoona had come to the Cambria County Fairgrounds to do a live remote on the late-afternoon news. He was on the stage as we did a run-through; as he asked Dean about life on the road with the band, we played and sang "Do It Again."

It's automatic when I think of old friends. . . .

"We just love it out here," Dean said. There was something about his speaking voice—it was a built-in uptick toward the end of most phrases, I don't think he could do a thing about it even if he wanted to—that always had a propensity to make him sound sarcastic whether he was trying to be or not. Today I couldn't tell.

. . . let's get together and do it again. . . .

The weathercaster turned toward his cameraman and, over our re-hearsal vocals, said the night should be windy but dry, and urged everyone watching him to come. On the way to the fairgrounds we had heard on the radio that an inmate named William Robert Armstrong, twenty-three, had escaped from the Cambria County Prison earlier in the day and was thought to still be at large. I didn't know if that would affect the attendance.

There was little likelihood of shrimp-filled canoes here. It was two days after Labor Day; the air was turning cool, the dingy, hardscrabble fairgrounds were scantly populated.

"School's started," Jason "Thumper" Silvasky, nineteen, told me as I walked around, those two words meaning: classrooms are bad for business. Wearing cutoff jeans and a red Budweiser cap, he sat on a stepladder in front of a he-man machine—one of those carnival devices that propels an object upward when someone smacks the target at the bottom with a wooden mallet. Thumper said he made his living by traveling to carnivals and county fairs around the country, serving as barker and proprietor for this particular attraction.

"Come on, man, I need a bell-ringer!" he called out, but right now there were no takers.

His machine was marked off with various levels of manliness: PUSS, WIMP, NERD, PUNK, BULLY, HE-MAN, HULK. Two hits for a dollar.

"I need a bell-ringer!" he called again, then: "Give you a free bandana just for trying."

A woman in a T-shirt with the inscription PERFECT BITCH glanced over, but did not approach. She was with her toddlers, a girl and a boy.

It was just after six P.M. "The first week of October, I go home," Thumper said. At Red's Lunch stand on the midway, all fourteen chairs—thirteen metal, one wooden—sat empty at the moment, waiting for the nighttime diners who might or might not arrive. Things were looking up: at the Berry-Go-Round, a ride for the youngest fairgoers, a line had formed, children waiting to twirl in cars painted to look like strawberries. I stepped up to Deedy's Dime Pitch, tried to make the dime I tossed stay put atop a glass ash tray, but it didn't have a chance. It skipped harmlessly into the dust, from where the proprietor retrieved it and banked it. "Getting chilly," she said.

When we strode onstage to sing, the place was full. The socialites in South Carolina, the weekday attendees at the down-at-the-heels fair here: all of them loved this music just the same. They sang along and smiled in the night. Two minutes and forty-one seconds, the record of "Surf City" had lasted. Here all the people were.

On High Street in downtown Ebensburg—the town had only three thousand or so residents—there was a restaurant with a light in its front window on an otherwise shadowy, shut-down-for-the-night block. The promoter of the show had arranged for the place to stay open for us, and a long table had been set up.

So we ate spaghetti and salads, and unwound as the hours passed; the show that had just ended had been loose and playful. Chris had meandered over to my microphone from his side of the stage and we had sung "I Saw Her Standing There" together; on "Barbara Ann" Dean threw an arm over my shoulder as we did a verse of the song as a duet. We were called back for a second encore; it was "Fun, Fun, Fun," and halfway through the song Dean pointed at me and said into his microphone to the audience: "Oh, he's playing in tune! Watch out!"

Now we were having our dinner, and on the way out of the restaurant Jan caught sight of something—a refrigerated glass display case with desserts inside. He asked the owner to wrap him a piece of coconut cream pie, and a piece of homemade chocolate fudge, to go; he wanted to eat them in his room back at the motel.

He carried them in a paper sack, and as we hit the sidewalk he showed me the bag and said, a little sheepishly: "This may make you die. But you might as well have fun in your life."

We waited for the van to pull up, and Dean looked down the darkened street of the little town—there was a furniture store, a law office, a gift shop of some sort—and said to me:

"This is what I like so much. Look at this. This is so unlike where I live. Sometimes I ask myself how it ever came to be that I find myself on a street like this, on a night like this."

We both knew the answer. Two minutes and forty-one seconds. That's how this came to be.

In the morning we turned our zappers back in at the front desk.

The news in town was that the escaped convict had been captured. The police had found him in the borough of Nanty Glo, nearly fifteen miles from the prison. He was seen at a coal-refuse pit near the Polish Legion Club, and was said to have surrendered without incident. All was right with the world again.

"Would you mind?" the desk clerk said to Jan and Dean.

He pulled down one of the old albums with which he had decorated the wall above the check-in counter.

Dean signed the jacket of the album, then Jan. "Thank you," the desk clerk said, and put it back where it had been.

As we departed I looked at it, with the signatures now covering the old color photo of the two of them, Jan so handsome and unharmed.

In Allegan, Michigan, during soundcheck, I was onstage by myself for a few minutes while the others were unloading their instruments from the vans.

The setting was so inviting—big stage, outdoor venue, cheerleaders practicing their high-kick routines in front of the seats that would be full of people within a few hours—that I turned my amplifier as high as its knob would twist and decided to unabashedly go for it.

I roared into "Louie Louie," the song I always felt most at ease with when warming up. The classic chord progression: A, D, E minor. Dah-*dah*-dah-dah, dah-dah, *dah*-dah-dah, dah-dah . . .

Just like the Kingsmen. That's how I was feeling. I roamed the front of the stage, a Kingsman at heart: Dah-*dah*-dah-dah, dah-dah. . . .

I was really into it, chopping the air with the neck of the guitar, hearing the song blast out, and I turned sideways and in the periphery of my vision I could see some guys standing on the back edge of the stage.

And I wanted to disappear. To evaporate.

It was the Kingsmen.

I'd forgotten that they were playing on the bill with us.

To say that they had been observing me with some amusement would be an understatement. I could feel my face flushing.

"I'm sorry," I said to them. "It's just that it was the first song I ever learned."

"Don't worry about it," the lead guitarist of the Kingsmen said. "It's the first song everyone learns."

I'd had trouble finding Allegan on the map. I had flown to Grand Rapids; the band had arrived the night before. We were staying at a Comfort Inn in Plainwell, halfway between Grand Rapids and Kalamazoo.

The hotel didn't have a restaurant of its own, but there was a Big Boy right across the parking lot. I called over to see if I could pick up some food and bring it back.

"Are you with the band?" the waitress who answered the phone said.
I said that I was.

"Just tell me what you want to eat," she said. "I'll bring it over. Some of us were hanging out with you guys last night."

So I placed my order, and in ten minutes or so there was a knock at the door. When I opened it I found the cutest waitress, clad in a Big Boy uniform, looking so sparkling that I wouldn't have been surprised if she washed her face fifty times a day. She just glowed.

She gave me the food; I gave her the money.

As I was closing the door she flashed an incandescent smile and said: "Say hi to Phil."

Oh.

The members of a classic-car club sat in their idling machines in front of the hotel, ready to drive us to Allegan for the show. The engines purred like healthy and impatient lion cubs.

The theme of the night was Drive-In Days, and these men and their autos were part of it. Each of us was assigned to our own car—there were high-performance sports cars, and souped-up hot rods. The sight of the Big Boy sign as we pulled away, the sudden nip in the air as the sun went down . . . this had an end-of-summer texture to it, and I thought of Thumper Silvasky, the midway barker, and wondered at what county fair he might find himself working tonight.

The men taking us to the show in their shiny cars were wearing purple-and-white Drive-In Days T-shirts, each of which featured a drawing of a billboard with a picture of Jan and Dean on it. Commemorating the evening, ordaining it to future dresser-drawer nostalgia before it had even happened.

This all felt like the last night before school starts again, hanging out with your buddies one more time, knowing that something is ending. When we got to the show we could see that members of the Plainwell High School varsity football team had come wearing their blue jerseys without shoulder pads—number 30, number 50, number 35—autumn heroes in repose, letting themselves be flirted with by the same cheerleaders we'd seen warming up before.

A light rain commenced as the Kingsmen started their set. They were singing the Rolling Stones' "Paint It, Black," and I worried that the show would be washed out by the time it was our turn to play, and that our final night of summer would be a no-go.

Dean and Chris pulled up to the stage in a rental car only ten minutes or so before we went on; they had skipped soundcheck and had spent the day in Ann Arbor at the Michigan-Notre Dame game, buying tickets from scalpers outside Michigan Stadium, then had hurried over here. I tried to envision Dean at the game, anonymous in the midst of more than a hundred thousand other spectators, the entertained and not the entertainer. I had only seen him when he was the main attraction, the one being stared at from the seats.

The drizzle stayed just that and nothing more until we got onstage. Soon it strengthened, but few in the stands left. As we sang "Help Me, Rhonda" I watched the rope-straight lines of rain cascade down through the bright cones of illumination from the spotlights that were aimed at us, as people danced and didn't seem to at all mind getting soaked.

Well, Rhonda you look so fine. . . .

We'd come to town and had made something transpire—this night, this music—that, however modest in its aspirations, had not been here the night before, and would not be here tomorrow; that, alone, had to have some value, had to count for something. Didn't it?

In the steady shower we made it all the way through to the encore, and as we were leaving the stage, my ears still ringing, I put my hand on Dean's shoulder—his surf shirt wet from the downpour—and said: "Thanks for the summer."

He said, "It has been a great summer, hasn't it?"

Then:

"The thing about summers is, they just keep coming around. That's the best thing about them."

And about this.

SEVEN

Over the winter I bought a guitar.

The impetus came from Randell, although I didn't realize it at the time.

During the summer I had been borrowing his spare, or Phil's, for every show. One night, after the concert had ended and I was giving Randell his guitar back, he said to me:

"Guitars don't like some people. You loan them to some people, and when they come back to you they don't want to play the same way."

He always had such a mystical way about him—he looked like the model for some character named Stretch McDougal in a long-ago novel for young people about a thin, lanky and sensitive would-be basketball star out on the lonely North Dakota plains—that what he was saying about guitars-with-vulnerable-personalities didn't sound out of the ordinary for him. This was, after all, the musician who carried his own sea salt into restaurants. So I just waited for him to continue.

"But you have a kind hand," he said. "This guitar comes back happy. It's OK. This guitar likes you."

"Thank you," I said, not knowing how else to respond.

Later, when I repeated the conversation to Gary and asked him to interpret it, he said:

"He means buy your own damn guitar."

"Really?" I said.

"It's as close as Randell will get to saying it," Gary said. "But that's what he means."

So, in the dead of winter back in Chicago, I did.

A black-and-white Stratocaster.

I felt like a kid buying a Louisville Slugger with Mickey Mantle's name on the barrel.

There was no name on my guitar. But I chose it because it looked just like the one Buddy Holly used to play.

Dean sent out itineraries for the first stops of the new summer, and there was something on them that I found just about perfect.

The itinerary for each show was printed on a form that was stored in a computer. There were key words that didn't vary.

Airline:
Boarding Time:
Hotel:
Soundcheck:
Doors Open:

Items like that. For each show, the specific information would be typed in after the relevant words. American Airlines, 2:30 P.M., Holiday Inn. . . .

What I loved was a small, probably inadvertent, touch. There were areas at the top and bottom of each page that summarized for the musicians what they were supposed to do on the current day, and then the next day.

TODAY WE: Fly to Minneapolis, then drive to Hinckley, MN

Or:

TOMORROW WE: Meet in lobby, drive to Fort Wayne

But on the day of a concert, as opposed to a day devoted to travel— this was what delighted me, the economy of the phrasing, and all that was conveyed in three words—there was this notation:

TODAY WE: Play

It was utterly factual—that was the agenda for show day: Today, we play.

How many adults are so lucky? How many adults, getting up in the morning to go to work, would do just about anything to be the recipient of a message like that, written or unwritten?

TODAY WE: Play

It was the essence of all this—the magical lure. And, on show days, I never tired of looking at the itinerary and seeing, once again, what was planned for us.

Only one thing—only one thing of importance.

Today?

Today, we play.

And iron.

At least Dean did, on show days.

He seemed quite devoted to it. What I'd first taken note of in Des Moines, when he had left dinner early to iron his stage shirts, I soon realized was almost an obsession with him. Whatever foibles or failings the Jan and Dean tour might have, whatever challenges or hurdles that existed in the band's professional life, Dean appeared determined never to walk onto a stage in a shirt that was less than fastidiously pressed. By him.

It didn't make much sense to me—surf music was, by definition, easygoing. Who would notice if a musician's Hawaiian shirt was a little rumpled? Rumples, you could argue, came with the beach territory.

Not for Dean. There was seldom a time when I visited him in his room that he wasn't ironing. Which is what he was doing before the first show of the new summer, in Chicago. The band had been hired to play at a party at the annual convention of the National Restaurant Association.

They were staying at the Hyatt—the hotels tended to be on the Hyatt level when the promoter was paying for rooms; when Dean was paying, the accommodations were a notch or three lower on the price scale. "Jan called me over the winter to say he needed a raise," Dean said as he ran the hot iron over the flattened-out sleeves of his shirt.

"What did you say?" I asked.

"I said no," Dean said.

I didn't question it. Life on the road with them, I had observed, was pretty close to the bone, as far as expenses were concerned. I was paying my own way; I was in it for the fun, for the memories in the making. On dates when the promoters, and not Dean, were handing out the hotel rooms, I often was given one on the house, the same as the rest of the band. Meals backstage at the shows were almost always provided. But no one on these tours was lighting cigars with hundred-dollar bills.

"I told Jan that the best way to make sure we keep getting hired is to keep our price down," Dean said.

A necessary dash of reality. But there were other, intangible benefits.

You could find one of them typed on the itinerary on a day like today. Today, we would play.

Jan was conducting.

Maybe it was just that he was so pleased for summer to be starting once again. Whatever the reason, during soundcheck, as we ran through "The Little Old Lady from Pasadena," he energetically waved his arms at us, as if he was Leonard Bernstein.

The show itself was an inauspicious start for the new touring season. We had been informed that we would play twice—at ten P.M. and again at midnight. That seemed rather late for a Sunday night, convention or no convention.

And indeed, by the second show we mostly were playing for men and women who appeared more interested in steering each other to the elevators and the Hyatt bedrooms upstairs—or in resisting the entreaties of their dance partners to do just that—than in listening to songs about surging waves and brute-engined cars.

"Sing 'New York, New York,'" a conventioneer, presumably from that city, yelled drunkenly toward the stage in the hotel ballroom.

Chris Farmer, rather than object, sang:

Start spreadin' the news,
We're surfin' today. . . .

The rest of the night was going to be a lost cause. That, we could tell.

"Bob, why don't you sing the lead on 'Surfer Girl'?" Chris called over to me.

At first I was flattered—Chris was the one who was never shy about pointing out my musical shortcomings. Maybe his invitation meant he thought I was making progress.

Right.

As soon as I started singing, I realized this was a practical joke, and not the most benevolent one, at that. I'd never attempted the lead vocals on "Surfer Girl"—and I found almost instantly that they require a voice with exquisite range and delicacy.

Try it sometime—especially the lilting tenor bridge:

We could ride the surf together,
While our love would grow. . . .

The remaining conventioneers were too intoxicated to notice. But the rest of the band was dissolving into tumble-to-the-floor mirth as I tried in vain to hit those Brian Wilson notes:

In my woodie I would take you,
Everywhere I go-o-o-o-o. . . .

"Very nice," Chris called to me, through his laughter.

"Play 'My Way,'" someone on the dance floor shouted.

Horne's department store, which for almost a century had stood imperially at the corner of Stanwix Street and Penn Avenue in downtown Pittsburgh, had recently been sold, its eventual fate cloudy.

Its exterior still looked the same—stately, austere, one of those imposing, bigger-than-life department stores that were once a fixture of

American downtowns. Horne's, as fashion editor Georgia Sauer of the *Pittsburgh Post-Gazette*, recalled it, "was a place of marble floors and shimmering chandeliers, a place with a bustling carriage trade and a doorman and a tearoom. . . . Women in their forties fondly remember dressing up when they were little girls to go shopping downtown at Horne's with their mothers, putting on their patent leather shoes and frilly dresses and their white gloves—always their white gloves. . . ."

By the autumn, it had been determined by the buyers of the building, Horne's would become something different, with a different name. Autumn was still a long way away, though; summer was just beginning, and from my room in the Pittsburgh Hilton I could see the venue where we would be playing: Three Rivers Stadium, home of the Steelers and the Pirates.

I had checked the newspaper and the local entertainment magazines; there were no mentions at all of the concert, no advertisements. The last thing the band needed was to find a sea of empty seats. There would be no way to hide a paltry crowd in that immense outdoor coliseum.

Jan and Dean were playing shows in two different cities today—one show in Ohio, then a charter flight in a small plane to Pittsburgh. Dean didn't want to give up the dual paychecks. I had come straight from Chicago to Pittsburgh.

I took a cab to Three Rivers, went to our dressing trailer beneath the stadium, then decided to go out and take a look at what awaited us.

And . . .

It was overwhelming. I couldn't process what I was seeing. More than forty-four thousand people in the blazing sun, in bikinis and cut-offs, tank tops and shorts. An opening act was already onstage; the colors of the crowd, the sounds of the guitar riffs in the ballpark . . . this looked like a Rolling Stones concert.

WWSW radio had made it happen—Pittsburgh's big oldies station had booked not just Jan and Dean, but Ronnie Spector of the Ronettes, and James Brown, among others, for an all-day, all-evening nonstop show from where the station was broadcasting live. Who needed newspaper publicity? Who needed advertising? WWSW had, for weeks, been sending its signal straight into the ears of the people in town who loved this music the most, telling them to come, and here they were, forty-four thousand strong.

And this is the strange thing:

I was happy—genuinely happy—for Jan and Dean.

It had come to that—I was happy for these guys that they would arrive here and not be disappointed. That no matter how many one-tenth-filled hotel ballrooms there were in their lives, today would be a day of good news for them.

They pulled up in a van that had met them at the airport, and as they got out I said: "Come here. There's something I want you to see."

I led them from the innards of the stadium out to the sunshine, and they caught sight of all the people, rising in the seats toward the sky. . . .

And they looked like children who had been given a great surprise. Their faces came to life.

"What the *hell*. . . ." Dean said.

Ronnie Spector was onstage, backed by the sound of a massive bass line as she sang:

Be my, be my baby. . . .

Women in skimpy bathing-suit tops danced as far back as the restraining wall behind the distant football end zone. Some were held aloft with their legs around the backs of their boyfriends' necks.

Be my little baby. . . .

James Brown was chauffeured into the stadium in a white limousine that had a hot tub built into the trunk.

And a license plate that read I FEEL GOOD.

The tearoom at Horne's was closed, presumably forever.

No one among us could even pretend to be blasé about this day.

As the technicians were setting up our microphone stands, we posed with our backs to the crowd so we could have a team photo with the full stadium as a backdrop.

In the wings, I stood with Jan just before the introductions.

"Philadelphia?" he said to me.

I didn't know what he meant.

He gestured toward the crowd.

"Pittsburgh," I said to him.

"Right," he said, nodding. He didn't want to say hello to the wrong city.

"*Ladies and gentlemen . . .*" the announcer boomed.

"Do you ever get nervous?" I said to Jan.

"All the time," he said.

And then we were on, and remarkably, it was not even that nervous a feeling, singing in front of that big an audience. There were so many of them that the whole afternoon simply didn't seem real—it felt like we were just up here together, singing for fun. A crowd of forty people, with forty individual faces, might have been cause for the jitters; forty thousand felt like a private dream.

During "409" my throat began to go dry, and I walked to the side of the stage where I knew there were cold bottles of water.

One of the bands that would follow us was a Beatles tribute group—there are many of them around the country, guys who make a pretty good living performing exact replicas of Beatles songs.

So in the wings, as I went to get the water, were the fake Beatles, in tight-fitting light-gray suits and ties. The fake Paul McCartney handed me a bottle, and, in a bogus Liverpool accent, said: "'ere you go."

I laughed out loud—how could anyone not?—and took a swig and then returned to the sunlight, telling myself not to forget a moment of this.

James Brown's bodyguards were barking like dogs.

I didn't know why; there seemed to be no reason for it.

But they were barking at each other. Not fooling around, not fighting, just barking.

James Brown, who would headline the day, had sent word that he'd like to see Jan and Dean. Which made sense—they were like old high school buddies, in a way, they had once lived right in the middle of musical fame together, competing with each new record for a spot in the national Top Forty. Never mind that, as marketed to the public, there had been no act meant to be perceived as symbolically blacker than James Brown, and no act meant to be perceived as symbolically whiter than Jan and Dean. They had been friends and competitors back then; they had a shared history, and were very much a jury of their own peers.

So after we finished our show the barking bodyguards led us up a concrete ramp, where James Brown, regal in a long purplish velour shirt, awaited.

"You got the big man there!" he said in his sandpaper voice. "You got the big man there!"

No one seemed to understand. But then Brown pointed. Dean—a graphic artist of genuine talent; that's how he had earned his living in the years before Jan recovered and they began touring again—had made laminated backstage passes for all of us to wear, with individual photos not of us, but of the Reverend Jerry Falwell, and Robert F. Kennedy, and Benito Mussolini . . . whoever came into his mind as he put the passes together.

One of us, by chance, was wearing a backstage pass with Frank Sinatra's photo on it.

"You got the big man there!" James Brown said, pointing at Sinatra's face.

The meeting was brief; we all shook hands, and posed for a group picture, and James Brown told Jan and Dean how good it was to see them again.

They had to get back on the little charter; I would be staying in Pittsburgh. As we said goodbye and turned to leave, James Brown said to them:

"Stay alive."

Such a peculiar thing to say—the words hung in the air.

"Don't die," he said to Jan and Dean, in that James Brown rasp.

There was complete silence. The bodyguards had ceased their barking.

"I hope you live to be two hundred years old," James Brown said, "and I live to be two hundred years minus one day. So I don't ever have to hear the news that Jan and Dean are dead."

We left quickly after that. The band departed for the airport in their van; I returned to the stage to watch the rest of the concert from the wings.

"You blokes were good," the fake John Lennon said to me.

I had been noticing something as I traveled:

People seemed to feel compelled to come up and talk as I carried my guitar in its black cloth case.

I'd been lugging around standard business bags—carry-on suitcases, briefcases—for years. No one ever said a word.

But as soon as I began carrying the Stratocaster, strangers appeared almost unable to help themselves. From the shape of the bag, there was clearly a guitar inside. People would approach to ask what kind it was, or to request that I unzip the case so they could have a look; every so often, at a boarding area, people would ask if they could take it out and strum it. As I would lift it into overhead bins on airplanes, women—sometimes passengers, sometimes flight attendants—would occasionally run their hands over it. The reactions seemed impulsive, involuntary.

I was surprised by this at first, and then concluded it was a daily testament to the continuing powerful mystique of the electric guitar—the fact of the instrument, the form of it, the symbolism of it—all these years down the line. Whatever the secret unspoken illicitness of rock and roll had been at the very beginning, this, I surmised, was a remaining touchstone, vestigial and vital all at once. I'd lay the guitar case on a conveyer belt to go through the X-ray machine, would walk through the metal-detection portal to greet it on the other side, and find a security worker absentmindedly stroking it. I'd never encountered anyone stroking my canvas overnight bag.

In St. Louis we were checking into our hotel before a show at the Riverport Amphitheatre, and Chubby Checker's band was checking in at the same time.

"These guys are real roadhogs," Gary Griffin said to me.

I could see what he meant. Chubby Checker's guitar players—pale, rawboned, tough-looking—more resembled members of a heavy-metal band, or a motorcycle gang, than backup musicians for the cheery, safe and smiling purveyor of "The Twist." They looked as if they could use a run through a carwash. Not their cars—*them.*

I was telling Gary my observations about traveling with the guitar.

One of Chubby Checker's guitarists, overhearing me, looked over as if what I was saying was the most self-evident thing in the world.

"Yeah," he said. "Of course. It's like carrying your dick through an airport."

What sounded in theory like an oddity—and an ill-conceived one, at that, these head-banger backup guys playing with Chubby Checker—turned out, in execution, to be inspired.

The concert in St. Louis was a package show, promoted with the hopes of bringing in different groups of fans of the multiple acts, and it worked: the outdoor concert hall was almost sold out. Dean, according to Gary, had long resisted these kinds of shows: "He used to say to us that if they don't want Jan and Dean alone, then they don't get to have us at all." But that had changed; by now, Dean was accepting, ardently or not, engagements that grouped him with other acts.

So Dion, who had first come to fame with Dion and the Belmonts, was on this show, too, and after he had sung I stood in the wings to watch Chubby Checker perform. I didn't know what to expect; he had always seemed like a novelty, and a frivolous one to boot, right down to the silly way he had created his stage name as a variation on Fats Domino.

But he walked out onto the stage with his band, and these guys—flipping their long hair from side to side, hitting rampageous, super-charged notes you'd think would be more at home in a basement metal club in New York or Boston, looking as if they were in self-induced frenzies—made his show a happily demented revelation. If you had asked me if I would even cross the street to hear a live rendition of "Let's Twist Again Like We Did Last Summer," my answer would have been no. But watching Chubby Checker sing it with that band behind him was a daft delight—try to envision the musicians in Spinal Tap, had the movie about them not been a comedy. That's what this looked and sounded like: Chubby meets Iron Butterfly.

At one point a blonde woman in the shortest of skirts, apparently over-wrought by the unexpected stinging seductiveness of all this, climbed from the audience and scrambled onto the stage, ran right at Chubby Checker, leapt at him, and wrapped her arms around his neck and her legs around his waist. It was all he could do to keep twisting.

I observed this as I stood next to the evening's master of ceremonies, flown in by the promoters to add a special touch to the night. Jerry Mathers. Yep. The Beaver from *Leave It to Beaver*.

There were evenings when the grand absurdity of all this verged on becoming too much to absorb. Mathers, in a baseball cap, stared at the woman who had wrapped herself around Chubby, wondering, as I was, if he would tumble to the stage floor. The guitarists, thrashing about and cranking their music ever faster and louder, seemed oblivious to their boss's plight. And there I stood, side by side with the Beaver, taking it all in.

The others always seemed, if not impervious to such moments, then mostly unaffected by them. It was as if they had been on the road with acts like these for so many years that they had developed a certain im-munity to the baseline weirdness of it. James Brown in Pittsburgh, Chubby and the Beaver in St. Louis—in the Jan and Dean world, these might as well have been the people working elbow to elbow with them on a factory assembly line.

I understood. But I was grateful that I had not yet reached the point at which this didn't enchant me. The very next night, for example, we were in Denver, for a show at Mile High Stadium. There weren't enough dressing trailers for each act to have its own, so we had to share.

Thus, Phil Bardowell and I found ourselves, in the hours before the concert, drinking beer out of the bottles in our trailer, musing, with each sip, about why a row of spangly gowns were hanging in the trailer's open closet.

"They look like the dresses the Supremes used to wear on *The Ed Sul-livan Show*," Phil said, even though he was too young to remember Ed Sullivan in first-run.

Close enough. The door to the trailer opened, and who should walk in but Martha and the Vandellas. Our roommates for the night.

"You want a beer?" Phil asked them, which seemed like the polite offer to extend.

"No, thank you," one of the Vandellas said. "But you guys are either going to have to leave for a few minutes, or turn the other way."

We turned the other way, as Martha and the Vandellas took off their street clothes and put on their stage clothes.

"OK, you can turn back around," one of them said.

"You look very nice," I said, sounding, I supposed, like Eddie Haskell complimenting Mrs. Cleaver, and wishing the Beaver had come along to this town with us so he could tell me if he agreed.

There were fifty-five thousand people in Mile High Stadium, which only a few weeks earlier would have floored me, but the experience in Pittsburgh had lulled me into thinking this kind of thing would come around all the time. Oh. Fifty-five thousand. Lovely day, isn't it?

So we sang—a short set, just thirty minutes—and were feeling pretty good about everything. The Mamas and the Papas were on the bill, and the band America; we were settling in to watch them when we heard the faint sound of police sirens.

The wail grew louder. From behind the stage, in the football parking lot where our dressing trailer was, we saw flashing lights. Squad cars accompanied two vans, which sped to within a few feet of where we were standing.

The van doors opened, and the Beach Boys emerged.

Carl Wilson climbed out, then some of their backing musicians, then Mike Love and Al Jardine. They caught sight of Jan and Dean and walked over.

The Beach Boys were in middle age, of course, and because of that it was easy to push aside, if only for a moment, just how important, just how new and fresh, they had been when every succeeding single they recorded was more urgent than breaking news to millions of kids who counted on them to provide the serial soundtrack of their lives. "Shut

Down" and "409" were not always oldies; "Be True to Your School" and "I Get Around" were once songs that you heard for the first time, as you and your buddies were driving around your hometown trying to break the Midwestern boredom. You didn't know a thing about the Beach Boys, once upon a time, except that they were living out in California in a world different than yours—better than yours—and that every time they made a record it was like a present, all wrapped up and ready to open. They never missed; every song they wrote and sang, for a long while, connected like a sharp line-drive double to center field. They understood that concept of being undefeated:

> We always take my car 'cause it's never been beat,
> And we've never missed yet with the girls we meet. . . .

It feels very distant, now—those days when the Beach Boys weren't nostalgia, weren't taken for granted, weren't part of anyone's memories. When their lives were as unformed and as new as your own—at least it felt that way, listening to their music coming out of your monophonic front-seat speaker—and when the tales they sang weren't delivered with a wink, but with the insistent narrative of a two-and-a-half-minute novel:

> It happened on the strip where the road is wide. . . .

Tonight they pulled into the football stadium parking lot surrounded by squad cars, and when they reached us Carl Wilson said that they had played earlier in the day in Salt Lake City and that their flight out of Utah had been delayed, which is why the police had to escort them from the Denver airport to here. They would headline, it went without saying; they were the Beach Boys.

"How you doin', Jan?" Mike Love said.

"Oh, I'm OK," Jan said.

There was a tenuous and breakable, all but imperceptible, feeling in the air, one I hadn't sensed before. Dean was a bit quiet. All of them had started out in California together, and had done quite all right for themselves. But the California boys who had just arrived had done a little better than the California boys with whom I was traveling. They were the Beach Boys.

They were due onstage; they had cut their arrival here just that short.

So they talked with us by the side of the stage while their roadies arranged their instruments, and then the promoter said it was time. I still had my guitar under my arm; as they started to climb the stairs to sing, Al Jardine said offhandedly to me: "How's the sound?"

"Good," I said.

I walked a few feet until I was alone. I didn't even want to attempt to tell the others what all of this was meaning to me. "How's the sound?" From Al Jardine. I looked up at the stars in the Colorado night. I put myself back in that car in the middle of Ohio, all those years ago. When much of this music was future tense, when the Beach Boys hadn't written most of it yet, and we waited for them to think it up and somehow get it to us. "How's the sound?"

The sound is wonderful, thank you.

Randell and I wanted to watch full-on instead of from the side, so we walked out onto the football field, which was shoulder to shoulder and belly to back with fans for every inch of where the chalked-off gridiron usually would be.

There was a rope running along the periphery—something about keeping the crowd away from some equipment for fireworks that would be set off to end the show—and he and I stood just behind the rope.

Out of darkness the colorful stage lights went up, and an impeccably modulated voice with the understated baritone authority of the public address announcer at Yankee Stadium said:

"From southern California . . . America's band . . . the Beach Boys."

The opening keyboard strains of "California Girls" filled Mile High. I looked around and thought about the man who wasn't here.

Brian Wilson, in whose heart this music was born, was not singing with the Beach Boys tonight because he practically never did anymore. Whatever the varying reasons for his continuing absence—the long-standing anxieties inside the same heart where the music had formed, the personal estrangement from some of the men on the stage—the absence was especially saddening on such a splendid June night as this. I looked at the fifty-five thousand—bathed in Brian Wilson's music, letting it take them to places of yearning and remembrance—and wondered where Brian might be.

Long ago he had painted his portrait of America—a Norman Rockwell portrait, I supposed, of a world he wished to be a part of, but that on a primal level he knew he never could. It was a country he ached to inhabit, a life he so wanted to live—idealized and happy and pure—yet the young man who wrote songs about the joy and excitement of high-speed cars was a person too fearful to drive; the young man who wrote about the bravura of surfing lofty waves was terrified to go near the water.

Tonight the people in Mile High Stadium were laughing and dancing to his music, joining hands as they ran together in long lines up and down the aisles; what had brought them here was the private vision, expressed in public music, that had once silently gestated inside that lonely heart. Like the dream nation of Rockwell before him, maybe Brian Wilson's perfect America had never truly existed. Perhaps what the two men had in common was a prayer that the America they imagined could somehow be real and sustaining.

If anyone should be here on this exquisite night in Denver, I thought, a night awash in his music, it should be Brian. As I thought about him, for whatever reason a passage by Herman Melville, from *Moby-Dick*, came to mind:

> This lovely light, it lights not me; all loveliness is anguish to me, since I can ne'er enjoy. Gifted with the high perception, I lack the low enjoying power; damned, most subtly and most malignantly! Damned in the midst of paradise!

The Beach Boys sang "Little Deuce Coupe" onstage. Randell suddenly grabbed my shoulder; something was going on on the other side of the rope.

A fight had broken out among a group of girls in their late teens; it appeared to be over a boy who was with them. The girls were swinging at each other; one girl was pulling another's hair.

A female security guard in uniform—she couldn't have been more than twenty years old, if that, this may have been a summer job for her—hurried over to see what was going on. As she encountered the fight, she tried to separate the girls and persuade them to step away from each other.

One of the girls—the one who had been pulling hair—wheeled on the security guard and in a fast, unbroken and terrible motion raked her long fingernails over the young guard's eyes, seeking to sink the nails in where they would do the most damage.

The security guard screamed—it was a shattering moment, all but drowned out by the amplified guitars from the stage. What I could hear was a sharp intake of breath from Randell, next to me. The guard raised her hands to her eyes; the hands came away red, covered with blood. She was in a panic, keening; from where Randell and I were standing, we couldn't tell if the girl's fingernails had actually entered an eye socket of the guard, but the guard was covering her eyes as if she could not see, crying out in her pain.

Within seconds other security guards were arriving to help the wounded young woman; they embraced her, but her sobs still sounded. The girl who had attacked her—and the other girls who had been in the original fight—ran into the crowd, trying to lose themselves among the thousands on the football field; one male guard ran after them in pursuit.

The Beach Boys, knowing nothing of this, continued their song:

Just a little deuce coupe with a flat head mill . . .

The guards led their young colleague away, her body trembling, her hands still over her eyes. The Beach Boys sang Brian Wilson's songs of untainted bliss. As soon as their show was over they got into their vans and were driven out the gates.

The fireworks started and Randell and I found Jan and Dean and the rest of the band. Our hotel was within a few blocks of the stadium, so with rockets and Pinwheels exploding in the sky above us we walked back, hearing man-made thunder.

EIGHT

"What is that you keep reading?" Phil said.

We were having a drink in the barroom of the Royal Sonesta Hotel in Cambridge, Massachusetts, before going across the Charles River to a show at City Hall Plaza in Boston.

I had the front section of that day's *New York Times* laid out on the surface of the bar. I was finding this whole day—the juxtaposition of the story I was reading in the *Times* with what I was about to do—more than a little disorienting.

"Here," I said to Phil, handing him the newspaper.

The fact that the band and I lived in different worlds when they were back in California and I was in Chicago might, in theory, have served as an impediment to any potential true friendship. Except that it didn't. Having little in common became the thing we had in common. It seemed to draw us together. Phil and I met for drinks and conversation before just about every show.

Phil scanned the story I had been reading. A justice of the Illinois Supreme Court, in a written opinion deciding a controversial case, had taken the unusual step of personally attacking the governor of Illinois and me. Legal scholars seemed surprised, even aghast—justices seldom, if ever, used court opinions to fling personal insults. It had caused such a stir that it was written about in a Page One story in that day's *Times*. That's what I had been reading as Phil and I, in our surf shirts, sat at the bar.

He skimmed the story, took a swig of his drink, and pronounced:

"What an asshole."

I had to laugh. I appreciated Phil's loyalty, but he didn't know anything about the case at hand, or about who was right or wrong. And what he said next—because he used no transition at all—made me laugh even harder.

"So you're going to do lead on 'Shut Down' tonight?" he asked.

From the dry-and-sober news account in the *Times* to tonight's set list with not so much as a pause. Gary had to miss the trip—there was a family obligation he was attending to. Chris Farmer was going to play Gary's keyboard parts; we were all going to divide up his vocals.

"Yeah," I said. "But I'm nervous. I don't know all the words."

I'd been hearing "Shut Down" all my life. But I'd never had to sing the lead—and I was realizing, an hour before the concert, that there were lyrics I wasn't sure of.

"Here," Phil said. He ripped a page from the *New York Times*, borrowed a pen from the bartender, and, in the white space surrounding the artwork in a half-page advertisement, wrote the lyrics to "Shut Down" for me.

Some of them, I wouldn't have gotten on my own:

My Sting Ray is light, the slicks are startin' to spin. . . .

And:

Pedal's to the floor, hear the dual quads drink. . . .

Chris, appearing in the door of the bar, said to us:

"You going to hang around here, or come to the show?"

We got up, leaving the rest of the *Times* and the day's news it contained behind, where it belonged.

We ate our dinner in a conference room in City Hall, which didn't even seem very strange.

Nothing did, when we were all together on the road like this; in the van we had passed Faneuil Hall, and what we observed on the street was not sightseers on their way to have a look at that landmark building full of

Boston politics and history, but sightseers on their way to have a look at us. They hurried past Faneuil to get good seats for the show.

This was the pleasing illusion that Jan and Dean dealt with each night they were away from home: the illusion that life's spotlight was always on them. Never mind that every touring band must feel the same way, feel ever the center of attention, the focus of every eye. It's one of the benefits of constant motion: being able to fool yourself into thinking that every evening revolves around you and you alone. The people are streaming past Faneuil Hall, aren't they? Forsaking it, for you.

So in City Hall, in a room where government officials presumably debated points of policy most days, we put our paper plates loaded with coldcuts and potato chips on the boardroom-style table and waited for the Kingsmen—they were opening for Jan and Dean again—to finish their set out on the plaza.

"Is there any band in the world you would stand in the rain for an hour to see?" Randell, apropos of nothing, asked the room at large.

"No," Dean said.

"*Any* band?" Randell repeated.

"No," Chris said.

"The Beatles?" Randell said.

"Yes," Chris said.

"Trick question," Dean said. "Not possible."

We ate and pondered such subjects, and there was a knock on the door. It was time to play.

From the perspective of the City Hall Plaza steps, Boston was lovely and inviting. I pulled Phil's "Shut Down" lyrics from my shirt pocket, intending to put them down by the base of my microphone in case I had to refer to them.

But I saw that there was already a piece of paper taped to the stage floor. There were words on it: "Matchbox." "Not Fade Away." "Shakin' All Over." "Little Latin Lupe Lu."

It was the Kingsmen's set list. One of their guitar players had taped it there to remind himself of their show's song order.

A few minutes ago, they had been the ones who could fool themselves into thinking they were the center of the world. A few minutes ago, all eyes and ears had been focused on them.

It ends each time the music ends. Now they were gone, and it was our turn. I tore their set list from the floor, replaced it with my words for "Shut Down." A few feet to my left Jan said, "Hello, Boston," and his amplified voice carried for blocks.

Sometimes, on the way to delivering memories to others, there were moments when someone among us would seek out memories of his own.

We were en route from Hartsfield International Airport in Atlanta to a planned community called Peachtree City, about half an hour to the south in Fayette County.

The promoter had sent a long limousine. It had a sideboard stocked with heavy glass tumblers, buckets of ice, and liquor in fancy decanters.

Gary, who was not usually a drinker, and never in the daytime, filled a glass with ice, then poured it full of bourbon.

He took a single ceremonial sip, then—this was the point—clinked the ice softly in the glass.

"Quick," he said. "What's the sound?"

None of us answered.

He clinked the ice some more. "Come on," he said. "This is easy. Where did you first hear this?"

More silence from us.

"You're a little kid," he said. "You're upstairs in your pajamas. It's a Saturday night. Your parents are having their friends over for a party.

"You sit at the top of the stairs and listen to them talking, and you hear the ice clinking in their cocktail glasses. . . ."

It was morning in Georgia. But he was somewhere else, inviting us to close our eyes and join him.

"Nights like this make me think we're pretty fortunate," David Logeman, his hands clasped behind his neck, said. "Just to find ourselves in a place like this. Who even knew it was here?"

It was hard to disagree. We were back in the woods, in a cabin that felt like summer camp and lightning bugs. We could hear crickets, and the rustle of the wind, and little else. This was our dressing room.

Peachtree City was a place I'd never heard of, and probably never would have, were it not for the Jan and Dean itinerary. One of the hallmarks of the town, we saw when we arrived, was a web of golf cart paths throughout—it wasn't a golf course community, just a place where the people who developed it had come up with an idea: this will feel more closely knit and protected if families can get around on golf carts in addition to cars.

So not only grownups, but children as young as twelve, chugged slowly around Peachtree City at the controls of the golf carts (the boys and girls that young had to have an adult in the cart with them). Our show was going to be in an outdoor amphitheater cut out of a thick forest. During soundcheck we had seen children riding their bikes alone on little trails that ran through the trees. It had both a tranquil and bucolic feel to it, a throwback remembrance of an America in which children habitually felt at ease doing such a thing—combined with a nagging and somehow ominous Hansel-and-Gretel feel: this was not, after all, that old-time America, and the woods were murkish and dense, the children small and solitary beneath the looming trees.

And at night here we were. When we walked together on a winding forest path to the stage, we could hear crunching beneath our shoes as we felt our way in the dimness. We arrived to find that the citizens of Peachtree City had filled the amphitheater.

Before the show there was an announcement by someone from the community, saying that no standing or dancing in the aisles would be permitted, so everyone in the audience could see the concert clearly. But during "Surf City" the people seemed unable to help themselves; many of the younger ones ran up toward the stage, pulled themselves onto it, and danced as we sang.

A uniformed Peachtree City police officer, standing in the wings, motioned furiously toward me. I cocked my head, as if to ask what was on his mind; he irritatedly motioned me over.

In midsong I walked to him.

"Go to the microphone and announce that the stage has to be cleared," he said loudly, so that I could hear him over the guitars.

"It's not my band," I said back to him. "I can't do that."

"Then I'm going to have to end the show," he said.

I spread my arms as if to say: Please don't.

"Look," I said, pointing to the people from the town who had come up onto the stage.

They were so happy; they were out in the woods on a flawless summer night, surrounded by neighbors they knew, dancing and singing along to music they loved.

"You don't have to worry," I said to him. "We don't pose any threat. We're old."

He laughed.

"We're a lot older than you are," I said, accurately. "I promise you. This will be fine."

He looked uncertain, but I made my way back to the microphone through the dancers on the stage, and picked up the song:

. . . *Surf City, here we come.* . . .

I looked over at the police officer. He had his arms crossed. I shrugged, and he shrugged and smiled, and I could see his mouth making the words as he sang along:

. . . *Surf City, here we come.* . . .

When the show ended and the crowd was dispersing, a couple who appeared to be in their forties walked up to the lip of the stage and handed me something.

It was two one-dollar bills.

"Someone must have dropped this in the aisle," the husband said. "Could you see if there's a lost-and-found in case they're looking for it?"

It was that kind of place, that kind of evening. Lost-and-found, all right. Quite a country.

In the Waffle House after midnight, I had a feeling I'd been here before. Even though this was my first Waffle House.

After the Peachtree City show was over, we were hungry; a female fan had followed us back to the hotel, and Chris had somehow persuaded her that she should let us borrow her car. I guess she was content to hang out in the hotel bar.

Dean was tired and said he was going to sleep; Jan and David were still at the amphitheater, where Jan was selling and autographing photos and merchandise as he did after most shows, and David was helping him out. So Chris, Gary, Phil, Randell and I drove in the borrowed car to the Waffle House.

We weren't in pursuit of waffles, but cheeseburgers, hash browns and Cokes. The Waffle House was the ideal place for it—cheeseburger heaven. "Could we have separate checks?" Phil asked the waitress as we settled into a Formica-topped booth, and that's when I knew why the place seemed so familiar.

It was just like the Toddle House, the cheeseburger place of my growing-up years, where my buddies and I would gather late each summer night just because we didn't want the day to be over yet. Probably, on some of those Toddle House nights, Jan and Dean had been on our car radios.

Tonight we had crowded into the car and driven over to here, with the music from the encore still echoing in our ears, and most of the world had gone to bed in preparation for the alarm clock that was going to sound too soon. Not us; here we were. None of us was ever going to be young again, but, at least for me, this was 1964, this was time and feeling recaptured. A summer night, and a bunch of guys you like to spend time with, and music and burgers and nothing to do but laugh and tell stories. . . .

Who would have guessed this? Who would have guessed you could ever have it again? We sat in the Waffle House in a town I'd never been in before, and I'd probably never be back to, and I thought of my old friends, and of what David had said in that cabin in the woods just before the show:

"Nights like this make me think we're pretty fortunate."

I didn't say anything about it out loud, though. Some things, you'd ruin them if you tried to tell anyone.

It doesn't sound possible for a man's eyes to be both dead and angry.

But Jerry Lee Lewis's were.

He walked past us, those lifeless, enraged eyes staring straight ahead, on his way to the piano on the hotel ballroom stage.

We were in Clearwater, Florida, playing at a fundraiser for a local hospital. We were scheduled to close the show, but, hearing that Lewis would be on the bill, none of us wanted to miss the chance to see him.

"He looks like someone told him to dress like a rush week chairman," Gary said.

Indeed, the man whose whole life had been soaked in trouble and turmoil looked tonight like he was trying to fit in at the Sigma Chi house, 1959. Blue sport coat, tan dress slacks, white shirt, striped tie . . . but there was a bottle on the piano, even though I had read somewhere that he had stopped drinking.

To greet the audience he brought his hands down hard on the piano keys, and it was like an electrical jolt. The simplest of acts: banging a keyboard. No one ever did it like Jerry Lee Lewis.

"It's good to be on the bill with Jan and Dean," he said. "They probably didn't know I was still living."

Bang, those fingers on the piano again, and he sang the words:

What am I living for. . . .

My mother wasn't especially overprotective, but when Jerry Lee Lewis had come to our town as part of a caravan show when I was eleven or twelve, and a friend's mother had bought tickets, she would not permit me to go along. My fixation with Elvis, she was willing to put up with. Not Jerry Lee. Elvis was theatrical danger. Jerry Lee was danger.

Those songs of his—jacked up by that pumping piano—were powered by a boogie-woogie beat that felt like a taunt, a dare. "Great Balls of

Fire," "Whole Lotta Shakin' Goin' On," "Breathless"—with his wavy dark blond hair flying he would kick the piano bench so it skittered behind him, or so it was said, and fights routinely broke out in the audiences of his early shows. At the height of his fame his marriage to his thirteen-year-old cousin sort of sealed the deal as far as America's parents were concerned, and the years that followed—alcohol and drug problems, erratic behavior with guns, battles with the Internal Revenue Service—sent him to the margins of the entertainment world.

"Is that who I think it is playing guitar behind him?" Randell said.

"I think so," Chris said. "James Burton."

Burton had been Elvis Presley's lead guitarist. But Elvis was dead; a guitar player has to play somewhere. It probably was logical that James Burton and Jerry Lee had found each other.

Jerry Lee sounded good, if weary:

You shake my nerves and you rattle my brain. . . .

From what I'd heard, his life was still unsettled. A wire service story from northwestern Spain had reported that he was jeered off the stage there after he kicked a cameraman. He had recently opened his home in rural Mississippi to tourists willing to pay to walk through, in an effort to satisfy his debts to the IRS.

"What are you doing *later*, Jerry Lee?" a woman in the audience with a goading, singsong voice called to him.

"Not tonight, darlin'," he drawled smokily, indifferently, into his microphone.

He mostly looked at the keyboard, seldom at the crowd.

He played not a minute longer than had been scheduled.

He walked off in his fraternity uniform, the eyes looking like the eyes of someone who had been insulted in ways no one could understand.

It wasn't often that we encountered reminders of American life as it had been when it was dotted with formality, grandeur, and an overarching sense of occasion.

Mostly we saw things like the T-shirt an attractive young woman in a Midwestern audience was wearing one night, with the words JUST EAT ME printed on the front. Apparently she had picked that shirt out of her dresser drawer before leaving the house, and had concluded it was a fine one to wear in public.

But this hotel in Clearwater was a lithograph from a different time. The Belleview, later the Belleview Biltmore, had opened its doors in 1897; constructed with a sense of scale almost beyond imagining, it was said to still be the largest occupied wooden structure in the world. Its buildings resembled the great and gabled hotel in the movie *Some Like It Hot*; as we checked in we could tell that it had seen better days, yet in the lobby I met a woman in her eighties who told me she had been vacationing here for fifty years.

Gary and Chris and I had wandered around in the hours before our show. There was a Belleview Biltmore museum of sorts in a first-floor alcove; mounted and framed was a typed letter from a manager of the hotel to a long-ago guest, confirming a reservation down to the smallest detail, courtly in its language, designed to make the guest feel that every member of the hotel staff was just counting the minutes until the guest's arrival.

According to the hotel's archives, the Belleview was erected at the behest of one Henry Bradley Plant, a prominent Florida railroad man. Workmen with mule-powered scrapers, wagons and carts cut down palmetto thickets to make space for the hotel, and when it opened on January 15, 1897, it "almost overnight became the favored winter retreat of railroad presidents, steel magnates, public utility tycoons and other industrial barons. As many as fifteen private railroad cars were parked at one time on the special siding east of the hotel. Recreations most prominently suggested were bicycling and walking, although casual mention was made of 'six sporty holes of golf, with shell greens.'"

In our new and unceremonious age, the hotel didn't seem to know quite what to do with itself; it had recently been sold to a Japanese concern. Before our show we had eaten beneath the steep ceiling of its elegant old dining room. David Logeman wore a tank top as he munched on a grouper sandwich, and his attire did not stand out, because no one seemed to expect dressiness from the diners.

A waitress approached him, but it was not to request that he put on a shirt with sleeves. Instead, what she said was:

"You're a drummer, right?"

He beamed that ten-thousand-watt smile at her, and said:

"How'd you guess? My muscles?"

"No," she said. "I overheard you talking to the others."

She tarried near him, in a room where once tuxedoed orchestras played as tuxedoed guests dined to the illumination of gas lamps.

We didn't wear tuxedos, but after our show, as we walked through parts of the hotel's two full miles of corridors, it was difficult not to wonder what would eventually become of this place. It was too big; it was too ancient. Yet to lose it would seem a shame.

We went to a reception in a suite someone from the sponsoring hospital had rented. His wife—she was wearing tight white short shorts, and had an Ace bandage wrapped around one of her legs from the ankle up to mid-thigh—did something:

She sat on a couch, pulled her legs up on the cushion so they were crossed in front of her, took a banana from a fruit bowl . . . then peeled it, made eye contact with one man after another, and, slowly and provocatively, ate it one small bite at a time.

She did this in a manner that might have made even Jerry Lee Lewis blush.

No one said anything, so I thought I might be the only one to notice.

But around two o'clock in the morning, when I was back in my room in bed, the phone rang.

It was Randell.

"I'm sorry if I woke you," he said. "I can't stop thinking about that chick with the banana."

Moments like these were the serendipitous signposts of the journey.

That summer ended late. There were stops in Nevada and Arkansas and Texas and Minnesota, and during a slow week Chris and Phil and David accepted an invitation from Mike Love. He—not the Beach Boys—was heading to Europe for a handful of shows, and he needed backup musicians. Few people knew the Beach Boys' catalogue better than the Jan and Dean band. "I'll see you when I get back from Amsterdam," Phil said to me.

On an October evening I flew to Jackson, Mississippi. In the airport I waited for Jan, Dean and Gary to arrive. Their cramped-looking little commuter connector plane pulled up to the terminal in darkness; I watched through the window as Jan limped down the airplane's stairs.

It was a forlorn sight on a forlorn night. Dean and Jan had had an argument on the way from California; as we waited for a Holiday Inn van to pick us up by the curb outside of baggage claim, Jan grabbed a metal luggage cart from Dean and pushed it angrily into the roadway.

"Now, Jan, go get that," Dean said.

Jan said nothing.

We shared the hotel van with a Delta flight crew. One of the pilots had the flu, but told his colleagues he was reluctant to take any pills that would make him groggy, because he had to fly again in the morning.

"What are you guys in town for?" one of the flight attendants asked us.

"Business," Dean said, in no mood to talk.

"If you're looking for something to do, I hear the state fair is going on," she said.

Dean said he knew.

A paper bag from Taco Bell by his feet, David Logeman worked out in the hotel's health club in the morning.

"We got in overnight," he said. He seemed in exuberant spirits. "Four days in London, two in Amsterdam," he said. "Mike Love really does things right. First-class air on Northwest and KLM all the way. It was cool."

Later Dean called us from the McDonald's next door to the hotel to say he was having lunch. We joined him; Chris, who also had arrived in Mississippi overnight, walked in wearing sunglasses and a T-shirt. "London was great. . . ." he started to say.

"Fuck you," Dean said. "I've never been to Europe in my life."

"You never have?" Chris said.

"Go get yourself a hamburger," Dean said to him. "We order at the counter here in America."

The late-afternoon October sun was bright and cold as we left the hotel for the fairgrounds.

Something was amiss.

Maybe it was Dean's unexpressed weighing of the possibility that his professional life could be subtly shifting; Mike Love had lured his band across the Atlantic Ocean, and even though it had just been for a few days, it might, in Dean's mind, be portending future difficulties.

Maybe it was the conflict between Dean and Jan; Jan had called my room in the middle of the night, and when I answered he had said: "About that episode at the airport . . ." In the annals of human discord it had been a trifling thing, but nevertheless awkward to witness. "I did it because Gary Griffin took my cart," Jan said on the phone, which made it all the more wistful: he was trying to protect Dean by revising the story. "I've been trying to call the others to tell them, but the hotel says they're not even registered," Jan said. No one had told him that they had gone to Europe.

Or maybe it was just the knowledge that winter was on its way. Whatever the reason, there was an intimation of brittleness during that Mississippi trip, an impression that fun had taken a leave of absence.

"This place is sitting empty," Dean said as we ate our catered dinner in a drafty hallway behind the stage in the Mississippi State Fairgrounds' indoor coliseum. "You'd think we could have played in here."

We weren't going to be. The stage was set up for the country act Brooks & Dunn, who either had played the night before or would play the night after; in any case, the coliseum wasn't being used tonight, yet Jan and Dean were scheduled to play in a canvas tent out near the midway. The band was being fed in the big coliseum, but wouldn't be performing in it.

One of Jan's hands was bleeding; I don't know what he had done to

103

it, but I saw it as soon as we were into our first song. The tent, sponsored by Budweiser, was muggy even in the coolish night. The volume of the speakers was turned up so loud that it was painful to the ears. It felt like it was doing damage song by song. There was a woman in the front row with a boy on her lap who was three or four years old, and his face was contorted, his tears making his cheeks slick. He shouldn't have been here, and assuredly not so close to the speakers. The noise was hurting him.

She did nothing. It was all I could think about during the first show. I saw that Gary had noticed, too; behind his keyboard he caught the woman's attention, pointed to his ears and then to the boy. The woman just smiled and waved back, as if Gary was flirting. I did the same pointing-to-the-ears motion, then pointed straight at the boy. The woman was oblivious.

Between shows we wandered the midway. It was by most measures a rugged-looking, even sullen, crowd. The T-shirts here were aggressive in their bellicosity. One young woman wore a shirt with the slogan: DON'T ASK ME SHIT. A young man's shirt bore the words: DOWN ON ALL FOURS FOR YOU, BOY. This was the summer and fall during which many people around the country had been wearing T-shirts and caps with an X on the front, inspired by a flurry of publicity about the life of the late Malcolm X; here on the fairgrounds I saw four different men in black T-shirts with the slogan YOU WEAR YOUR X AND I'LL WEAR MINE, above a color reproduction of the Confederate flag, with its crossed bars.

Gary bought a leather wallet at a booth. When we returned to the tent for the second show we were relieved to see that the woman with the little boy was gone. Jan had not tended to the wound on his hand, which continued to bleed.

Just one night before, David and Chris and Phil had been sleeping in a luxury hotel in Amsterdam. The music can transport a person to many places, some of them happier than others. During "Surfin' U.S.A." I looked over at Dean as I always did when the song reached a certain verse:

We'll all be planning that route, we're gonna take real soon,
We're waxing down our surfboards, we can't wait for June. . . .

He looked back at me. Maybe the coming of winter was all it was. Maybe that was the explanation for how everyone was feeling.

We'll all be gone for the summer, we're on safari to stay. . . .

Another summer was ending, and we didn't want it to. Maybe it was as simple, and as complicated, as that.

NINE

Some men endeavor to find the answers to the great conundrums of the cosmos. What is life? What is truth? What is the square root of 2?

Others of us have more modest quests.

In suburban Maryland before a show, I was hanging around a dirt infield in front of the grandstand when I saw a man whose face looked vaguely familiar.

Gary U.S. Bonds.

For me, it was a "Dr. Livingstone, I presume" moment.

During the summer of 1961, Gary U.S. Bonds—he had come up with that name for himself in the hopes that his songs would get more airplay if radio programmers and listeners mistakenly assumed he had a connection to United States Savings Bonds—had the number-one record in the United States, an irresistible mixture of rhythm and blues and rock and roll called "Quarter to Three." It came out of every juke-box, every car radio—you couldn't miss it:

Don't you know that I danced, I danced till a quarter to three. . . .

But aside from the purely musical aspects of the tune, there was another factor that fueled its success. The record began with the sounds of a raucous party in progress. Underneath the party noise, you could hear—barely—a certain phrase being uttered by someone at the party. The phrase was so salacious that it crossed the line to filthy. Which, of course, is why every kid snapped to attention every time the first few seconds of "Quarter to Three" came on the radio.

I hadn't thought about Gary U.S. Bonds in years.

Now here he was. Part of the same week-long festival that had brought us here.

I approached him.

"Mr. Bonds . . . there was this rumor, see, and I don't know whether it was just a central Ohio rumor, or whether it was a national rumor. . . ."

Gary U.S. Bonds exhaled softly, resignedly.

"It was a national rumor," he said.

"Then you know what I'm talking about," I said.

"I know what you're talking about," he said.

"It's the phrase at the beginning of the song, right?" I said.

"Right," he said.

"What was the phrase people thought was in there?" I said, wanting to make completely sure that he knew what I was talking about.

"The phrase they thought was in there was . . ." he said.

And then he said a phrase that was every bit as dirty as the one I had in mind.

But it was slightly different. Same filthy idea, slight variation in words.

"So was it in there?" I said.

"No," Gary U.S. Bonds said. "Absolutely not. I mean, my *mother* was at the recording session where we did 'Quarter to Three.' Do you think I would say something like that in front of my *mother?*"

He seemed quite sincere. He said he was aware of what everyone thought they were hearing at the beginning of the song.

"I have listened to that record over and over again, for years and years," he said. "I have tried to hear it. I'm telling you—that phrase was never in there."

We shook hands solemnly.

The first customers were filing into their seats, the summer sun not yet descended below the vista of the skyline.

We were with Jan so much, and witnessed the involutions and vexations of his life on such a regular basis, that sometimes it was easy to forget just how fundamentally brave he was.

To do what he did—to travel the country, knowing, somewhere inside, what people saw, and thought, as they looked at him. . . .

There was an unquenchable courage there—something inside him that was so determined, so ambitious in the face of everything, that to consider it was to feel humbled. Despite all that had happened to him, he got out of his house, and he got on the planes, and he climbed onto the stages, and he did it.

In Florida after a show one night the rest of us were hanging out in the hotel bar. When we walked in from the concert there was a slight argument with the bartender; backstage at the show, the promoter had provided a plastic garbage can full of ice and beer. Chris had grabbed a couple of six-packs, had taken them in the van back to where we were staying, and when we walked into the bar he said to the bartender: "Do you think we could just get some glasses?"

"You're kidding, right?" the bartender said.

"Come on," Chris said, in that velvet-lined corporate-communications-director voice. "We won't tell anyone."

"What we do here is *sell* drinks," the bartender said. "You can't bring your own beer in here."

But Chris somehow prevailed—he always did—and so we were drinking the beer sometime after midnight when the phone rang behind the bar, and I heard the bartender call over:

"Is there a Bob Greene here?"

A call like this, late at night, was highly unusual. Puzzled and more than a little concerned, I went to the phone.

"Don't tell the others it's me," the voice said.

It was Jan.

"I'm in room 710," he said. "Come up to my room. Don't let the others know where you're going. Don't tell Dean."

I made an excuse to the guys at the table. I rode the elevator to the seventh floor, knocked on his door once, twice, three times.

Finally he answered.

"Bob?" I heard his voice say. "Just a second."

He opened the door wearing shorts, knee-high support stockings, and no shirt. He smiled and told me to come in.

In the closet, his Hawaiian stage shirts were neatly hung. He seemed to realize he should be wearing more clothing; he went to his suitcase and put on a yellow tank top.

"I want you to hear something," he said. "But I don't want the others to know I'm doing it."

On the night table was his portable tape recorder.

"I've been writing some new songs," he said. "Someone back home has been helping me record them."

He pushed the "Play" button . . .

And there they were—Jan Berry songs no one had ever heard, new songs about surfing, and driving cars, and hanging out at spring break. I listened to his voice on the tape recorder singing about the old joys of his young manhood, and I saw the man battered to the pavement by life sitting in front of me, and it was all I could do not to cry.

"Listen here, to the percussion," he said.

Then: "There's a starlight sound coming up in a few seconds."

He still, apparently, had the ear. I could see what he must have been like as a cocky young writer/singer/producer. His confidence, as he was breaking down the individual elements of the music to me, was absolute.

"This next song has a harder sound than the rest," he said, holding his hand in midair.

The vocal performances had many of the limitations that his onstage singing did. But he was trying so hard.

"What are you going to do with these songs, Jan?" I said.

"I don't know," he said.

"If you find someone to bring them out, will they be Jan and Dean records?" I said.

"No," he said. "Just Jan."

We listened for a while.

"What do you think of the album?" he said.

Before I could answer, he said:

"Do you think it sounds out of date?"

I wanted him to go to bed feeling proud.

"I think it sounds like a brand-new Jan and Dean record," I said.

"Thank you," he said.

"Why does it matter so much to you that you make a new record?" I said.

He paused for just a second, then said:

"Because it shows that I'm a person."

We listened some more. A cable news show was playing silently on the television set in the room.

I was getting tired. I said that I probably should head for my own room and get some sleep.

He stood to walk me to his door.

"Don't tell the others," he said one more time.

"They know that we talk, Jan," I said.

"Then say we were talking about something else," he said. "Don't tell them I'm trying to make a record."

I said I'd see him in the morning. As his door closed, his voice from the tape recorder was still singing.

He wasn't the only one with thoughts not easily revealed.

Because of the implicit agreement in the band to let life on the road constitute its own universe, it seemed to come out of nowhere one night when Dean chose to share a piece of his other world—his private world—with us.

We were near Washington, D.C., in a hotel restaurant after a show in the new summer. Everyone had been hungry as the concert ended, and the plan was to order several platters of appetizers before heading for bed.

So we were passing around plates of onion rings and quesadillas and chicken wings—the basic nutriments of our time together—and Dean was quieter than usual.

With no preface he said:

"My little one has something wrong with her heart."

His wife had given birth to a new baby: a daughter. He had told us at the time she was born, but had said little since.

Now, this.

"How long have you known?" Chris said to him.

"We found out Friday," he said. "They tell us it's a heart murmur."

He hadn't said a word. An hour or so before, he had been onstage working to get the crowd into a good mood, doing his every-night lead-in patter to the various segments of the show. Before the car-song set, in a peppy voice: "So do you have a drag strip here in town?" Before "Honolulu Lulu": "Who wants to take a little trip to Hawaii?" Before "Let's Dance" and "Do You Wanna Dance": "It's *time* for the semi-famous Jan and Dean dance party." His demeanor then had divulged nothing.

"What does this mean?" Gary said to him now.

"I don't know," Dean said. "Maybe an operation, maybe not."

I had no idea what these men did for health insurance; there wasn't some employer of record providing it. Sometimes when the audiences were small I could see Dean wordlessly counting the house. This—the money he brought home from these tours—was his family's livelihood. This was it. Abandoning the road—even on a week like this—was not an option.

"You know," he said, in a voice that sounded suddenly far away, "when my wife gets sick, I probably don't help as much as I should, because I never used to get sick, my whole life. It's nothing I've had to deal with."

He had been one of the golden ones. He had gone through his young manhood as Dean Torrence, with all that implied.

"I guess I told myself that the reason I didn't get sick was because there were girls to meet, guys to hang around with," he said. As if, when he was young, he had been able to delude himself into thinking his robust health was a choice, not a piece of random fortune.

He had learned since then. First from Jan, who for a time had seemed even more golden, more invincible.

Some women at a nearby table had been whispering and looking over; one of them worked up the nerve to approach.

"I loved your show," she said. "We were singing along with every song." She asked for autographs, and said: "Do you all have families?"

Some at the table answered her, some didn't. "Do you?" she said to Dean.

"Yes," he said, his tone neutral. "I have a wife and two daughters."

"Do you have pictures of your kids?" she said to Dean.

He told her he didn't have his wallet with him. I don't know if he did or not. She went back to her table and soon enough we went upstairs.

In the first baseball stadium where I ever set foot, we got dressed in an oversized storeroom.

Jet Stadium, it was called back then—home field of the Columbus Jets of the International League, farm club of the Pittsburgh Pirates. My father had taken me to a ballgame. I was so young that, during a full count on the batter when the crowd had chanted *Three-and-two, what'll he do? Three-and-two, what'll he do?*, I'd had no idea what the words had meant.

The Jets had been succeeded by the Columbus Clippers, the outfield grass had been replaced by AstroTurf, the name of the park had been changed to Cooper Stadium. But here we were, on West Mound Street, getting ready to sing.

Quite a battle broke out before the show, between a fake Ringo and the woman who was promoting the event.

There were a number of acts on the bill—us, Lesley Gore, the Drifters, a different Beatles tribute group than the one we had played with in Pittsburgh.

The stage in front of second base had been set up with all the various groups' instruments in place. It was a crowded arrangement; it looked as if fitting all those guitars, keyboards and amplifiers onto the stage floor had been like piecing together a jigsaw puzzle.

Someone apparently had made a decision: the drummers for all the acts would face sideways. Instead of drumming from the rear of the stage, the drummers would look across from the three o'clock position.

Ringo—today's fake Ringo, in the standard-issue gray Beatles '64 suit and black Beatle boots—was irate.

"Listen!" he screamed at the promoter, a woman, even as the fans were coming into the stadium. "You can't do this! Ringo didn't play to the side of the guitars!"

"I understand that," the promoter said. "We're doing the best we can. Just try to make it work."

"No!" the fake Ringo screamed.

"Yes," the promoter said calmly.

"Ringo would never drum facing sideways!" Ringo screamed.

"But you're not really Ringo now, are you?" the promoter, all sweetness and light, said.

That did it.

"Bitch!" he yelled at her.

"Oh, quiet, asshole," she said to him.

"I'll see you in court!" he shouted.

"Fuck you," she said.

The stage manager told them that they had to clear the area. The show was going to begin in a few minutes.

Lesley Gore strode vigorously to the microphone to sing her hits. She sounded strong and overflowing with self-assuredness on all of them—"It's My Party (and I'll Cry if I Want To)," "Judy's Turn to Cry," "You Don't Own Me"—and, in this Midwestern minor-league infield, she had the noblesse-oblige bearing of a woman returning a diamond bracelet to the counter at Van Cleef & Arpels.

The fake Beatles came on next, and I stood with David Logeman as we watched the fake Ringo, sitting sideways in full profile, singing "Boys."

"Are you going to play sideways, too?" I asked David.

"I guess," he said. "If that's what they want."

"Why don't you stand up for your rights the way Ringo does?" I said.

"I wonder," David said.

Then:

"Do you think he'll really take legal action against the promoter?"

"Right," I said. "I can just picture it. The fake Ringo in Franklin County Common Pleas Court."

He was flopping his hair back and forth on the right edge of the stage as he drummed and sang:

. . . take a trip, around the world. . . .

"He's actually not bad," David said. "One of the better Ringos I've seen."

Jet Stadium was one thing. There was another ballpark, though, that I had never visited. Growing up in Columbus, it always seemed impossibly distant.

We were supposed to have a show in Wheeling, Illinois, on a Friday night. A few days before, I got a call from Brian Williams. Tom Brokaw was still anchoring *NBC Nightly News* at that point; Brian was his principal fill-in, and was sitting in for Brokaw that week.

On the Friday night in question, Brian wanted to do a self-contained essay about the decline of sportsmanship. He'd read something I had written on the subject. His idea was to make the piece a one-on-one conversation. He asked if I would come to Yankee Stadium to tape it with him.

I had never been there. Yankee Stadium, to me — to a lot of people, I imagine — had always stood as the pinnacle, the rung beyond which there are no more rungs. If the world is indeed a stage, then Yankee Stadium has long represented the largest stage of all. My whole life, every stadium I ever walked into, no matter how pleasing or impressive, the thought was: This is nice. This is big. But it's not Yankee Stadium.

I flew to New York and rode over to the Bronx. The Yankees weren't in town, but arrangements had been made to open the ballpark for our taping. I went to the appointed gate, and the people who were supposed to let me in pointed me in the right direction. Even that seemed odd — it seemed that you would need an escort in that place, you shouldn't be allowed to wander around as if you were in some strip shopping center.

I walked into the stands. I looked around and I thought:

This is nice. This is big.

But it's not Yankee Stadium.

There was a rock-and-roll analogy: I had once read a story about the early days of rock, and of some of the early groupies. One young woman, or so the story went, had set a goal for herself: to sleep with Mick Jagger. She slept with a lot of rock stars, the way she related the story; some she liked a lot, some she didn't like much at all. But every time she would sleep with a famous singer, she would think: He's cool. He's fine. But he's not Mick Jagger.

And then, at least according to the tale, she finally did get to hang around the Rolling Stones, and she finally did sleep with Mick Jagger.

And found herself thinking:

He's cool. He's fine.

But he's not Mick Jagger.

I stood in the seats along the first-base line. The street address was correct. This was, objectively, Yankee Stadium.

Yet it wasn't. It was a big ballpark with seats made of some blue plastic-like material, and advertising signs wherever they could be sold, and solid metal railings. I looked at the pitcher's mound and tried to see Don Larsen throwing the final pitch of his perfect game, tried to see Yogi Berra ready to run into his arms, and I realized that the Yankee Stadium that came out of the radio of my childhood back in Ohio was more real than the real thing.

If there is, indeed, a top rung of that ladder—if there is a finish line—then perhaps you're never supposed to see it. If you see the finish line, it's not really the finish line. Which is a good piece of knowledge to have. For all the people who spend their lives trying to make it to the metaphorical Yankee Stadium, it's not so bad to find out that, when you get there, it's not there at all.

Brian Williams was waiting with his camera crew in the box seats. We did the interview. Afterward, with my guitar case in my hand—I had brought it from Chicago; I'd be flying straight back to do our show—I walked out to right field.

I stood on the grass, looking toward home plate, trying to see what Babe Ruth must have seen on all his New York afternoons in right. I wondered if he felt like he was ever here.

By late afernoon I was sitting in a priests' residence in Wheeling, a town north of Chicago.

Our concert was part of a church-sponsored celebration; the priests' living quarters—it was a one-story ranch-style house—was going to be our dressing room and dining hall.

Dean was trying out a piano in the living room. I didn't know he could play; he was doing a pretty creditable job on "Surf City." Jan was watching. "What's the name of this tune?" I said to Jan, and he grinned.

The television set was tuned to the local NBC station, and at five-thirty P.M. Chicago time the network news from New York began, with Brian Williams in the anchor seat. We all sat and watched.

There was Yankee Stadium. There we were.

"Hey," Jan said.

It seemed less than real. Had I been there, today? In a few minutes it was over.

Dean left to go to the stage area to commiserate with the event's organizers. I walked around a little carnival that had been set up on the church property, and sensed, from the side of my eye, some commotion back around the priests' residence.

I hastened over there. Jan had walked outside for a moment, then, on the way back in, had tripped on the metal runner of a sliding door. He had fallen flat onto his face.

He was embarrassed, lying on the floor near the piano. Several people were kneeling next to him. "I'm all right," he was saying. "Give me a glass of water, my medication, and some bread." Someone told me that I should go find Dean.

So I did. He was by the stairs to the stage; I pulled him aside, so the organizers would not hear exactly what had happened.

He sighed.

"You know, back home, time goes by the regular way," he said. "Here, it's like every minute is an hour."

He made a sluggish sweep with his arm, like the hand of a clock moving in the slowest of slow motion.

"If anyone ever told me that I had six weeks to live, I know what I'd do," he said. "I'd go on tour with Jan Berry. It would seem like forever."

He started over to the house to talk to Jan. Soon we all, Jan included, were onstage, singing "I Get Around."

It would be hard for anyone on the outside—the people in the audiences, the promoters and booking agents, the airline flight crews and local van drivers—to delineate exactly what the shifting dynamic between Jan, Dean and the rest of the band was, not just ongoing, but on a given day or night.

To say that this group of musicians faced a distinctive set of circumstances was self-evident. All touring bands deal with their own states of affairs, each seemingly unique. But this, it was probably safe to conclude, was unlike anything else.

Sometimes, relievedly, it managed to verge on the comical. We were in an airport in Iowa one morning, waiting to make a connecting flight, and Jan came up to me excitedly with something in his hand. He'd been at the airport snack counter.

"These are new," he said with great enthusiasm, showing me what he had purchased: a six-pack of Famous Amos–brand cookies made in the approximate style of Oreos, which apparently had just been introduced.

"What are they?" I said.

"Rolaids," Jan said.

David Logeman, seeing the cookies, said to him: "Right, Jan. Remember to take them every four hours."

Phil Bardowell said, "How many milligrams are those, Jan?"

Jan, realizing his mistake, laughed and put his palm to his forehead.

"Not Rolaids," he said. "I know."

And Dean, for all his consternation about his lifelong singing partner, clearly felt on some level an empathy and affection for Jan of the kind sometimes seen in longtime marriages, marriages in which one half of the couple has been beset by a mishap that, they both know and no longer have to discuss out loud, has transformed things forevermore.

Dean wasn't a person to articulate such feelings—he seemed much more comfortable making frustrated little asides to us about Jan's eccentricities. But if you looked, you could see, in quiet moments, something bordering on love.

In another airport one morning, we were milling about, waiting for a plane to pull up to the gate so we could board and head to the next city. Dean craned his neck around and, with an exasperated edge we'd all heard before, said: "Where's Jan?"

He was always doing this at flight time—looking to see where Jan had wandered. I saw Dean get up, check the adjacent gate areas, then walk quickly down the concourse. I decided to follow.

Jan was in a little restaurant-cafeteria, sitting at a table all alone. On his less-than-good days, I knew that the ostensibly simple act of ordering a meal must not be easy for him; onstage he heard cheers and applause, because in that context he was Jan Berry of Jan and Dean, and the guitarists were playing and the music was terrific and Dean Torrence was standing beside him . . . onstage he was a star, one of the men everyone had come to see.

Alone, though, on the difficult days, when his bouts of confusion were at a high ebb, he must have seemed, to restaurant workers who saw him limping in and who had no idea who he was, something somewhat different. Jan had to know this.

So there he was, a man in his fifties with a cafeteria tray in front of him, having breakfast by himself.

Dean saw him. He walked to the table and sat in the chair across from Jan.

The two men talked quietly. Then—Dean didn't know I was observing this—something close to tender happened.

Dean reached across the table for Jan's tray. He picked up the miniature containers filled with jelly and butter and, with the plastic utensils, spread them on Jan's pieces of toast. Then he cut the toast so it would be easier for Jan to eat. He slid the tray back to Jan. I saw Jan nod toward Dean in gratitude.

So I probably should not have been surprised by what Dean said to me late one night.

We were somewhere in the Carolinas. It was after one A.M., and I was having trouble sleeping after a show. I was thirsty; I grabbed the ice bucket in my room and went to look for an ice machine.

In the hallway, walking around with his own ice bucket, was Dean.

His eyes were red and tired. This had been one of those days when he and the band had flown across the country from the West Coast.

"I thought I saw a sign before that said 'Vending,'" he said.

"I don't know," I said. We walked up and down the hall; we couldn't find an ice machine. We rode the elevator to the lobby together; the overnight desk clerk told us what floor to go to.

We did, and found one of those little closet-like areas in which there are candy and soda pop machines, and a loud, clanking ice machine behind a door to muffle the sound. We stood in that compact room together, and Dean seemed a little discomfited by what he asked me.

"Do you think you could get some information about the Rock and Roll Hall of Fame?" he said. "About their rules and procedures?"

He didn't want to make the call himself. I got the impression it would have made him feel crestfallen. Jan and Dean had not been selected for induction into the Hall.

"I probably can," I said.

"I just think it would be so nice for Jan," Dean said. "He was so much more talented than so many people who are getting in."

I'd never heard him say such a thing so directly.

"I don't even care if I get in," Dean said. "Oh, I'd love it, obviously. But if they just elected Jan for his songwriting and arranging and producing, I'd be so happy for him. Because the guy deserves it, and I don't think he's ever going to get it."

He said that, because of the accident, people in the music business tended to define Jan only by that: he was the guy who had had the "Dead Man's Curve" collision.

"But they never saw him when those records of ours were being recorded," Dean said. "Jan was just brilliant. He could do anything in a studio. You know how he can be so difficult now? It's not really all that different than how he was before the accident. He went into every situation thinking he was smarter than anyone else, which was sort of hard when you were the other person. But the thing is, he was right. I don't know what the definition of 'genius' is, but I think he probably was one. I wish all you guys could have known him back then."

The two of us stood there with our ice buckets. I told him that I would make some calls; I was sure I could get some sort of packet from the Rock and Roll Hall of Fame.

"I don't even know what I'll do with it if you get it," Dean said. "It would just be good to have the information. It would make the guy's whole life, to be able to walk across that stage."

We rode the elevator back to our own floor.

"Long day," Dean said as he opened the door to his room. "See you in the morning."

TEN

In Cassapolis, Michigan, the IDCOs were out in full force.

That, I had learned early on, was the band's acronym for the question we heard over and over, in every city, and also the affectionate acronym describing the people who asked the question. IDCO—Is Dean Comin' Out?

We'd hear it each night as we made our way back and forth between the stage and our dressing area. Dean usually didn't mingle for long periods of time among these most tenacious and resolute of fans, because if he made a practice of it he'd end up doing little else.

So, always, men and women would be lined up with old Jan and Dean albums in their hands, with vintage fan magazines and dog-eared posters. When, on our way back to the dressing area from soundcheck or on our way to get food, we would pass them, there the words would be, usually uttered with studied offhandedness, unchanged from town to town:

"Is Dean comin' out?"

"Probably later," we would say.

When Jan would be selling merchandise after the shows—this was his private enterprise—it was the most common sentence in the air there, too: "Is Dean comin' out?"

It was instructive, a reminder: Oh, yeah. This is the legend part, isn't it? People have brought their artifacts many miles and have stood for many hours, because this man means something important to them.

In Cassapolis, north of South Bend across the Michigan-Indiana border, the fairgrounds were muddy and sloppy, and the IDCOs stood patiently behind a rope that was guarded by security personnel.

"Is Dean comin' out?" a fellow in a feed-supply-company cap asked as I passed the rope.

"He will, sooner or later," I said.

And he always did. The IDCOs always got their man.

In our dressing trailer in a mud-covered field, Dean was showing Jan how a card game called Uno was played.

Some of the people outside caught sight of him through the open trailer door, and began to chant:

"We want Dean! We want Dean!"

"Can't imagine why," Dean said under his breath, dealing the cards to his old partner.

When it has reached children this young, in a place this small, then you have to fear for what is coming our way.

Before the show I went for a walk around the fairgrounds. The Cass County Fair was about as modest in scale as such gatherings get; there were a few rides and a smattering of livestock exhibits, but I had seen a lot of county fairs by now in my travels with the band, and it was hard to imagine one much more compact than this.

At a restroom near the midway I saw a little boy, perhaps eight years old, coming out the door in a hurry with a frightened, troubled expression on his face.

He was white, as were more than 90 percent of the people I'd seen so far at the fair.

Out of the restroom came six other boys, following him. They were black, and I would say their ages were eight, nine, ten—perhaps the oldest was eleven. These were little kids, not teenagers.

The black children immediately surrounded the white child, pinning him in.

He tried to walk away. Everywhere he turned, the black boys stopped him from getting out of the circle. He looked like he was about to weep.

One of the black children raised his fist. The white boy tried to break out of the circle again, and failed.

They were so small, all of them. Why was this occurring?

"Hey, guys," I said.

They all looked up toward my voice.

"What's going on?" I said.

"He called me a nigger," the boy who had raised his fist said, in a flat, not especially convincing tone.

"No, I didn't," the white child said, his voice trembling. "I didn't say anything to him."

He looked at me with imploring eyes. He said he and his brother had gone in to use the restroom, and his brother had left first. That's when these other boys had started to pick on him, he said.

"He called me a nigger," the black child said again.

It was hard to imagine. The child in the middle of the circle was outnumbered, slight, shy and scared. He would have been out of his mind to have called one of the boys that name. What this looked like to me was a boy being bullied because he was alone and afraid, and one of the bullies coming up with an excuse for it. But what did I know? I didn't see what had happened in the preceding minutes; I was just some middle-aged white guy in a surf shirt who had turned a corner on a rural fairgrounds and come face-to-face with this.

The boy in the middle of the circle kept looking up at me, pleading in his face. He tried once more to find a way out, and once more he failed.

"Come on, guys," I said to all of them. "Let's all be friends."

The words sounded obtuse and oversweet as soon as they left my mouth—they sounded like I was trying to be a dad from a Golden Age of Television sitcom.

Whoever was lying—and someone was—when the hatred and distrust start this young, in a place this seemingly out of the way and tranquil, when children so little walk around with this lodged in their hearts, either locked into those hearts already or forming there on a night like this one and settling in for a long and bitter stay . . .

"Hey, guys, stop it," I said. "Listen, guys, why don't we just . . ."

The black child who had been talking the most shoved at the white child, and the white child found a hole in the circle and tried to run, and the black children followed right behind him. I saw a county sheriff's deputy, and pointed him toward the children; he ran after them, caught up, separated them and started to talk to them. I joined him.

"All right," he said. He told the white child: "You go find your brother." The boy walked off, as quickly as he could. The deputy told the black children: "Come on, now. Leave him alone. Everyone's supposed to be at the fair having fun." The deputy stood with them until the white boy was out of sight.

If the black children were being untruthful, then they had already learned that accusing someone of using that word was a way to try to escape blame themselves. If the white child was being untruthful, then he had already learned to use that word to hurt others. Either way, it was all lousy.

With tinny and tooting carnival midway music sounding, I walked back toward our trailer, the evening already ruined.

"Is Dean comin' out?" someone at the rope line said. Showtime was minutes away on a muddy Michigan night.

The singing was everything.

I had first begun to understand this the summer we had been in Iowa, on the night everyone gathered to sing "Don't Worry, Baby" at the hotel-corridor piano in the hours after the show. No one ever talked explicitly about the act of singing, just as they never talked about the craft inherent in playing their instruments. Phil and Randell and Chris on their guitars, Gary at his keyboard, David behind his drums . . . they were so good at what they did—so proficient, to use a too-dry term—that it never occurred to them to discuss it. They played their instruments as seemingly effortlessly as most people talked. The music was their language; they didn't have to think about the mechanics of it any more than other people have to think about the kinetic process of forming words in daily conversation.

Once in a while, I would prompt them. Chris and I were sitting at breakfast one morning; he was gloomy, because Jan's demands and erratic outbursts, I could tell, were getting to him. Chris was a stickler for order and rigid ritual; Dean joked that he considered Chris to be his H. R. Haldeman. Someone was five minutes late to the lobby, Chris would be the one to call the room with an admonition. We would get up from a pre-show meal, Chris would be the one to say, "Bus your plates, everyone." He couldn't help himself; he should have been a career Marine.

At breakfast this day I asked him: "What do you think about when you're playing your guitar?"

He smiled. "Paying the mortgage," he said.

"I'm serious," I said. "Do you think about where your fingers are on the strings?"

"Nah," he said. "It's automatic. I'm not all that good a player, by the way. I enjoy the singing."

And about that—about the singing part—I knew he was telling the truth. I watched every face onstage. Whatever the work part all of this was for these men, whatever the drudgery, that dropped away when it became time for their vocal solos. Maybe they wouldn't have admitted it, but it was the most fun part of their day. It was what made the trip worth it.

Even a trip like the one that brought us to Framingham, Massachusetts. Some sort of computer software company with more money on its hands than it knew what to do with had hired Jan and Dean to play at a picnic for the firm at a conference center. The journey from California had not been stress-free; Jan was angry about some imagined slight, and had not shown up for the second leg of the flight in Minneapolis. He had arrived in Boston eventually, but nerves were frayed.

And then we got to the conference center to find sixty people in a tent.

That's what the audience was going to be. Sixty. The company evidently had the cash, and had felt like hearing some surf music.

Before we went on, some executives of the company—males—got onstage in grass skirts and stuffed bras and lip-synched to a tape of "Surfin' U.S.A."

Dean turned to me. "We flew three thousand miles, for this," he said.

Yet even on such an afternoon, the singing mattered. The singing was the fun. No one sloughed it off.

For me, it was dreamlike every time. It was once again the gift be-
stowed, the chance to do this. What surprised me was that the others,
quietly, regardless of how many times they had done this, seemed on
some inner stratum to feel the same way. Each of us had his own wedge
monitor in front of our microphones every night, so we could hear our
voices being angled back up at us, and thus stay in tune. It was a team
sport; the songs never sounded exactly the same from night to night, because there was always some variation in the way someone would hit a
guitar chord, always a slightly different sound to the alloy of the backup
vocals, or the inflection someone decided to put into a certain word . . .
it must be what a long-running stage play is like, with the script being
constant, but each night's performance having a life of its own.

When you sang, you were *making* something; that's what it felt
like—your song might last only two and a half minutes, but because it
was live, because the others were all pitching in on a new stage in a new
city, because the song was coming through different setups of speakers
than it had the night before, and the week before, and the month before, that two-and-a-half-minute song was unlike any version of itself
that you had ever sung before or you would ever sing again. Three seconds before your solo began, you could not know exactly how it would
come out this time around. That was up to you, and to the men standing by your side.

I always looked over at the others as they sang their leads, tried to
discern what was in their eyes. I wished they could see themselves.
They were happy during those minutes. Maybe they would have told
me I was nuts for thinking that. But it was the truth. Sixty people
watching or six thousand, it made no difference. This is what they had
been doing since they were boys, this is what gave value and pride to
their lives. Their day, their night, turned happiest when it was their turn
to sing.

I wasn't present for the blowup.

We drove to Boston to sleep after the Framingham show. The band
would be getting up for an early flight; I would be going to Chicago later.

Gary called to tell me about it after it was over.

At six-thirty in the morning, in the lobby, Jan told Chris that he thought he had left his little tape recorder on the stage in Framingham.

He told Chris to call the promoter and find it.

Chris, according to Gary, had said there was no way he was going to call the promoter at six-thirty A.M.

Jan insisted.

Chris said, "No, we'll deal with it later."

According to Gary, Jan then shouted: "Fuck you. You don't care about me."

And in the van to the airport, Gary said, Jan continued to yell at Chris. Apparently what he yelled was:

"You're fired. Davy's the new leader."

"David Logeman?" I said to Gary.

"Yeah," Gary said. "I have no idea what Jan was thinking."

"So what's going to happen?" I said.

"Who knows," Gary said.

During all this I met Frank Sinatra.

In Chicago I ran into Tom Dreesen, the comedian who had been Sinatra's opening act for years. Sinatra was in town for a sold-out stand at the Civic Opera House. Dreesen invited me to be his guest at the Saturday night performance.

From the audience I watched Dreesen do his stand-up routine. There was an intermission; I went backstage to thank him for the ticket.

He hesitated for a second and then said: "Come with me for a few minutes."

He led me down a cluttered hallway, past a table with a coffeepot on top. We rounded a corner.

A door was ajar. Standing alone in a small room, wearing a tuxedo, his back to us, was Sinatra.

"Frank, there's someone I wanted to introduce you to," Dreesen said.

Sinatra turned fully toward us. He had not been expecting visitors.

For just a moment—not even a full moment—I considered saying to him, as a joke: "Hey, I'm a singer, too." Just to give myself the story to tell. Just to get dinner table laughs for the rest of my life.

But Sinatra looked at me with those famous eyes, and I knew there was no chance I would say it. He was seventy-seven. The eyes were not wary, not annoyed, just waiting to see what this was all about.

He extended his hand and I shook it. Without having thought about it in advance, I said, "May I ask you a really stupid question?"

"Go ahead," Sinatra said, in Frank Sinatra's voice.

"Do you practice?" I said.

Maybe it's the word that confused him. Maybe "rehearse" would have been the proper word. But in fact it was practice I was interested in. The singer of the century—I just found myself wondering whether, after all the years, he still felt the need to practice the fundamentals of his trade.

"Practice?" Sinatra said.

"Singing," I said.

He looked surprised at the question, but not offended.

"Sure," he said. "Sure I do. I practice all the time."

We talked for a few minutes—nothing earthshaking—and I thanked him for taking the time, and on the way back down the hallway Dreesen told me two things.

The first was that Sinatra did, in fact, practice: "Just about every day," Dreesen said. "He genuinely works at it."

The second thing Dreesen told me was that it was no coincidence that Sinatra had been standing when we encountered him. After putting on his tuxedo in his dressing room each night, Dreesen said, Sinatra never sat down before going onstage. The reason was that he did not want to crease the trousers; he worried that it might make him look slovenly to the men and women in the audience. So, at seventy-seven, he stood until the time he was called to the stage.

I went back to my seat and watched him come out and sing those songs no one else will ever own: "I've Got the World on a String," "All or Nothing at All," "Street of Dreams."

What he was doing up there in front of his orchestra was so qualitatively different from what I had been seeing on the road that it might as well have been classified as a separate line of work. That was my first impression.

But then I thought:

Even with all that was different, there were certain things. . . .

I saw him standing in that tuxedo, the one he had not permitted to wrinkle, and I remembered Dean Torrence in all those hotel rooms, ironing the stage shirts even though no one would care if he didn't.

I saw Sinatra singing, and I knew that he was reading some of the lyrics off a TelePrompTer, because, as it had been widely reported, he had found that with age he was beginning to forget some of the words. I thought of Jan Berry, having to relearn his own songs again every night. Maybe that was why Jan had been so distressed about having left his tape recorder on the stage in Massachusetts; maybe he was afraid of what would happen to him without the tape.

Sinatra was Sinatra, the one and only; the work he did had nothing in common, in almost any meaningful respect, with the work done by the men with whom I had been spending my time.

But perhaps some things are universal. I looked at him up there, singing his heart out, and I wondered:

Is this the happiest time of his day?

St. Louis Union Station had everything going for it:

Nearly a million square feet of space, stretching farther than the eye could see. Escalators and wide stairways and elaborately painted high ceilings. Five different highways linking it to the rest of the St. Louis metropolitan area. A Hyatt hotel right in the terminal, and more than a hundred shops and restaurants: a Disney Store, an Eddie Bauer, a Banana Republic, a movie multiplex.

And it was gleaming. One hundred fifty million dollars had been spent to make it sparkle and shimmer. It probably looked better now, as we arrived for our show, than it had when it first opened on September 1, 1894. On that day it was said to be the largest rail terminal in the United States, and by the 1940s more than a hundred thousand passengers a day passed through it, arriving and departing from all corners of the nation on forty-two working tracks in an unbroken rank on a single level. During that era it was pridefully proclaimed in St. Louis that one-sixth of the world's population eventually set foot in downtown's Union Station.

And here it was, polished to perfection. Union Station, today, felt like the ultimate hub.

It lacked only one thing:

Trains.

There were none. It had been redeveloped as a "shopping, dining and entertainment destination." We had been brought in to sing outdoors where the tracks once had hummed.

The new Union Station was part of an effort, like those in so many American cities, to bring people back downtown. Downtowns across the country, withering and facing desertion each sundown, had become beggars—elegant beggars in some cases, dressed up and trying their hardest, but beggars still. All of the handsome physical facets of a place like Union Station, all of the painstaking promotions and twilight concerts and special events, combined to form a single unspoken word:

"Please."

Please come downtown. Please don't abandon the soul of the city.

I checked into the Union Station Hyatt and called Dean's room. A woman answered.

"So I get to meet you at last," her voice said.

"Is this his wife?" I said.

"It'd better be," Susan Torrence said.

She had flown here from California to meet him for the show. I went to their room; she was slim and pretty with a ready smile, and Dean was softer-spoken than usual, almost bashful, around her. He didn't seem like a rock-and-roll star.

The rest of the band was at a Cardinals afternoon baseball game. At dusk Dean and his wife and I walked to some classic railroad cars, attached to no working engine and able to go nowhere, that would serve as our dressing rooms. Jan was already there, in a Pullman compartment, eating a sandwich.

The band arrived and we climbed onto a stage and saw, where the trains once were, eight thousand people looking back at us—fewer than the hundred thousand who once came in and out on the overland rails each day, but not bad at all for a weeknight in downtown St. Louis.

The Katy Flyer used to pull into this place, bearing travelers; the Wabash Cannonball, the Banner Blue Limited, the Southwestern Limited: all of them came over the horizon and into the station, and people from faraway cities and states stretched their legs and stepped into the heart of a real and thriving downtown.

"It's like you can see ghosts arriving with their old suitcases," Phil said to me between songs.

We finished our show with "Barbara Ann" and then went for a late snack at the Union Station Hooters. The patrons were all relaxed. No one had a train to make.

Chris quit the next day.

The band was scheduled to have a show in Essex Junction, Vermont. I wasn't going. They all flew to Albany, New York, and then had a long van ride.

Jan, who had flown separately to a small Vermont airfield, was already in the parking lot of the hotel, in a cab. He was upset about the arrangements—it wasn't clear what the problem was.

But, according to those who saw it, he immediately lit into Chris. He not only was screaming—he took a swing.

Chris, they said, yelled back, and resigned from the band on the spot.

The cabdriver, waiting to be paid, said to all of them:

"Welcome to Vermont. Now go home."

Chris apparently told Dean he would work through the end of the summer, but then would depart the band, and would not return. Life, he said, was too short. During the show he did his singing next to David's drum kit at the rear of the stage. He didn't want to be anywhere near Jan.

"Plus," Gary said, "all during the show, we kept hearing this amplified announcement from out on the carnival grounds. Some barker kept shouting: 'Come see the world's largest rats. Come see the hundred-pound rats.'

"So all in all, I'd have to say it's been a really delightful trip."

On Labor Day weekend, to say goodbye to summer, we flew to Roanoke, Virginia, for something billed as the Beach Festival, to be held at Victory Stadium, a local football field.

A "best tan contest" was scheduled. People were encouraged to bring coolers, flip-flops, beach chairs and beach towels. The Drifters and the Kingsmen were going to open for Jan and Dean. All this promotion was fine, but what was on our minds as we arrived was the fact that Chris had meant what he said: this weekend he was fulfilling the final part of his commitment to Dean, but that was going to be it. He was leaving after the summer.

At the football stadium we were led after sundown to a cinder block locker room, so we could wait while the other bands did their sets. Chris seemed becalmed, quite at peace by now with his decision; he was being civil to Jan, and Jan, on some level feeling abashed about the whole thing, was being civil in return. Everyone understood: what had happened to Jan in that car all those years ago had changed the course of his life so wholly and irrevocably that it did little good to dwell too long on all the ramifications of the aftereffects. One of those ramifications, we all knew, was the impending absence of Chris Farmer.

I left the locker room and went out to the stage during the Kingsmen's concert. I always liked listening to them; their taste in music, judging from their set lists, was very close to mine, and over the course of these summers I had become a fan of their live shows. When I reached the stage tonight they were into a driving version of the Rolling Stones' "The Last Time."

They were hitting that hypnotic, bending guitar line that runs like an exposed electric current through the song, and the vocals were as entrancing as they had been thirty years before when Mick Jagger first sang them. I stood there and thought: I'm home. Isn't this something? I've never been to Roanoke in my life, I don't know anyone in town other than the guys I'm traveling with, and I'm home. This music—all of it, all of these songs I have loved for so long—is reliable, is shelter, and has been since the first moment I heard it.

Who could have known it at the time—who could have known how long this would endure? On the loneliest nights, on the most joyful afternoons, during the sultriest summers and frigid winters, the music, since it was new, has been so profoundly and consistently welcome. In the very worst of times, and in the very best, this music—structurally uncomplicated, four chords in most of the songs, lyrics usually basic and bare—has been like a friend, something to be counted on and treasured. Magic: just guitars and drums and vocals, yet it has always been, without my even having to think about it, the most loyal and steadfast of companions. Wherever I have been, I have needed only to hear three or four seconds of any of hundreds of these songs, coming out of a radio or a loudspeaker or merely out an open window on a city street, and I'm instantly somewhere I've been before, somewhere I want to be, familiar and somehow safe.

The Kingsmen were up there singing:

. . . Don't try very hard to please me. . . .

Then the lurid mystery of the twisting guitar line.

. . . with what you know it should be easy . . .

So many songs, still with the power to make me feel this way. Even now; even all this time removed from when I logically should have stopped loving them. I was in Virginia tonight, and because the songs were here too, I was less alone. I guessed that as long as the songs were around, that would always be true. And I knew I would never say any of this out loud to anyone, because I would feel foolish unless I could know for sure that they felt the same way.

I went back to the locker room. The band was sitting around on football benches, waiting for the Kingsmen to finish up. I heard Chris's voice, echoing from somewhere.

"Hey!" he called to the others. "Come in here! This is great!"

He was in the shower room, standing there in his stage clothes.

"Listen to this reverberation!" he said. As in most shower rooms, the acoustics were such that his voice was bouncing off the walls, sounding rich and full.

The others went in and, without any preliminary discussion, stood together and started to harmonize.

Their voices, always, were so graceful; they had sung together for so long, knowing how to commingle those voices in just the right way, that sometimes I had to stop and remind myself of how prodigiously skilled they were. I had become spoiled, getting to hear those voices onstage every night.

In the shower room they were singing, without the accompaniment of any instruments, a version of the old gospel hymn "I'll Fly Away."

The hymn, the way it was written, begins:

Some glad morning, when this life is over,
I'll fly away. . . .

As Chris and Gary and Phil and Randell and Dean sang it tonight, the words were different:

Some glad morning, when this gig is over,
I'll surf away. . . .

The voices, in five-part barbershop concordance, were so lilting and lovely, they might have been those of a church choir. The guys weren't kidding around with the words or treating them as whimsy, and I could tell that this version was not new to them, they had, somewhere, sung the revised-for-themselves hymn this way before. And it was not some sort of sentimental sendoff to Chris, at least not intentionally so. They had simply found this shower room this evening and apprehended that the sound it would provide was just right for an a cappella song, and so their voices sought out and found each other, each making the others better.

I'll surf away, oh glory,
I'll surf away. . . .

Out on the stage in the end zone of the football field the Kingsmen were still at it, their amplified guitar chords making it into our locker room. But the singers in the shower room were easily able to override that; the tiled walls in the close quarters boosted their voices to a resounding crescendo.

I'll surf away, oh glory,
I'll surf away. . . .

In fifteen minutes they would be out in the stadium, singing for a paycheck, singing for an audience.

Until then, they were doing it for themselves.

The singing was everything. The singing was life.

It probably would have made them self-conscious to talk about it, and because of that I knew I never would. But the singing, the promise of being able to do it anew, together, was what got them up each morning. It waited for them.

ELEVEN

The winters, in the main, were something to be endured and not dwelled upon.

The barrenness intrinsic to them, when placed against the summers of endless touring, could be summed up in a few words. Sometimes the words were unexpected.

In the Cincinnati airport I stepped off my Delta flight on the last day of May. I had talked several times with each of the guys over the winter months. I was a few feet into the terminal when I heard a public-address announcement saying my name. The voice from the airport ceiling said I should report to a certain area in baggage claim.

I didn't know what this could be, but I followed the directions. There, waiting and grinning, sitting on his suitcase, was David Logeman.

"The promoter sent a van to take me to the hotel," he said. "The other guys took a later flight—they don't get here until late tonight. I asked the driver to wait for you."

A nice thing for him to do, I thought. We went to the van, and the driver checked his clipboard.

"I've got one more passenger to pick up," he said. "It says here 'Freddy Cannon.' His plane's supposed to get in in ten minutes."

What a great harbinger of summer, and of the days and nights that lay ahead. Freddy "Boom Boom" Cannon. If you've got to wait around an airport. . . .

David and I leaned back in the van and caught up on things, and then, hurrying across three lanes of access road traffic, carrying his guitar case, was Freddy himself—a star from the late 1950s whose fame and whose hits had pre-dated Jan and Dean's: "Palisades Park," "Tallahassee Lassie," "Where the Action Is," "Abigail Beecher (My History Teacher)" . . . just thinking of the titles made me smile.

I'd never met him, but his face, all pointy planes and tough juts, was as familiar as an older uncle's. Freddy held the record for the most appearances for a performer on *American Bandstand*—one hundred ten—and he climbed into the van already fast-talking in an old-time sales hustler's hard-East-Coast accent, more the speaking voice of someone you might imagine being in the business of pushing platters at *Blackboard Jungle*-era disc jockeys than of someone who sang on the records.

"Hey, guys, sorry I'm late," he said. "You know anything about the hotel? Is it close to here? I'm starvin'. Starvin'!"

I don't know what Freddy ended up doing for dinner, but David and I found a rib place.

Which is where I heard the words that summed up his winter. The words I wouldn't have anticipated.

I asked him how he had spent the months since September.

"I took a telemarketing gig," he said, trying to sound casual.

He had a son to support. He had found work in one of those boiler room operations where people sit at phones all day and make cold calls to people who don't want to hear from them.

"How was it?" I said.

"Don't ask," he said. Then: "Brutal."

But that was during the cold months. At the turn of midnight, it would be June. He was a rock-and-roll drummer on tour again.

In the morning I went to a bank of pay phones near the Holiday Inn's lobby to make some calls.

I heard music.

Behind the closed wooden door of a conference area called the Athens Room, a voice was singing:

She's my transistor sister,
and, boy, you've got to love her a lot. . . .

Freddy. I hadn't heard "Transistor Sister" in years.

From the other side of the door I could hear, accompanying Freddy, the steel strings of electric guitars that weren't plugged in to amplifiers. I knew what was going on: he was rehearsing his local band, teaching them his songbook.

My phone calls were finished. But I pretended to have more to make.

I just stood there, with the receiver to my ear, talking to no one, listening to the private concert.

Freddy was a taskmaster—that, I could hear.

"C'mon, guys," his voice said. "Pick it up! Pick it up! We're not gonna be playin' at a funeral, we're gonna be playin' at a rock show!"

I felt vaguely sheepish, standing there listening, but nowhere near sheepish enough to leave.

"Again, now!" Freddy's voice commanded.

Instantly the steely strings.

And his voice:

. . . she's my transistor sister,
playin' her radio. . . .

Winter seemed suddenly a distant memory.

The disc jockeys from the Cincinnati radio station called themselves "The Good Guys," which was only perfect—a radio phrase just as evocative a throwback as was Freddy Cannon himself. The station still employed jocks named Rockin' Ron Schumacher, Tom Cat Michaels, Dr. Boogie, Dangerous Dan Allen, Cool Bobby B . . . and the Good Guys kept the show moving on the big outdoor stage next to the Ohio River.

This was the Chuck Berry concert—the one to which he would show up at the very last minute, cutting short Jan and Dean's second show of the day. We didn't know anything about that during our first set. Randell was taking over for Chris full-time, and he and Phil cranked their razor-wire-sharp guitar lines toward the forty thousand fans in the blazing sun. One person always stood out in every crowd—this afternoon it was a woman in a traffic-cone-orange bikini top, sitting on her boyfriend's bare shoulders, swaying back and forth to "Help Me, Rhonda"—and I could see that there was a rusty barge floating in the Ohio River near the stage.

During "Dance, Dance, Dance" we brought about twenty people from the audience to join us, as we always did. One woman in her forties gyrated in front of the drum kit next to another in her twenties—"My daughter," she explained, shouting over the music—and it was the mother who was wilder, showing all the moves of a premium-priced stripper, and David Logeman, a telephone huckster no more, laughed like a boy on the first day of vacation as he pounded his drums.

After the show we all went to a restaurant called O'Charley's in the Holiday Inn parking lot. It was jammed, and when the hostess called out "Torrence, party of seven," we walked past those who were waiting, including one man who, with some annoyance, said: "Hey. I've been standing here longer." Freddy, alone. Cannon, party of one.

In the morning as I was getting ready to check out there was a knock. "Housekeeping," a woman's voice announced. I opened the door . . . and the two of us stared at each other. It took a second for it to register for both of us.

I didn't recognize her in uniform. "You guys were good," she said, standing by her cart. "So were you," I said. She was the dancer from the stage—the mother in the mother-daughter duo. Life can light you up.

I rode to the airport in a van with Sam the Sham. Like Freddy, he was another man I'd never thought I'd meet: the originator of "Wooly Bully." He'd been a big hit during yesterday's show—there's no one who doesn't love that song—and now, in the van, he was talking about an old concert at which he'd had a run-in with Dennis Wilson of the Beach Boys.

"Dennis said something to me about 'Karma's gonna get ya,'" Sam said, in a scratchy, early-Wolfman-Jack voice.

He balled up his fist like a prizefighter, beaming as he recalled the day. "I told him, 'Hey, karma's not gonna get *you*—*I'm* gonna get you.

I'm karma." Sam the Sham thrust his fist forward like a punch, and his band members in the van laughed and laughed, and it was summer, all right, it was summer being born all over again.

We were all eating cheeseburgers in the middle of the afternoon at a little restaurant in Winthrop Harbor, Illinois. That was one thing about these summers: I was eating more cheeseburgers than I'd eaten since I was a kid, and I am a person who has had a few cheeseburgers.

Randell walked in late, surveyed our burgers, and said to the waitress: "Do you have . . ."

He paused as if to ruminate.

". . . beef Stroganoff?"

Everyone stopped and stared at him.

"What's wrong with you?" Phil said.

Randell reached into his pocket and pulled out a container of pepper. Of course. That was the personal condiment he was carrying with him every stop of this trip.

They all looked like hell. I had pulled off the tour and hadn't seen them in a few weeks, but they had been traveling steadily since then. The day before, in Lac du Flambeau, Wisconsin, their bags had not shown up; it had happened again this morning at O'Hare in Chicago. The temperature was nearing one hundred degrees, and they had not slept.

"If she can afford a Corvette, you'd think she could afford teeth," someone said, as if no preface was necessary.

I knew the context without asking: the reference was to a woman we'd seen at a show several weeks back. The waitress pretended not to hear.

Dean came in, looking as haggard as the others. Straight off the plane, luggage and fresh change of clothing missing, he had been required to ride in an afternoon car parade through town: powerful Chevys and solid Mercurys, big-engined Pontiacs and cocky Thunderbirds.

"They put me in an open convertible," he said. "There was no sign on the side of the car. I was waving to people who had no idea who I was. I felt like an idiot—waving for blocks to a sea of blank faces.

"Tomorrow night I'll be back home in California at the dinner table, trying to explain it to my wife and kids."

We went to the hotel, a twenty-seven-room place with carpets that made you afraid to step on the floors, even with shoes on. Gary and I watched a White Sox game in his room, he on one of the two lumpy beds, me on the other, as the afternoon sun beat against the window, easily vanquishing the air conditioner. He fell asleep in the fourth inning. It felt like languid Saturday afternoons when I was fourteen, killing time with buddies, wishing we had something fun to do.

An Elvis impersonator—Vegas Elvis: white jumpsuit and wraparound shades—said to me: "Do you write books?"

We were behind the stage; the Winthrop Harbor show, the nautical name of the town notwithstanding, would be in a big, dry field.

"Yes," I said, trying to look into his eyes and seeing instead my own reflection in the lenses of his sunglasses.

"Did you write *Hang Time?*" he asked.

His hair was jet black, his lip curled. I was very pleased to have what appeared to be a reader, but this was incongruity incarnate.

"I did," I said.

"I just got done reading that," he said, Memphis marinated into every syllable. I made myself take a mental snapshot of the moment: standing with the Elvis impersonator, his giant metal belt strapped around his waist, listening to him drawl encouraging words. "I enjoy your work, sir," he said.

"Wait till you hear me sing 'Little Honda,' " I said. "Then we'll see how much you enjoy it."

I had lately been singing lead on that one—I thought the song sounded great when the Beach Boys had performed it at Mile High Stadium, I had suggested to Dean that he add it to the show, and one night he did, nodding toward me to sing lead. Things were a lot looser with Chris gone; we were like a discipline-impaired family on a long vacation trip after the stern dad has unexpectedly been called away. I was onstage the whole show now: no more being beckoned on midway through.

Dean was always generous passing the leads around: he seemed to prefer singing harmony, and even though he and Jan were the draw, his sense of self-regard didn't require the solo spotlight. So now I was singing lead on "Dance, Dance, Dance" and "Little Honda" and co-lead with Randell on "I Get Around" and, sometimes, "Help Me, Rhonda." Chris would never have allowed it; he would have talked Dean out of it, on the basis of me being not good, and his case would have been airtight.

The Elvis imitator did his set, and then in darkness we took our places in front of the mikes and monitors.

Just before Jan and Dean were introduced I turned to Randell and said:

"Beef Stroganoff?"

"It's a really good dish on a hot day," he said, which made no sense at all—cold fruit is a good dish on a hot day; a chilled salad is a good dish on a hot day—and then we heard the words: "Ladies and gentlemen, all the way from California . . ."

I looked down beneath the side of the stage, where Elvis was looking back. He gave me a thumbs-up. And why wouldn't he?

Gary was sweating as he played, and during the dance-segment part of the show as I was about to sing he yelled toward me:

"Bring that blonde in the dress onstage to dance."

He gestured toward the audience, in front of the other side of the stage.

"She's been smiling at me all night," he yelled.

So when the time arrived to invite people onstage, I pointed at the woman I thought he was referring to—she pointed back at herself, and mouthed: *Me?*—and I nodded yes, and motioned to the side stairs, where other would-be dancers were coming up to join us.

She came onto the stage and danced and Gary didn't even look at her, which surprised me. During the encore he came over to me and said: "You got the wrong blonde."

"Does it matter?" I said.

After the show, as we were getting ready to depart, a fan—an IDCO; Dean had gone into the dressing trailer and was nowhere to be seen—

cornered Gary and started earnestly asking a long series of detailed questions about the music, and the history of the band, and past concerts to which the man had traveled. Gary was being polite, but his eyes were glazing.

Suddenly there appeared, in a summer dress, a beautiful woman with blonde hair who walked up to Gary and said:

"I loved your singing tonight. I was looking at you the whole show."

She flashed him a dazzling smile and then she was gone.

"*That* was the right blonde," he said to me.

The IDCO hit Gary with his next question: "So were you with the group back in eighty-four, when they played up in Milwaukee. . . ."

Gary followed the retreating woman with his eyes, until she disappeared.

"And I'll never see her again," he said.

Such moments, rare to nonexistent in the real world in which most men reside—including, I was sensing, the real world in which the band resided when they were back at home, not touring—were commonplace on the road. The rules of life seemed to change when the music was playing.

At the White Water Bay water park in Oklahoma City—twenty-five acres, thirty water slides and pools—you might have thought we were combat pilots spotting enemy aircraft, if you'd overheard the clipped dialogue as we walked to the stage for soundcheck on a triple-digit-temperature July afternoon. "Quick—three o'clock." "Ten o'clock, blue bathing suit." "Six o'clock, straight ahead, the two in red." Outwardly, we might have appeared to be weary guys lugging musical instruments across broad expanses of pool decks; inwardly, we had all the maturity of a team of eight-year-old soapbox derby racers on their first trip out of town. The women in the vicinity of the Big Kahuna raft ride and Castaway Creek were so plenteous, and so skimpily dressed, that if we'd been cartoon characters we would have been drawn with our eyes attached to Slinkys, boinging in and out.

We were tuning up onstage when David said, "Top of the tower."

We turned. There was a ladder leading to a tall slide, and at its summit was a woman so staggering, in a minuscule yellow bikini, that it almost hurt to look—it was like staring at the sun. In any other setting, no one would have dared to say a thing.

Randell, guitar in hand, yelled to her: "Hey, yellow!"

What a thing to say, in the real world. But this was anything but.

She turned to look. In the real world, she might have ignored the call, or been offended. But seeing the band onstage, she smiled and waved.

"Is that your son or your brother?" Randell called to her. She had a little boy with her.

"Neither!" she called back. Then: "Play something!"

Gary hit the first chords of "Yellow Submarine."

She laughed, and we sang:

We all live in a yellow submarine,
yellow submarine, yellow submarine. . . .

She jitterbugged in place before sliding down the chute.

At one point during rehearsal, the park's P.A. system played one of my favorite songs: Bobby Darin's "Dream Lover."

Darin was long dead, but his voice filled the water park, and, my microphone live, I started to sing along with him.

Dream lover, where are you. . . .

Gary and the guitarists and David joined in with their instruments, adding a new tier of sound to Darin's long-ago band, and in the sunshine I continued the duet with Darin:

I want a dream lover,
so I don't have to dream alone. . . .

All this was mixed with an overlay of waterfalls and splashes and screams from the raft rides. There were some people in swimsuits watching us soundcheck, and a young woman said to someone on the stage:

"Are you going to sing tonight?"

"Only if you come."

The young man with her said: "She wants your phone number."

"Do not," the young woman said, blushing like a character in an old true-romance comic book.

The rules were separate here. They traveled from town to town, like a piece of trusty stage equipment.

In the lobby of the La Quinta Inn, after we had showered and were preparing to head back to the water park for the evening show, the desk clerk said to me:

"Mr. Berry keeps asking me to call a One-Way Records in Albany, New York. I don't know what to do."

She said that Jan, in his room, was repeatedly phoning the front desk, imploring someone to call One-Way Records for him.

"I've checked directory assistance in Albany, and in New York City," she said. "I can't find anything. But Mr. Berry's getting very insistent."

I knew what this was: he had told me that he was beginning his efforts to find a record company to release his new music. He didn't have an agent; he was trying to do it all himself.

"I'll talk to him," I said to the clerk. "He gets a little confused."

"It's seven o'clock at night here, so it's eight o'clock in New York," she said to me. "It's Fourth of July weekend. I don't think anyone's still going to be at work at a record company, even if I find the number."

"Don't worry," I said.

Her phone rang. She picked it up.

"It's Mr. Berry again," she whispered to me.

"It's time for him to go to the show anyway," I said. "Don't worry."

It was one of those concerts you don't want ever to end—the Oklahoma heat had us drenched by the second song, the sound system was booming, the people at the water park swarmed to the concert area like bugs at a picnic to spilled jam, still in their bathing suits and dripping as they danced the evening away.

At the end there was a nice moment as we left the stage. None of us felt like we wanted to stop singing, but there was no announcer around to call for an encore. So Gary knelt behind the stage where no one could see him, took Jan's wireless hand microphone, and, in a Top-Forty disc jockey voice, shouted:

"Have you had enough, Oklahoma City?"

"No!" the crowd howled, having no idea they were listening to one of the band members.

"Do you want Jan and Dean to leave the park?" Gary, still kneeling and hiding, yelled.

"No!"

"Should we ask them to do one more song?" Gary yelled, not mentioning that he was one of the "them."

"Yes!" the crowd screamed.

"Then let's hear it!" Gary yelled in the D.J. voice. "Let's hear it! Let's hear it!"

The crowd was out of its mind, chanting for the band to come back, and Jan, watching Gary do this, laughed, really laughed—he liked being in on the joke, he liked being included—and Gary handed him his microphone and we returned to the stage.

Afterwards, there was an example of how the rules on the road may be bendable, but that some breaking points should not be passed.

Two women, drunk on beer and wearing almost nothing, approached us as we were leaving.

Apparently they had known a touring singer or two in their lives, because one of them said:

"B. J. Thomas told us that the names of the hotels where a band stays is confidential."

"La Quinta!" three of our voices said in unison, playing along.

But then both women moved a little closer, and started rubbing up a little bit, and one of them said to one of us: "How'd you like to help me lose five pounds tonight?"

It wasn't a bad line, except that she followed it up by jeeringly saying—her tone was sadistic—that her husband was impotent because of some medication he was taking. And then she turned to a three-year-old girl who was wandering around—her daughter, whom we hadn't noticed—and said: "Mommy's going to go have a good time tonight."

Another daughter—around fourteen—looked at her mother approvingly, which made it worse, and, even as her mother continued to stand way too close to us, the older daughter said: "I won't say nothing at home if you don't say nothing." She said she would take care of the younger one while her mom was out.

The three-year-old was crying, and one of us said to the mother, "You should go with your daughter." She did.

We ended the night having our daily allotment of cheeseburgers at a Shoney's.

"I think all of us should be very proud of telling those women to stop," Randell said.

"Yeah," Gary said. " 'Stop . . . stop . . . in two minutes. . . . ' "

"I wonder if they have ice cream pie here," Dean said.

Weirton, West Virginia, was an old steel town; we were staying there for a show at the Coca-Cola Star Lake Amphitheatre, across the Pennsylvania line in Burgettstown. I checked into my room on the second floor of the Best Western Inn and looked out the window to see, just below me, Dean, Gary, Phil, Randell and David playing a slow-moving game of volleyball on a makeshift patch of dirt and sand. The window was thick enough to keep out all sound, so I could see them talking as with lassitude they hit the ball back and forth, but I could hear nothing. Beyond the sand volleyball pit was a bleak industrial plain that led ultimately to a Wal-Mart and a Kroger's grocery store.

We would be playing with the Monkees. On the way to soundcheck, in a van, the driver said that the Monkees had already gone over in a stretch limousine.

"So we didn't get a limousine?" Jan said.

"The Monkees had it in their contract," the van driver said. "You didn't."

There was something I had been carrying around, waiting to show it to Jan.

It was a letter that a woman had written to me after the show in Winthrop Harbor.

He was riding in front. "Jan," I said, "I have something I think you should read."

I reached to give the letter to him, but he said, "Could you read it to me?"

It was probably better that way. I wanted the others to hear it.

The woman wrote that she had noticed a "sudden transformation of the crowd's attitude after 'Dead Man's Curve.'" I read aloud:

Anyway, I myself have been diagnosed at the ripe old age of forty-one with Parkinson's disease. . . .

She wrote that, because of her illness, she had found herself becoming much more sensitive to other people with disabilities, especially ailments that were readily observable. She wrote that she noticed people talking louder to her, as if they assumed her hearing was impaired; she wrote that people seemed not quite to know how to act in her presence.

Jan, in the front seat, listened as I read. It was a long letter.

When the woman had first seen Jan onstage, she wrote, she had been worried for him. But by the end of the performance, he had inspired everyone in the audience. The best part, she wrote, was when she sensed Jan realized "that we appreciated him for who he is, and not for who he was. It took me a year or so to get my family members to do the same."

There was silence in the van.

I reached a part of the letter where she asked me if I had some way of passing on to Jan her gratitude—and the gratitude of the audience. She was certain, she wrote, that in the years ahead there would be other members of the audience that night—people who didn't yet know it—who would find themselves in situations similar to Jan's, and who would be able to use the memory of his perseverance as an example for themselves as they tried to recover.

And, she wrote, there was a final moment at the concert that was the most meaningful to her. She had been standing in line at the table where

Jan was signing autographs; all she had with her was her pocket Bible. It was the Bible she used when she was in particularly rough shape, and she decided to ask him to sign it. That way, whenever she turned to her Bible for help, she would also pray for Jan.

So, she wrote, Jan had signed it. As he did so, she began to tremor from her illness.

He said to me, "God bless you."

With that, I finished reading.

"Could I hold the letter for a minute?" Jan said.

I handed it to him.

No one said anything for a few moments, and then Randell said, "Jan, you're a very lucky man."

"I know it," Jan said. "I know I am."

The Star Lake Amphitheatre was like a big outdoor cash register built for maximum summer revenues: theater-type seats for top-dollar ticketholders, long expanses of lawn for those who wished to pay a little less and bring blankets, tables with waitress service for corporate sponsors. National acts just about every summer night: memories in, memories out.

There was a private commissary for the bands to get their meals. I stood in a buffet line with Micky Dolenz, Peter Tork and Davy Jones, each waiting with plates in hand. They were the draw tonight; Jan and Dean were billed as "special guests," which seemed to irritate Dean.

Maybe it was that the Monkees had come along after Jan's accident, and were an unmitigated creation of television; I knew that there was a Jan and Dean weekly TV series in the works before Jan had hurt himself. Maybe it was just that Jan and Dean had been Number One before anyone had ever dreamed up the Monkees, and Dean didn't like being second-billed to them. In our dressing room Jan asked Dean for a copy of tonight's song list.

"It's the same songs in the same order you've been singing them for twenty-five years," Dean said.

"But I want to tape them on the floor in front of me," Jan said.

BACKSTAGE IN TULSA:
Front: Phil Bardowell,
Jan Berry, Dean Torrence
Back: David Logeman,
Gary Griffin, Chris Farmer,
Bob Greene
(Gary Griffin collection)

Jan and Dean (Lori Brown collection)

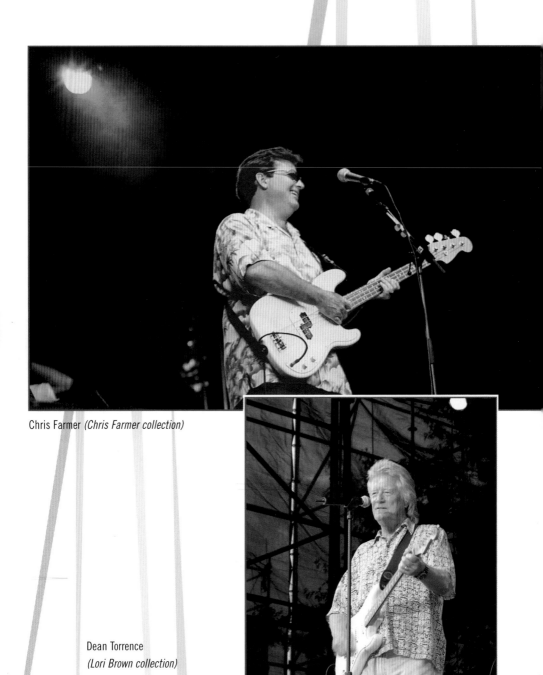

Chris Farmer *(Chris Farmer collection)*

Dean Torrence
(Lori Brown collection)

David Logeman *(Lori Brown collection)*

Randell Kirsch
(Lori Brown collection)

Don Raymond leading fans onstage during "Dance, Dance, Dance" *(Lori Brown collection)*

Phil Bardowell *(Lori Brown collection)*

Gary Griffin, Phil Bardowell, Bob Greene, Chris Farmer at Three Rivers Stadium, Pittsburgh
(Phil Bardowell collection)

Gary Griffin *(Gary Griffin collection)*

Matt Jardine *(Matt Jardine collection)*

Jan and Dean with hit albums *(Dean Torrence collection)*

Jan Berry *(Dean Torrence collection)*

Dean Torrence at Three Rivers Stadium *(Dean Torrence collection)*

Union Station, St. Louis. Dean Torrence, Bob Greene, Randell Kirsch *(Travis A. Curd, II)*

"No," Dean said. "If you forget, I'm right next to you, and I'll tell you. I don't want you looking down at the stage all night."

It seemed to matter to Dean that the band do well. "We really have to be aggressive tonight," he said to everyone. He seemed to regard the evening as a competition. I hadn't heard him quite this way before.

But the Jan and Dean set was cut short by the Star Lake stage manager to allow maximum time for the Monkees. On the back of the stage was a mammoth lighted Monkees logo in the shape of a guitar, in the same typeface as on their television show. They had vendors in the amphitheater selling full-color souvenir booklets for eighteen dollars a copy.

We left the stage after our truncated set so they could come on. Randell wanted to watch their show from the wings, and stood there with a paper plate of commissary lasagna in his hands. Peter Tork, before he and the other Monkees were announced for their entrance, gave Randell a withering look, meaning: Leave.

Jan wanted to talk to Davy Jones after the Monkees were finished; apparently they had been friends years ago.

But the Monkees' dressing room was closed, with Star Lake security guards posted outside, and so Jan waited and waited, sitting on a folding chair by the Monkees' door.

When we went back to the hotel in Weirton, Gary told me, "Add another show to your schedule. Lima, Ohio has been added for Labor Day weekend." He presented it as neither good news nor bad—just another chance for a payday for the band.

We all had a drink at a hotel bar called Annie's Lounge, but no one was in very good spirits—the shortened show had disappointed everyone—and soon enough we headed for our rooms.

Gary and Randell and I stood waiting for the elevator. We saw, down the first floor corridor, on his way to his own room, Jan. He had stopped and had leaned against the wall to rest. He was just standing there, waiting to gather strength.

TWELVE

When the news of the outside world was especially bad, as it was on the day of the Ozark Empire Fair—faraway bombings dominated the front pages—there were always tiny moments that came upon us to serve as a reminder of just what an elixir this parallel universe of ours was. Just what an antidote to heartache.

None of these moments were newsworthy; they came and went in an instant. But they had a way of staying with you, maybe for longer than anything that ever warranted a headline.

One such moment occurred in the St. Louis airport, where I was switching planes to get to Springfield, Missouri.

I was looking for the right gate, carrying my guitar case, and a flight attendant, out of nowhere, said:

"Sing pretty tonight."

So much sunniness packed into three words. And then, at the Quality Inn near the little Springfield airport, as I was putting the key into the lock of room 1015, the young housekeeper working next door in room 1013 called to me, Ozark-hill-flavor in her voice:

"I haven't gotten to 1015 yet. It's not made up."

She walked out into the hallway and said:

"But it's prettier than 1013."

Now . . . I knew that room 1015 was going to look almost exactly the same as room 1013; she knew that room 1015 was going to look almost exactly the same as room 1013. But why not put a little optimism in the day? I thanked her and let myself into 1015 which was, in fact, untended to; in a few minutes she came over and we talked as she made up the room, and it was prettier just because she said it was.

We all met to go to soundcheck; according to the Ozark Empire Fair schedule, we were one of the few rock acts booked into the ten-day event. Most of the headliners were country singers: Mark Collie, Ricky Van Shelton, Wade Hayes.

"I don't know why it is," Randell said in the limousine. "But these country guys all sing like they've got brass balls."

Out the window we saw some attractive young women heading toward the admission gate.

"Those girls are here for the country music stage," Dean said.

He pointed across the road, at a small herd of bored-looking cows in a pasture.

"Those are our fans."

Tiny moments. We soundchecked; the fences around the grandstand were locked. The audience wouldn't be allowed in until later. So we were onstage in an outdoor arena empty except for fair workers and sound technicians. We sang a few songs, the guitars turned all the way up. From behind my microphone I could see it happening:

Dozens of people, then scores, then hundreds, gravitating from all over the fairgrounds.

The people were leaving what they were doing and approaching the fence, pressing up against it, listening. All these years later, and rock-and-roll music still has this magnetic effect—the teasing wail of the electric guitars, the pounding of wooden sticks on the drums, the mixing of the voices: the pied piper immemorial. It's not that we sounded good or that we sounded bad; this was just a rehearsal. But thirty seconds into "I Get Around," and there they all were, with more coming to join them.

I sang and I saw them against the fences, present because they wanted to be. Small moments. Destined to stay in the memory for years.

"Is there a town where we haven't seen it?" Phil said to me.

He was playing his guitar next to me onstage that night. Gary was singing lead on "Shut Down," and Phil was looking toward the third row in the audience.

A woman in her late teens or very early twenties, about eight months pregnant, sat with her parents. There was no husband or boyfriend with her. It was a scene we witnessed at every small-town fair:

The young women with their babies and their own parents. Or the young women, pregnant, sitting with their mothers and fathers. These families stood out because they almost never smiled. A part of their world had collapsed around them; the young women had gotten pregnant, and the young men had evidently taken a powder.

The parents and their daughters had come out to see a show. But they seldom sang along; they seldom demonstrated any joy. We were probably wrong about what we were seeing some of the time; maybe, in some cases, we were incorrectly deciphering what was in front of us. But it happened too often: the pregnant young women, or the young women with babies, and the older parents. Just sitting, with sad and worn-down faces. Realizing belatedly that the concert is not a cure.

"You wonder where the fathers are tonight," Phil said, not missing a stroke on his guitar.

"With their buddies, right?" I said.

It was a courteous and quiet crowd; they had come over to the grandstand from the Houseplant Extravaganza inside the Food & Flowers Building, from the Master Gardeners exhibit sponsored by the University of Missouri extension campus. They seemed honored to have Jan and Dean on the premises, too well-mannered to yell.

After the show, as Jan was signing memorabilia, a girl of about sixteen—not in the same category as the melancholy young women we observed from the stage—was in line with her family, and said to me: "Bob, do you know if Gary is coming out to sign autographs?"

I couldn't remember having met this girl anywhere, but she answered my question before I could ask it.

"I heard Dean say your names onstage," she said.

"And you want to see Gary?" I said.

"Yes," she said, all stern formality. "I think he's cute."

It was such a sweet scene—proper and prim. I went to our trailer and said to Gary, "There's a girl with her family who wants to meet you. She thinks you're cute."

"Yeah, right," Gary said.

"I'm serious," I said. "Don't let her down."

It took a few minutes to convince him I wasn't pulling his leg. I walked out with him, went up to the girl and her family, and said to her: "Look what I brought you."

"Hi," he said. "I'm Gary."

She extended her hand to shake his, solid as a Rotarian.

"Rose Pennington," she said.

They shook, and I wished Frank Capra were around. Rose Pennington, first name and last, in an era of Heathers and Tiffanys. Shaking hands at the Ozark Empire Fair.

"Hon, I can't take your money," the waitress at the Waffle House said.

Gary and I had gone over there after the show. It was just a short walk from the Quality Inn.

"You have to settle up at the counter," she said. "The manager told some waitresses that he thought they were stealing."

"How great was that girl and her family?" Gary said. "So much decorum. Made you feel like cheering."

We paid for our meal and I noticed a sheaf of white forms on the counter. I slipped a few into my pocket.

"Here," I said to Gary as we walked back to the hotel. "Just in case this whole Jan and Dean thing doesn't work out."

I handed him one of the forms. It said:

WAFFLE HOUSE MINI-APPLICATION

There was a place for name, address, phone number, best time to call. Questions: "Have you worked for Waffle House before?" "Please indicate the days and hours you're available to work."

"You think you get free meals?" he said. "That alone would make it worth it."

As we walked he stuck out his hand to me. I knew what was coming.
"Rose Pennington," he said, as we shook.
"Rose Pennington," I said.
"The Waffle House and Rose Pennington," he said. "Perfect night."

The streets of Reno, Nevada, were jammed, all but impassable. Hot
August Nights was beginning: Reno's annual bacchanal of rock music,
souped-up cars, public drinking and tens of thousands of revelers roaming from dawn to dawn. I asked the cabdriver at the airport to drop me off
in front of the Flamingo Hilton. He said he didn't want to attempt to navigate the congestion, and called me "asshole." I thanked him for his can-
dor and overtipped.

We weren't scheduled to play until the next day, and decided to have
an early dinner in town. The two options we discussed were a topless bar
on Lake Street, and the National Bowling Stadium on Center Street. We
went with the National Bowling Stadium, which had in its four-story
lobby a bronze statue sculpted with the solemn majesty used for the Marine Corps Iwo Jima Memorial outside Washington, except that this
sculpture depicted a frolicsome family on its way to bowl.

To get back to our hotel we fought through the crowds in the searing
streets: the scorched stink of sweat, the unsolicited touch of bare sticky skin,
the stench of spilled stale beer. We passed an outdoor White Castle stand,
erected just for Hot August Nights. The grill cooks couldn't steam the slid-
ers fast enough; from the way people were grabbing for them, you'd have
thought they were silver doubloons, not meat squares topped with onions.

In the casino of the Flamingo I saw Glen D. Hardin, Elvis Presley's
old piano player, and I was about to speak to him when, at one of the tables, standing with a pile of chips in front of him, I saw Jan.

I supposed it was legal. But was Jan really a man who should be putting his money at risk at a casino table? He had an excited look in his
eyes, and he seemed at the same time exhilarated and bewildered by all
the noise and motion around him.

"I know," I heard a voice next to me say, as if reading my mind.

It was Randell.

"I went up to him and asked him if he was all right," Randell said. "He said he was."

"Does he have any idea what he's doing?" I said.

"I can't imagine," Randell said.

I walked over to the table.

"Jan, you think maybe it's time to go up to bed?" I said.

"This is fun!" he said.

I looked at him for a long moment.

"You don't want to lose all the money you're in town to make, do you?" I said.

He didn't look up from the table. I saw him push some chips forward.

At Mackay Stadium—the football stadium of the University of Nevada at Reno—Don and Phil Everly stood backstage next to two upright trunks that apparently held their wardrobe. The trunks were of the old-fashioned sort that travelers once took with them on oceanliners.

The Everly Brothers said nothing, just waited. They looked just like the Everly Brothers of your memory—Phil, his face long and mournful, Don, his face rounder but carrying no more mirth. I wished they weren't here. They deserved better.

The Everly Brothers, I thought, did not belong on some oldies package. They were . . . well, they were the Everly Brothers. In the context of every other act out on the road, they might as well have been Thomas Jefferson and Benjamin Franklin, standing there in the heat. I asked Dean if he would introduce me, and he did. The Everly Brothers were polite and gracious, Phil saying hello in a high-pitched speaking voice, Don in a baritone. I didn't know where they belonged—Carnegie Hall? The Kennedy Center?—but it had to be somewhere other than on a multi-act bill at Hot August Nights.

Mary Wilson from the Supremes sang, and the Crickets, and us, and when we were finished Phil Bardowell and I stood on the stage steps to watch the Everlys.

The crowd wanted their hits—"Bye Bye Love," "Wake Up, Little Susie," "All I Have to Do Is Dream"—and eventually would get them. But the Everly Brothers seemed to be singing for themselves as much as for the audience; they started out with the languorous country song "Bowling Green," about their native Kentucky, almost daring the crowd to object. To hear their voices from that close a range—to see each brother seeking out the other's voice, to listen as those voices intertwined and mixed, the voices finding each other and forming a sound pure enough to make your heart humbly pause . . . to hear the sound of the Everly Brothers, through the stadium loudspeakers and, at the same moment, without amplification, from a few feet across the stage . . . to hear that was to witness the irrefutable rebuttal to the idea of atheism. A sound so lovely comes from somewhere not entirely of this earth.

Phil Bardowell turned to me and said: "They're so good, it's like they don't make their living doing the same thing the rest of us do."

Except they did. They sang in the August sun, on the same boards where, undeservedly, we had stood.

"Bobby?"

I heard the word from somewhere over in the football stands.

It was being directed at me. A man yelled it again: "Bobby?"

He motioned at me.

I reluctantly left the place from where I was watching the Everly Brothers. No one had called me "Bobby" since high school.

The man—I didn't know him—said that two women in the seats had asked him to summon me.

I thought maybe they had, in fact, gone to school with me. If I was "Bobby" to them, that had to be it.

They came down the aisle to the restraining wall. I didn't recognize them.

"We love your work," one of them said.

They did?

"We have all your records," the other said.

All my records?

"I can't believe we're really meeting Bobby Vee," the other said.

Oh, my. He was on the bill, too. They must have had distant seats, with bad sight lines. "Rubber Ball," "Take Good Care of My Baby," "Run to Him," "The Night Has a Thousand Eyes" . . . I should *think* they'd love my work.

"We're two big bundles of fun," the first one said.

I went back to watch the Everlys, whose voices, on "Let It Be Me," sounded like angels softly crying.

"We think we know who you really are."

A group of four more women came up as we were leaving the football stadium.

The Bobby Vee experience had left me dumbstruck. I didn't know what to say to this new group of spectators.

"We have a bet," one of them said. "If we're right, do you promise you'll tell us?"

After the Elvis imitator in Winthrop Harbor telling me he'd read *Hang Time,* I was ready—all right, hopeful—to be flattered again. The Elvis imitator had made me feel like William Faulkner.

"Who do you think I am?" I said, waiting to bask in the moment.

"You played Little Ricky on *I Love Lucy,*" one of the women said.

I stood there. Faulkner could rest peacefully.

"Are we right?" one of them said.

"Yes," I said. "Yes, you are."

I stayed in town an extra day, and the next night I went to see the Beach Boys, who were playing on an outdoor stage at the Reno Hilton. Chris Farmer had joined their band, making more money than he had with Jan and Dean, working more concerts. Some people are destined never to miss a beat.

He'd left me a ticket; I sat in the audience and watched him up there. Same the-house-always-wins pit-boss smile, same voice as on all those Jan and Dean stages, but now he was Chris Farmer of the Beach Boys. We're all, in the end, interchangeable parts. It's probably best not to think too much about it.

Just ask Bobby Vee. Or Little Ricky.

His laconic manner notwithstanding—sometimes, even in the middle of a show, he seemed so relaxed that we were tempted to check for a pulse—Dean had certain dreams.

He would mention them to us at odd times. In a car, over beers, even right before an encore, he would tell us, out of the blue, about his latest scheme.

They never involved music. They had nothing to do with singing. Maybe that's why he dreamed of them.

Casinos: that was one, and a pretty constant one. Dean was always talking about putting together groups of investors to construct and open casinos in parts of the country that, he said, were underserved by such enterprises.

Then there was something about a man walking on a tightrope across a big river in China. I could never get the particulars straight on that one; Dean's interest had something to do with persuading a big American corporation to sponsor the tightrope walker, maybe televise the crossing of the river internationally.

In Warren, Ohio, he had a new one for us. We were staying at the Park Hotel—"circa 1888," its brochure said, and the place felt like it; the three-story red-brick structure was the kind of place where salesmen on their Ohio routes must have stopped for the night when they stepped off the intercity trains in the early years of the Twentieth Century. The guest rooms, the hotel proclaimed, were furnished in "true Victorian style," and that, we could see, was factual, literally.

We were sitting around the hotel, killing time before going over to our show at the local auditorium, and Dean sprang his latest idea on us.

He drew a rectangle, and in the middle of it he printed:

DSI4

"What is it?" he said to us.

We just looked at it.

"Come on," he said. "What is it?"

Silence from us.

"It's a license plate," he said. "Now: What does it say?"

More silence.

"'Decipher,'" Dean said. "It says 'Decipher.' D-SI-4."

We waited.

"It'd make a great TV game show," Dean said. "That's what I'd call it: *DSI4*. The contestants would look at letters and numbers inside of license plates in the TV studio, and try to decipher what they mean. Everyone drives. Everyone looks at license plates. I'm trying to get a meeting with Dick Clark to pitch it to him, and ask him to produce it."

He drew another rectangle. This time we knew it was supposed to be a license plate.

He wrote inside the rectangle:

TTTTTT

"What is it?" he said.

"'T-T-T-T-T-T'?" Gary guessed.

"No," Dean said. "'Sixties.' The answer is 'Sixties.' Six T's. See?"

He knew the TV show would be a hit, he said. He just had to convince Dick Clark.

He dreamed these dreams all the time. They seemed to be his escape.

Mark Ward was a real-estate appraiser in southern California, but he used to be a guitar player and vocalist for Jan and Dean. He had left the band years before to enter the grownup world of business, and he was doing well. No complaints.

But here he was, with Gary and me in a booth at a place called The Mocha House on High Street in Warren. Dean had asked him if he would fill in on this trip; with Chris out of the group, Dean was experimenting with the lineup, seeing what sounded best.

So Mark Ward had appraised his last property of the week and had flown to Ohio with the band. I could see the delight in his face. He had left Jan and Dean in the first place because he knew that staying with the group was no way for a responsible adult to lead his life. But. . . .

"So you miss it, right?" Gary said to him.

"I miss this," Ward said. "The guys. The hanging out."

"And you don't want to come back full-time?" Gary said.

"No way," Ward said. "Not possible."

Yet here he was, on a Saturday afternoon, whiling away the hours before showtime, and he looked like a man who had been trapped for years in a stuffy attic and was finally breathing pure oxygen. Dean may have had his own dreams, but I had to guess that, on dark nights, Mark Ward dreamed of this.

"I saw Chris in Reno," I told Gary. I filled him in on the Beach Boys show I had stayed for.

"Did he seem like he fit in?" Gary asked.

"Well, he didn't seem to be running the show onstage, like with Jan and Dean," I said. "He seemed a little like the new guy. But he played well and he sang well. I thought he was good."

"I'll never forget the first time I played with the Beach Boys," Gary said.

He had performed on keyboards with them when, as a young man, he had initially moved out to California.

"I was supposed to play the lead-in to 'California Girls,' to begin the show," he said. "You know—those first instrumental chords to get the song, and the show, started.

"So there I am, a kid from Cincinnati, so nervous. So eager to do well. I can hardly believe it—I'm playing 'California Girls' with the Beach Boys. And I hit the first few notes. . . .

"And Dennis Wilson, from behind his drum kit, yells: 'Too fast, motherfucker.'

"That was my introduction to the Beach Boys."

"How long did it take you to feel like you were a Beach Boy?" I asked.

"That's the point," he said. "You never do. You may play with them, but you never are a Beach Boy. Chris will find out. You are not a Beach Boy."

On the way back to the Park Hotel to get ready for the show, we walked past an Army recruiting office, and a clothing store, and when we were about to pass a light pole Gary wrapped one of his arms around it and began circling it.

"Quick," he said. "What's this remind you of?"

Mark and I stood watching him. He kept circling the pole, almost swinging on it, his arm still tethering him there.

"Acrobats at the circus?" I said.

"Monkeys at a zoo?" Mark said.

"Think harder," Gary said. "You'll get it."

We watched him.

"So obvious," he said. "The opening title sequence of *Leave It to Beaver*. When he and Wally are walking down the street."

"Are you sure?" I said. "I don't remember it."

"Trust me," he said. He half-hummed, half-sang the show's theme tune:

"Dee-*dee*, dee-*dee*-dee-dee dee, dee-*dee*, dee, dee-*dee*-dee-dee dee-*dee* . . ."

He continued to circle the pole, and Mark joined in and circled it too, and so did I. A car on the streets of Warren slowed down to see what this was all about, but all it was about was three grown men on a weekend afternoon in a town they'd probably never find themselves in again, circling a lamp post and as they did it laughing at themselves, and at life.

We'd play that night, and on Monday Mark Ward would be a real-estate appraiser once more. It was the judicious thing to do.

The summer had been a jumble of cities—Watertown, New York; Vallejo, California; Red Wing, Minnesota; San Diego; Lancaster, Ohio—and each city had its unexpected moments. In Warren, after the show, two female desk clerks asked Gary, Mark Ward and me if we would mind going upstairs with them to deliver some champagne. Someone had booked the honeymoon special package, and the champagne was part of it, but the clerks detected something they felt was a little weird in the voice that had phoned downstairs to request the delivery, and were wary. So we went up and stood with them as they knocked on the door—which was answered by a honeymooning couple who seemed quite traditional, if a little surprised to find their bottle transported by two desk clerks in uniform and three men in surf shirts.

The moments, we encountered on our own; the towns in which the moments awaited us were the result of the efforts of Bill Hollingshead. He was the longtime booking agent for Jan and Dean—a one-man operation based out of Santa Ana, California. As the summer came to an end, he joined us in Albuquerque for the New Mexico State Fair. Hollingshead was a white-haired fellow of indeterminate years with the face of a perennially and irrevocably debauched leprechaun. I suppose if you're the booking agent for the Rolling Stones or Paul McCartney, you just announce that your act is ready to go out on tour and then sit back in the high-rise offices of your international talent agency and wait for the calls to come in. Hollingshead's vocation was somewhat more complicated, and more difficult, than that.

To book Jan and Dean, and the Kingsmen, and the Surfaris, and the other groups he handled, he had to know the top man at every county fair in the country, the general manager at every minor-league ballpark, the local chairman of every small-town summer festival. What Hollingshead did was labor-intensive—he had to work at getting the dates for his acts. And one of the ways he rewarded himself was to come out and perform whenever he could find the time.

He was a saxophone player, apparently from way back. Because of this, the band referred to him almost exclusively as "Honk." He would put on a white suit and a white Panama hat and, for several numbers, come onstage with his horn and do backup. He had a showman's presence; the audiences never knew exactly who the man in the white suit was, but he carried himself with such an air of importance that they always assumed he was someone big.

So we were in Albuquerque with Honk and because of Honk. As with the other cities we passed through, we would not have been in town had Hollingshead not managed to arrange it. Whatever memories we took away from these summers, he had put us in place to find them. "Looking good, Honk," Phil Bardowell said to him as we headed for the stage, and Hollingshead's expression said: Of course I am.

Some memories—some moments—are better than others.

At least for those among us who as boys listening to 45 rpm records never had reason to think such moments could ever conceivably happen.

The New Mexico State Fair concert was in a rodeo arena—big and
drafty and high-ceilinged, full of echoes and shadows, an ideal place to
play a rock-and-roll show, if not necessarily to hear it. The acoustics may
be muddy and soft in an arena like that, but everything about the
structure—the dimness, the smoky haze wafting through the cones of the
spotlights, the sight of the audience as it rises in the rows of seats into
blackness, the way you can hear your voice rebounding to you—
everything feels like your first fantasy of what it must be like to perform on
a traveling rock tour.

And so it was, as we were into "Little Deuce Coupe," that we noticed
a small commotion by the side of the stage.

A young woman in a flannel shirt and jeans had pushed her way past
a security guard, had scrambled up the stairs and onto the stage, and now
was running straight toward us as we sang.

She ran past Randell, past Dean. . . .

And right up to me.

She threw her arms around me and hugged me.

"I'm sorry," she said into my ear. "I just had to do this."

The crowd was roaring. I don't know if we were still singing or not. A
security man hurried over and grabbed her arm firmly and led her away.
I was stunned. The audience was cheering and clapping for the woman
as she was taken from the stage.

Dean looked at me, shook his head, and mouthed the word: *You?*

Gary left his keyboard and walked the three steps to me and said,
"Oh, quit trying to look so cool. If she could only read the words in the
cartoon balloon above your head. *Please, Miss, don't leave! Please, stay!
Please don't go!*"

We finished the show and in the van back to our hotel the band
wouldn't let up.

"It had to be a sorority initiation prank," Randell said.

"'You girls are assigned to go out and see the lamest oldies act you
can possibly find,'" Phil said.

"'And you don't get credit unless you stay for the whole show,'" Dean
said.

"'And you, young lady,'" Gary said, imitating the voice of a pledge-master. "'You don't get to be initiated unless you run onto the stage and kiss the ugliest one.'"

"Say what you want," I said. "No one can take it away."

"She's already forgotten it," Gary said. "You never will."

Some moments do stick around, like the warmth of long-remembered laughter.

But there were so many moments to choose from.

That's what made all of this so precious.

In the van that night, Jan said, "I heard there's a karaoke bar near our hotel."

"So?" Dean said.

"I want to go," Jan said.

"Why?" Dean said.

"To sing," Jan said.

Summer was ending again. The show was over. And Jan wanted to keep singing.

"Jan, we're not going to a karaoke bar," Dean said. "We have an early flight out of here in the morning. And why would you want to sing in front of people at a karaoke bar?"

"I don't know," Jan said. "It might be fun."

"We're not doing it," Dean said.

"They might have some of our songs, Dean," Jan said.

No one wanted it to end. Ever. Though most of the time, the wish went unspoken.

Bill Hollingshead was riding in the van, and someone said to him:

"Keep the summer alive, Honk."

Meaning: Keep finding the fairs. Keep finding the festivals. Keep finding the stages and the lights.

"I do my best," Hollingshead said.

We rode in silence the rest of the way, through dark Albuquerque streets, the sounds of the concert in our ears.

THIRTEEN

There was a word that was seldom spoken out loud on tour, partly because it didn't need to be said, but mostly, I sensed, because there are certain things, if you talk about them, you fear they will go away.

The word was friendship.

It was so much the basis of all this that no one seemed to want to jinx it by discussing it. These were people who genuinely liked each other's company. Maybe, for a young rock band on its way up, shouted artistic clashes and bitter personality disputes and raging flare-ups are part of the standard script. But for the men in this band, at this stage of their lives, the time on the road would be pretty unbearable—hardly worth the effort—if the friendship wasn't there. It was the bedrock of everything.

One of the places where we had stopped before the summer ended was Salt Lake City. At the Utah State Fair I bought a watch from two guys at a card table set up near a corn dog stand. The watch looked spiffy—it had a black face and gold-colored trim—and it cost only ten dollars. What sealed the deal was that the men offered a warranty on the watch—for ten dollars, you might expect a watch to break before long, but they said they were serious about the warranty, and wrote their home telephone numbers on the back of the warranty slip in case the watch conked out and I needed it replaced. (The same guys were selling, at the same card table, ten-dollar vibrators, which made the whole thing a little less wholesomely pastoral. As far as I could tell, the midway vibrators did not carry warranties.)

Still, though, the Utah State Fair had an overabundance of charms; I had one of the best meals of the summer inside a tent put up by the Utah Cattlemen's Association where its members custom-cooked you a steak sandwich from local prize beef, with your choice of side dishes. For five dollars.

As a tribute to the fair, we thought about singing the seldom-performed Beach Boys album cut "Salt Lake City."

Down in Utah, the guys and I dig a city called Salt Lake. . . .

We were working on it, and every time we got to the falsetto bridge I sang:

The girls, the girls, they've got the cutest of the Western states. . . .

Which is what I thought the words were. Those had always been what I thought the words were; it's how they had sounded to me on the *Summer Days (and Summer Nights!!)* album in the summer of 1965, when the song was new.

But the third time I sang the words in rehearsal, Gary slammed his hand on his keyboard and said, almost angrily: "Why are you singing that?"

"Singing what?" I said.

" 'The girls, the girls,' " he said, imitating my falsetto.

"Because those are the words," I said.

"Those are *not* the words," he said. "The words are"—here he went into falsetto—" 'girl for girl.' "

"What are you talking about?" I said.

"The words are 'Girl for girl, they've got the cutest of the Western states,' " he said.

"That's ridiculous," I said. "You mean like a boxer? 'Pound for pound he's the best middleweight in the business?' Why would the words be 'girl for girl'?"

"Because they are," he said.

Every time I sang it the way I knew was correct—"the girls, the girls"—it was like fingernails on a chalkboard for him. It was as if I was purposely misquoting a line from *Hamlet*; it offended Gary's sense of the world's order. But I wouldn't change, because I knew that there was no way that the Beach Boys had written "girl for girl." The rest of that summer—sometimes out of nowhere, in an airport or at dinner—he would look at me and shake his head and say, with scorn, "the girls, the girls," as if disdainfully uttering a blasphemy.

The winter came.

And one day in Chicago an envelope with a California postmark arrived, and inside it was a set of sheet music. For "Salt Lake City."

I didn't even know there was sheet music for most of these songs. I had never thought of rock songs being committed to the dry pages of sheet music. I'd assumed these songs just kind of existed, like the afternoon sky.

But there it was: "Words and Music by Brian Wilson," with a tidy black-and-white arrangement of notes and clefs and staffs like on a marching band's rehearsal sheets.

And lyrics.

. . . Girl for girl, they've got the cutest of the Western states. . . .

He'd gone out and found the sheet music.

And purchased it, and, with no note of explanation, put it in the mail to me.

On a cold winter day in Chicago, it was like a campfire.

Friendship: something none of us ever felt we needed to discuss.

Why run the risk of scaring if off, by saying the fragile and sacred word?

We had a show scheduled in the rural mountains of West Virginia. The night before was dotted with thunderstorms across the Midwest, and by the time our delayed series of flights got us to Chuck Yeager Airport in Charleston and we made it to the hotel, the restaurant and room service were closed until morning. So we walked down the street to an all-night gas station and dined on Slim Jims and Lance peanut butter crackers.

An accident on the route up into the mountains had blocked all lanes of traffic the next day. Our van, like every vehicle on the road, was stuck in place for over an hour. People were getting out of their cars, walking around, introducing themselves to each other; Randell hiked into the brush by the side of the asphalt and looked for something to eat among the berries and vegetation, which seemed a little excessive, even for him. We weren't stranded in the African bush, this was just a traffic jam.

When we finally arrived at our concert destination we knew at once that it had been worth the trouble getting there. This was an annual outdoor music festival in a meadow nestled high in a range of green and luxuriant mountains, with the stage giving us a majestic view of vistas that felt like places where residents of heaven might choose to go on their summer vacations. Our dressing area was a wooden cabin with multiple bedrooms featuring bunks and mattresses. The Coasters ("Yakkety Yak," "Searchin'," "Charlie Brown," "Along Came Jones") were sacked out in several of the bunks, wearing their stage suits, catching some shuteye and snoring away before they were summoned outside, to paradise, to sing.

In the hour just before the concert began there was, as part of the festivities, a parade of spotlessly polished high-performance cars. From our elevated cabin you could stand at an open window and observe the sparkling cars roll slowly by.

Which is what I was doing, as I stood next to a female sheriff's deputy who was in full uniform, including hat and gun. She had a West-Virginia-hollows accent so lush that it almost made you drunk just to hear it. We looked together out the cabin window at the parade, and as one especially gorgeous car purred just beneath us, she said:

"Damn. Well, there goes another commandment down for me."

I was puzzled only for a moment.

She nodded toward the car.

"Covet, covet," she said.

Moses himself would have laughed in delight, with the tablets in his hands on a different mountain, long ago and far away.

In **Blue Ash,** Ohio, Felix Cavaliere of the Rascals finished his opening set that was filled with the group's keyboard-heavy hits—"Good Lovin'," "I've Been Lonely Too Long," "How Can I Be Sure"—and then, just before Jan and Dean came on to headline, a local disc jockey approached the microphone with a sheet of paper.

David Logeman had given it to him. Logeman had written it out in longhand back at our hotel, as he had lately been doing every night.

"Ladies and gentlemen," the disc jockey read aloud, just as Logeman had instructed him to do, "in 1966 Jan Berry had a near-fatal accident. . . ."

It served two purposes:

It prepared the crowds for what they would see when Jan walked onto the stage. For years, Dean had assumed that everyone knew the story of Jan's accident, and thus would understand the lingering aftereffects. But with the passage of time, fewer people recalled what had happened, and we could tell that there were many each night who were confused: why was one of the singers moving unevenly, why was his speaking voice sometimes slurred and unsteady? Jan was getting heavier, and perspiring a lot during humid outdoor performances; Dean thought that it would be a good idea to prepare the audiences for what they were about to observe.

The other purpose was to inform the crowds, before the show began, that Jan would be signing photos and albums afterward. Jan would get almost frantic worrying about that—it was a profit center for him, something he didn't have to share with Dean, and he had been regularly stepping on the impact of the end of the shows by trying to promote the signings even as the last songs were building to a climax. We'd be singing the final words of "Surfin' U.S.A." and Jan would already be pumping for his autographing sessions. The band would be hitting the high melody:

Everybody's gone surfin'. . . .

And at the same moment Jan would be hurriedly saying into his microphone:

"Good night, I love you, and don't forget the concessions. . . ."

The concessions? The crowd, if they could hear him over the guitars, often had no idea what he was referring to.

So the pre-show announcements became a nightly staple. Logeman was in charge of making sure they happened because he was the one who worked with Jan at the autographing tables—it was David who lugged around the canvas bags full of CDs and T-shirts and eight-by-ten glossies, who sat next to Jan and counted the money, who relayed the fans' special requests to Jan as Jan signed. The announcements turned out to be a doubly good idea:

They set up Jan's story as inspirational—even heroic—before the audiences ever set eyes on him. This was no small thing: the announcements helped turn Jan's limitations into a strong feature of the show, a selling point, instead of a distraction. Because of the way the announcement was worded, the audience was on Jan's side—often on their feet and cheering—as soon as they saw him.

And the announcements dramatically increased the length of the lines at Jan's autograph tables after the show. Because the audiences were expressly told, before the concert ever began, that Jan would be signing (and selling), he didn't have to rush to inform them of the idea at the end (although he usually did anyway—Jan didn't trust the audience to remember).

So because of the announcements, even as the band was playing the first chords of the "Ride the Wild Surf" instrumental stanza that brought Jan and Dean themselves onto the stage, the crowd knew the narrative of Jan's struggle—and they also knew that they would be able to meet him after the performance.

". . . and he's made it all the way back from Dead Man's Curve to be with us here tonight," the disc jockey in Blue Ash continued, reading the words that David had written on a piece of hotel stationery.

Jan made his entrance, to an ovation.

"**Thank you for** coming to Gulfport! This will hurt your feelings!"

The voice was Jan's. It was on my hotel voicemail.

We were playing two nights at the Grand Casino in Gulfport, Mississippi. A stage had been erected for us on the sand next to the Gulf of Mexico. The show the first evening had gone well—enthusiastic crowd, expertly run sound system, the lights of the casino tower glimmering mirrorlike off the vast surface of the water.

We had played and then gone out to dinner after the concert, and when I woke up in the morning the red message light on my phone was blinking.

I groggily punched the button to listen to the message, and that's when I heard Jan's voice.

That it had gone straight to voicemail was not a surprise; his middle-of-the-night calls to members of the band were becoming so frequent that in many hotels the front desk staff had been instructed when we checked in: Don't connect Jan with any of our rooms after mid-evening, no matter how much he insists. Just have him leave his message with the desk, or, if you can, put him on voicemail without ringing the room.

The subject of his message, though, was one I would not have foreseen:

"Thank you for coming to Gulfport! This will hurt your feelings! On 'Dance, Dance, Dance' you were *low* and *flat*. I told you it would hurt your feelings, and it does. Ciao!"

Now . . . I had no doubt that my voice was occasionally low, and flat, and flawed in all kinds of ways. But I didn't think I had been especially off-tune in Gulfport. And Jan, most of the time, was a genuinely sweet person. Even if he'd thought that, it was out of character for him to say it.

I called Gary's room to tell him about the message.

"Well, Jan has a pretty good ear for stuff, if it's not him," Gary said. "He's still a producer at heart. He hears everything onstage. He probably heard something while you were singing last night that he didn't like. You never know what sticks with him."

I phoned Jan's room and decided to overplay it.

"I got your message," I said. "I know I'll probably have to quit. I just don't have the ability."

"What do you mean?" Jan said. I could tell that I had awakened him. He had very likely been up all night, and then drifted off to sleep at dawn. That's what he often did.

I told him about the message, which he seemed to have no recollection of having left. He sounded mortified when he realized that he had, indeed, left it.

A few minutes later he called me back.

"You were only flat on 'Dance, Dance, Dance,'" he said. "Dean is flat on *everything*. And the band plays too loud—it's their fault. They make it so you can't hear yourself when you sing."

He was like a little boy who had been caught doing something he regretted, and was trying to blame someone, anyone, else. It was Jan at his most winsomely appealing—a nice man, lost.

"Tell the band not to play so loud," he said. "They won't listen to me. Maybe they'll listen to you. Tell them to harmonize."

I thought of him sitting at home in the days and weeks between shows, just waiting to go out on the road again. If the hour onstage was the most important hour of the day for all of us—the reason for all the travel—it was so much more so for Jan. It was all he had, all day. It was all he worked toward. He sat in his room relearning and rehearsing his songs, and by the time the show started every fiber of his wounded body was ready to try its best. It mattered terribly to him that he do well.

And the fact was, most nights he did manage to do remarkably well. His voice, on most of the songs, was on key and in register—which shouldn't be a point of pride for a professional singer, but in Jan's case justifiably was. Because he was, in fact, a professional—his absolute belief in that was what kept him going. His name was on the marquee. And the good part of his day—the part he literally lived for—began with the first minute of the show and ended with the last minute of the encore.

"You're a good singer," he said, even though I wasn't. "Tell the band not to play so loud."

And with that he hung up. I knew he'd be going back to sleep, to awaken again at sunset. We had another show scheduled on the sand next to the Gulf, and he would be ready.

His memory might have been faulty on some things—it had to vex him awfully that the words to the hit songs he had written almost always abandoned him after each concert—but he remembered certain matters in a way that made me understand how much he really did want to be liked.

In Midland, Texas, we played a strange show at some sort of car dealer's convention—we were in a big civic arena, and someone had come up with the idea of placing the automobiles between us and the audience.

So we stood on the stage and sang to the equivalent of twenty rows of steel, chrome and glass. Usually when we sang, we could see the eyes of the people in the front of the house; in Midland, we saw headlights and windshields and hood ornaments.

The real audience—the humans—were seated at tables well behind the cars. It made for a very disconnected experience onstage. We could barely make out the men and women we allegedly were performing for. They were out there in the distance. The best seats in the house were given to the autos.

Everyone in the band was thrown off a little by this, and in the morning, when I was getting up to head for the Midland airport, my message light was on again.

The hotel operator said it was a text message.

"Mr. Jan Berry called for you. The message is: 'Fantastic. Know what I mean, jelly bean?'"

"Pardon me?" I said.

"'Fantastic,'" she repeated. "'Know what I mean, jelly bean?'"

Then she added:

"Mr. Berry is the one who said, 'Know what I mean, jelly bean?' I'm not asking you that on my own, sir."

I laughed. "I didn't think you were," I said. "Was there anything else?"

"Just that he asked you to call him when you got home," she said. Jan and Dean and the band had already left the hotel to get an early flight to California.

So when I returned to Chicago I called Jan, and asked him what his message meant.

"You know," he said. "You know."

I didn't, really. But I supposed that it was his way of trying to be kind. "Fantastic." Meaning the performance in Midland. Meaning my singing. He was still attempting to make up for the critical voicemail he had left in Mississippi.

"I know what you mean, jelly bean," I said to him over the long-distance line, and he said he'd see me soon.

The kindness cut both ways.

There was something that Gary did onstage every night that warmed my heart. He had started doing it long before the decision was made to add the pre-show announcements about Jan and his accident; as far as I knew, he had been doing it for years.

He did it in the split second after Jan finished singing "Dead Man's Curve" each show. The song was the most haunting moment of every concert; I don't know what must have been going through Jan as he performed that number again and again. The audiences had probably forgotten—if they ever knew—that "Dead Man's Curve" was written and recorded two years before Jan's accident, that it had been a fictional lyric written by a strong, handsome, whole and healthy young man.

So Jan would stand in the spotlight and say the words near the end of the song:

Well, the last thing I remember, Doc, I started to swerve. . . .

And he would complete the soliloquy, and then we would join in to sing the last verses, and the song would conclude.

There would be a quiescence in the audience. People didn't know how to react.

Which is when Gary did the thing I thought was so merciful.

Instead of just letting Jan stand there, Gary would yell into his own microphone:

"Jan Berry, ladies and gentlemen! Jan Berry! He wrote that song!"

At which the audience would erupt in cheers, would stand and applaud for Jan.

For whatever reason, Dean never showed a sliver of emotion during "Dead Man's Curve," never said a word to the audience. Maybe it was because the song reminded him of what might have been, for his career and for Jan's, had Jan not gotten into the car that day. They had the television series lined up, they had their hit records, they had beach-party movie interest . . . and then Jan climbed into his car, and everything changed. Maybe that's why Dean shut himself down when Jan sang the song each show; maybe it was too difficult for him to think about.

So Gary was the one who turned the song into a moment of victory for Jan. "Jan Berry, ladies and gentlemen!" I knew I probably wasn't supposed to do it, but I applauded for him every night, too. Right there onstage, I turned toward Jan and I clapped my hands and when he looked over I raised my fist to show him that I was a fan of his, as much as any person out in the audience. "Jan Berry!" Gary would shout. "He wrote that song!" I applauded for Jan, and almost every night he would look at me and silently form the words: Thank you.

In Huntington Beach, California, there were Lucille Balls and Jackie Gleasons spread out before us.

Actually, they were Lucy Riccardos and Ralph Kramdens; the waitresses and waiters were dressed in character: the Lucys in housedresses, the Ralphs in gray bus-driver uniforms. This was at an outdoor dinner party in the swimming pool area of a hotel—the theme had something to do with the early days of the television industry. So the Lucys and the Ralphs arranged the table settings as, with the sun still hovering in the end-of-the-day sky, the guests arrived and were served cocktails.

The way the evening was planned, the rest of us would do a set first, without Jan and Dean, and then later the two principals would join us for the main concert. We couldn't do any of the Jan and Dean or Beach Boys hits during our opening set, because we had to save those for the second show. So it was an even more unconstrained atmosphere than usual as we sang anything that came to our minds. We just threw the titles of songs out to each other and then performed them; we sang Buddy Holly's "Rave On" and the Beatles' "Eight Days a Week," and it felt like a bunch of guys standing around in front of live microphones and having fun. Which it was.

I had flown out that day for the show. When we finished our

Jan-and-Deanless set, and had a short break before the real concert, Randell called me aside.

"There's something you should do," he said.

"What?" I said.

There was a street separating the hotel's pool deck from what waited across the way: the Pacific Ocean.

"You ought to take your shoes off and go over there and step in the water," he said.

"Why?" I said.

"Because you were in Chicago when you woke up today, and now it's not even dinnertime and look where you are," he said. "Why would you want to travel all this way and get this close to the Pacific Ocean and not feel it?"

Randell was always getting semi-spiritual like this, and usually I did my best to brush it off. Which I did again this time. "I can see the ocean," I said to him. "I don't have to feel it to know it's there."

But then, a little later, just as we were about to play, I realized that what he had said made pure and shimmering sense. And I told him so.

He and I crossed the street—the Pacific Coast Highway—and walked over to the ocean. And, just for a moment, I stepped into it.

You do owe it to yourself to pause once in a while, to stop and tell yourself that these things really are happening—these things our grandparents never permitted themselves to dream about, things that don't even make us blink. From the Midwest to the Pacific Ocean, all in the course of a day, as if this is the way it has always been.

Randell was right. Every now and then you need to remind yourself to feel it all.

FOURTEEN

When the schedule indicated we would be going to the New York State Fair, some visual images came to mind.

Carnival booths set up in the shadow of the Empire State Building. Midway rides on blocked-off streets in Greenwich Village. Food concessions winding through the ethnic neighborhoods of Manhattan, Brooklyn and Queens.

I knew such a setup was unlikely. It was just that I had never considered the existence of a New York State Fair, and had no idea what to anticipate.

The fair, it turned out, was in Syracuse, exactly where it had been for the entirety of the Twentieth Century. And—the words "New York State Fair" aside—it made you feel as if you were in Ohio or Illinois or Missouri.

Those of us who don't live on the East Coast have a certain stereotype when we hear New York mentioned, and the stereotype does not include the parts of the state outside of New York City. The other New York—the rest of the state—is a place the world at large seldom thinks about. It took me no more than a few minutes on the fairgrounds to realize something:

The people in charge of marketing New York—the state, not the city—would do well to try to persuade Americans to come visit during fair week. The visitors would see the secret New York.

On the fairgrounds, Granny Nichols's needlework, crochet and hands-on jump rope demonstrations were scheduled on the front lawn of the agricultural museum. Gary Gerken presented blacksmith lessons in the reconstructed 1868 Harris Blacksmith Shop. There was the historic train and railroad exhibit, the Tom Williams shoemaking presentation, storytelling with Molly McIntosh in the horticulture building, the Youth Dairy Goat Show. . . .

The New York State Fair felt, for want of a better word, Midwestern.

Which is the greatest compliment I can give. But when I ran into Roy Bernardi, the mayor of Syracuse, on the fairgrounds before we sang, he rejected that analysis.

"I think the New York State Fair does feel like middle America," Mayor Bernardi said. "But that's not the same thing as Midwestern. The fair feels like middle America because that's what most of New York State feels like. We never feel like Manhattan up here."

Syracuse, he said, had approximately 160,000 residents, a number much smaller than most people suppose. The misapprehension was a byproduct of the New York syndrome—anything associated with New York is presumed, by the rest of the country, to be bigger than it likely is.

"If you drive around this state," Mayor Bernardi said, "you'll find many more places that feel like this than feel like New York City. I wouldn't want to live anywhere else."

All across the fairgrounds, as we were getting ready to play, visitors were saying "please" to vendors and vendors were saying "thank you" to visitors. Young people with brooms were everywhere, keeping the fairgrounds clean.

In my head I paraphrased the line from the movie *Field of Dreams:*
Is this Iowa?
No. It's New York.

One thing I prized was that the time on the road was a postgraduate course in the music I loved, with professors who knew the subject better than anyone else in the world.

The morning after our New York State Fair concert, we were leaving the Syracuse airport as that night's main attraction—Gene Pitney—was arriving.

I had always wanted to meet him. If heartache had a voice, it would be his.

During those years in the 1960s when most of the music coming out of American car radios was big-beat British Invasion rock, Pitney—born in Connecticut—was singing anthems of unconcealed pain and despair. Tens of millions of young hearts were breaking every week, and Pitney was the spokesman for their anguish.

His voice was almost operatic. There was something about that voice, and its range, that made people cease whatever they were doing to pause and listen more carefully. It was a voice that sounded as if it were on the verge of real tears. If your heart had been hurt, there were certain Gene Pitney songs—the last thirty seconds of "I'm Gonna Be Strong" is the best example—that were simply too much to take. You had to turn the radio off.

How interested was I in his craft? Given a choice between asking Plato how he came up with the language in *The Republic* or asking Gene Pitney about the chord changes in "The Man Who Shot Liberty Valance," I'd go with Pitney.

And here he was in Syracuse, gray-haired and affable as could be. When I asked him what he thought it was that set his voice apart, he laughed and said one critic had written that "only dogs can hear some of the notes I hit." But that had worked out to his advantage: "As soon as you hear a song of mine, you know immediately who's singing."

He had written some memorable songs for other singers: "Rubber Ball" for Bobby Vee, "He's a Rebel" for the Crystals—but I wanted to ask him about the Gene Pitney hits, almost all of them written not by him, but by other composers and lyricists. I just wanted to know a little of the stories behind his singing of each song. He said to ask away.

About "Town Without Pity": "I was frightened of that song. I saw that song and thought, 'How do I sing it? What do I do?' I decided to sing it as slowly as I possibly could."

"It Hurts to Be in Love": "I knew it was a hit. You have 'listeners' ears' when you're first starting out, and your 'listeners' ears' tell you what will work. You lose those ears later, when you break songs down into production elements too much."

"Only Love Can Break a Heart": "That one frightened me, too. . . . I didn't think it was a hit record—I thought it had too few words. I was wrong."

"Twenty-Four Hours from Tulsa": "The 1960s was a very strange time to have a hit with that kind of song. I remember a girl sitting in the front row while I was singing that song, and I could read her lips as she said to the girl sitting next to her: 'Isn't he *different?*'"

"The Man Who Shot Liberty Valance": "I thought I was recording it for the movie. But in the middle of the recording session I found out that the movie had already come out. Here's a movie with Jimmy Stewart, Lee Marvin and John Wayne—and the song doesn't get into the movie. People tell me that they saw the movie on TV, and that someone cut my song out. I say, no, they didn't. The song was never in it."

"I'm Gonna Be Strong": "What a song. That last phrase in the song— . . . *how I'll break down and cry* . . . —how the notes change within that last word. All these years later, and I still get goose bumps every time I sing that song."

Was he really as despondent as his songs?

"Nah," Pitney said. "People tell me all the time that I must be so sad. I never was."

He wasn't a lonely man?

"'Solitary' is a better word," he said. "I always feel that it's great when you can be by yourself. That's not a bad thing."

Graduate school in music, all right, with the classrooms moving from town to town. I never got tired of it.

"Where were you this morning?" Randell said.

I knew why he was asking.

"Walking around the streets of Chicago," I said.

"Amazing world, isn't it?" he said.

It was around midnight. We were standing out on the Bonneville Salt Flats, where Utah approaches Nevada—the harsh and endless floor upon which countless lonely racers have tested the very limits of speed. This felt like the most desolate and remote part of the world, separate from everything. We were taking a few minutes' break from our long drive across the highway; we were on our way west into Nevada, our eventual destination the town of Elko.

From where we stood in bright moonlight it appeared that, about a hundred feet away, there was a short white wall and then a body of water. It was the optical illusion of the salt flats beneath the moon. The flats seemed to go on forever, but because such a thing is not possible, the expansive void played tricks on the eye.

"No noise at all," Randell said.

That morning, in Chicago, I had listened to traffic sounds, to the impatient honking of horns and the intertwisted jumble of the voices of hundreds of people on the sidewalks, the jackhammers of construction and the whistles of hotel doormen. That was at breakfast time.

Now—same day, different America—we were in this empty and silent part of Utah, with the stars in the black sky so white that they, too, appeared to be part illusion.

"You shouldn't be able to do all of this in a day," Randell said, although by the sound of his voice I knew he meant the opposite: I knew he was saluting the wonderment. It was the same way he had sounded in Huntington Beach, when he had urged me to cross one more road and feel the Pacific Ocean.

Chicago in the morning, the stars above the salt flats at night, and no people in the history of the world ever had it quite this way before: to be able to look at a map of the continent and find the map not only undaunting, but effortlessly inviting, as simple, as possible, as a shrug. A cross-country journey, in a handful of hours? Nothing.

And everything.

"Just listen to the stillness," Randell said, and we did, and soon enough we were back on the road.

The Stockmen's Hotel and Casino in Elko was rough-hewn and hardscrabble, devoid of all airs. We'd be playing there for two nights; that's what it said on the hand-lettered sign on Commercial Street. As we walked in from the darkness to register, I heard a rather vivid pickup line. A man at the bar said to a woman:

"You want to have a drink? I've got to wash some of this gold dust out of my throat."

There was, in fact, some sort of gold rush in the area. The Nevada Division of Minerals had gone so far as to issue a warning to new arrivals: "Do not fall for claims of new 'secret' processes. . . . Precious metals do not mix. Claims of a mine site with high levels of platinum along with gold and silver is almost a certain indicator of fraud. Platinum has not been mined in Nevada since 1919. . . ."

Golden moments in Elko were not limited to mining, though. We found that out quite unexpectedly the next afternoon.

There were some suburban-patio-type tables by the small outdoor swimming pool, and Gary, David and I were hanging out there while, inside, the musical equipment was being set up.

In a room on the first floor of the hotel was a one-chair local barbershop. The entrance must have been on Commercial Street. The barbershop was a little incongruous, in this no-frills place, and we looked into it from the equivalent of its rear window.

"Look at the kid's face," Gary said.

A boy of about five was in the chair—he was way too small for it. We couldn't hear a thing; this was like watching a silent movie. But from his scared expression, and his ramrod-stiff posture, we wouldn't have been surprised to learn this was his first visit to a real barbershop.

"Look at the dad," David said. "Big day for him, too."

The father, looking on, might have been a rancher.

"Perfect," Gary said. "The boy's reading a comic book."

It could have been 1955. This—or at least it seemed to us—may have been a family turning point. A genuine barbershop for the boy. A stride toward being a man.

The barber cut the boy's hair short—the boy stared straight ahead, as if afraid to move. The father and the barber exchanged a few words. The boy read his comic book—or pretended to read, he was that young—trying his best to make this seem routine. Which, soon enough in his life, it would be.

"Here it comes," Gary said.

The barber removed the cloth from where it covered the boy's neck, patted some talcum, whisked with a stiff-bristled brush—the boy winced a little—and then . . .

"The reveal," Gary said.

The barber turned the chair toward the mirror, and the boy, for the first time, saw himself—saw the results of the haircut.

His mouth made an "O"—one of his hands went up to the top of his head and he ran his palm over his scalp.

"Going to the barbershop with your dad," Gary said. "He'll remember it fifty years from now."

The father and son left the shop. We got up and headed for the showroom to rehearse. Gold is where you find it.

We ate cream pie in the casino's all-night coffee shop after the last of our shows in Elko, and the waitress told us about the brothels.

"You ought to go look," she said. "They're only five minutes from here."

We didn't, that night, but in the morning—just after dawn; we were due in Salt Lake City for early flights—we asked the van driver to swing by.

There were four of them, down around Third Street. Squat and dull and unexceptional, grungy little houses with industrial-strength air-conditioning units grinding loudly away, we wouldn't have known what they were had the driver not pointed them out. They could have been anybody's dilapidated homes on the wrong side of any tracks.

They were legal and licensed by the state, the driver told us. Elko County permitted them, and if you knew how to find them, here they were.

"OK, I want to kill myself," Gary said.

They were just that depressing. The idea of men, in the dead of night, being so desperate and so lonely that they would willingly drive down to here, all so they could share a bed with whomever was toiling inside those weary walls. . . .

"Think about walking out of one of these places at this time of the morning," Dean said.

That would be the worst moment of all: a new day just beginning on a cruddy block in the desert, the sun inching up, and you walk out the door and glance back and think of the hours just past—and of the years that have led you to here.

"Somebody must like them," the van driver said. "They do a good business."

We headed toward Salt Lake. "How many years before that kid in the barber chair hears about those places?" Gary said.

"Don't say it," I said.

"You know he will," Gary said. "You know his buddies will talk about it."

"Don't say it," I said, the sun higher now through the windshield.

The home of the Pee Dee Pride minor-league ice-hockey team was the Florence, South Carolina, Civic Center, a gleaming arena of recent vintage. ("The Pee Dee" was how this part of South Carolina referred to itself; the name, I was told, was a reference to the Pee Dee River.) The arena where we would sing fronted on Radio Drive—a nice touch, I thought, as we arrived for the concert—and most of its 7,400 seats were filled.

The show was a touring package production called a Lovin' Feelings Concert—Jan and Dean were one of many acts, including Johnny Rivers and Ben E. King. The stage was run with stopwatch punctuality—each band was told exactly how many minutes to perform, and there was no leeway. The result was a fast-moving shuffle of singers, with multicolored spotlights sweeping back and forth over the audience and a general atmosphere reminiscent of what the itinerant rock shows of the Fifties must have felt like, with a palpable sense of bigness and motion and something akin to drama.

We played and then Gary and Phil and I decided to watch the rest of the acts from out in the audience. We found a few seats open on the side.

In the darkness we sat next to a group of women in their late thirties or early forties. The woman directly next to me was attired quite nicely—heels, the kind of dress she might wear to an expensive restaurant, jewelry. There were a lot of jeans and T-shirts in the audience, but she had treated the evening as one not to be attended casually.

She was wearing a light floral perfume. She stared at the lighted stage—because the seats were to the side, she, and we, were seeing the performers in semiprofile—and she didn't say much to her friends. There was just something in her eyes.

During a set change, the house lights went up. She saw us in our surf shirts, and realized that she had been watching us sing half an hour earlier. She said she had enjoyed it.

She and I started talking. Her voice was a little empty, the slightest bit subdued. I asked her what had made her decide to come to the show tonight, and she said, "My friends thought it would be good for me."

This was her first night out since her divorce, she said. The end of the marriage had been her husband's idea; she had not wanted it to end.

"I haven't been going out at all, and my friends said it was time," she said. "But I don't know."

Her children were home with a babysitter. She and her friends had gone out to dinner before the show. And here she was, and—she didn't have to say it—her new aloneness was hitting her hard.

"For so many years, we automatically went as a couple," she said.

Her friends had told her the music would cheer her up, that she would be surrounded by thousands of other people enjoying the evening. But here in the arena I could tell that, thousands of people or not, this was a lonesome night for her.

"It's nothing against your music," she said, as if afraid she had offended me.

"I know that," I said. "I just hope you're not wishing you hadn't come."

"Well . . ." she said, with a little attempted lilt in her inflection.

Then:

"You know what the hardest part was? Getting dressed. I was at home getting dressed to go out, and I thought: Why?"

Ice hockey arenas, even on nights when no one is skating, seem to have a chill to them, a tinge of frost that floats in the air and that you can feel beneath your shoes. It's as if the ice has never melted, even when it has.

It felt like that tonight, and Phil, Gary and I watched the rest of the show, with the woman and her friends in the seats to our left. Some of the songs were sad songs; music has forever depended on that. Her friends hadn't taken that into consideration, I would have ventured; if the purpose of the evening was to gladden her spirits, there were plenty of songs just about guaranteed to do the contrary.

We all listened and I could smell her floral perfume the whole time, and I thought about her putting it on at home before saying goodbye to her children. I thought about what she would tell them later tonight, or tomorrow morning, when they asked her how her evening had been.

The show ended and the lights came up and we were due in the van that waited behind the arena. Not knowing what else to do, I shook her hand, and said it had been nice meeting her.

She said, "I hope I didn't talk too much."

Not at all, I said, and then I said, "Your husband doesn't know what a mistake he's made," which I intended to be a compliment, something that would make her feel a little better, but which I feared, as soon as the words had left my mouth, may have done just the opposite.

We had another Lovin' Feelings concert scheduled the next night in Augusta, Georgia, and the promoters had decided it would make more sense to travel the one hundred fifty miles by chartered bus instead of flying all the acts over.

So at breakfast time in Florence all of the bands piled onto a coach that sat with its engine running in front of our hotel. It was sort of a kick—this really did seem like the old Cavalcade of Stars tours, riding on a bus with rock musicians booked for a series of one-night stands.

It was going to be two and a half hours on the highway. David Logeman broke out a pack of cards and recruited some players from the other bands. David tended to be loud when he was playing cards—I'd seen it in airport boarding areas; I don't think he even noticed the levels his voice reached, it may have been a byproduct of being a drummer by trade, and of assuming that everyone around you welcomes noise—and it was early enough in the morning that I didn't especially relish it.

I looked for a seat closer to the front of the bus, and saw that there was a vacant one next to Ben E. King.

He had been lead singer for the Drifters in the late 1950s, and later had gone out on his own; among his indelible vocal leads were "Stand By Me," "There Goes My Baby," "Spanish Harlem" and "I Count the Tears."

On this bus ride, though, there was another song I felt like talking with him about. The night before, as we had sat next to that woman in the Florence Civic Center, he had sung, as part of his set, "Save the Last Dance for Me."

You can dance, every dance with the guy that gives you the eye,
Let him hold you tight. . . .

The young teenagers who had made that song a number-one hit for the Drifters in the fall of 1960 had done so because the idea of the last dance—the final song before going home from a party—was something with which they could readily identify.

But in Florence, as I had watched the audience watch Ben E. King, I saw that most of the people were in middle age and beyond. No more high-school gym dances for them; no more proms or homecomings.

They had listened as he had sung:

. . . but don't forget who's taking you home,
and in whose arms you're gonna be. . . .

Last dance seemed to mean something else now. A new realization: that the opportunities life offers were no longer limitless, that choices were becoming more important, that the last dance—in every sense—was closer and more critical than it had been before.

. . . so darling, save the last dance for me. . . .

I thought about the woman at the concert, and about what she was thinking right now as she made breakfast for her children after her night out on the town. And I asked Ben E. King if he ever noticed what I thought I had noticed.

"Every time," he said. "Every night. You think about what the last dance used to mean to you—all the dances you went to when you were young—and then you think about all you've gone through in life, what's behind you and what's ahead. All your years of setbacks, all your years of hope.

"And you think how important it is for you to get the rest of your life right—to do it in the right way, with the right person. From the stage, I can see the faces in the audience. The glow in the eyes of the people. And I know that they're thinking about the same things I'm thinking."

He brought up another song he sang each night.

"'Stand By Me' makes me think a lot, too," he said. "About how important it is to have at least one person in your life you can count on. Someone you can call when there's no one else to talk to.

"You may think you're all alone, you may even choose to be alone—put the walls up. But even when you do that, you know that you need at least one person who you know, no matter what, will stand by you."

The bus, on a cloudy Carolina morning, was crossing the Broad River, toward our show in Augusta. On some nights, King said, as he sang "Save the Last Dance for Me" he would notice people who were all by themselves in the audience. Who had come to the show with no one.

"There are always couples holding each other during that song," he said. "But my eyes go to the people who are out there alone in the audience. I look at them, and I know what's going on inside them."

*. . . so don't forget who's taking you home,
and in whose arms you're gonna be. . . .*

"The people who are alone are the ones I can't look away from," he said. "I'm pulling for them."

FIFTEEN

The cardiologist in the next seat said that he had heard of the casino, although he'd never been inside.

This didn't surprise me; the doctor, careful and conservative in the way he conducted a conversation, didn't look like the kind of guy who might depend on magic.

That was the name of the place where we'd be playing: Casino Magic, in Bossier City, Louisiana. The doctor and I were on a Delta flight heading for Shreveport, the next town over.

As another new summer began, these casino dates were starting to overtake those at county fairgrounds. It was probably just a reflection of America itself.

What had historically been condemned as one of the nation's cardinal vices—organized gambling—had been almost completely co-opted and embraced by state governments. The days of police racket squads hunting down dice players and numbers runners had morphed into a cheery montage of smiling governors at bill-signing ceremonies authorizing legalized casino gambling within their borders or on their rivers. At the beginning of the Twentieth Century, Americans were told from the pulpit and from city hall that the surest path to degradation and ruin was a life of indolent gambling. By the end of the century, state-run lotteries—the officially endorsed versions of the old numbers games—were so ubiquitous as to be no longer controversial. Once the lotteries took hold, the casinos followed— the citizens had not only been assured by their governments that it was now all right to gamble, they were aggressively prodded to gamble by those governments. Buy a lottery ticket—you can become a multimillion-aire by the end of the weekend. We—the state, the same state that once threatened to arrest your grandparents if they dared to gamble—we're the ones pantingly peddling the tickets.

So once the lotteries were an established part of the social landscape, the casinos soon started springing up like neon-and-mirrored-glass toad-stools. It seemed, on one level, like an abject surrender by state and city governments. If you can't raise enough taxes by attracting manufacturers and merchants, if you can't create jobs and revenue by producing goods that actually matter to people, that improve their lives and give them a sense of worth . . .

Well, license a casino. Just pick the pockets of your citizens.

"I'm on my way home from seeing my daughter in Virginia," the car-diologist in the next seat said to me. "She was acting in her college play."

I told him he was welcome to come to our show at the casino that night; I said I'd leave him a ticket. He said thanks, but he planned to spend the evening at home.

He offered to give me a ride to my hotel before going to his medical office. When I was dropped off, there was a note at the front desk: the band had gotten in from California before I arrived. I should meet them for lunch at Joe Cobb's barbecue.

"So, Joe, how long have you owned this place?"

Randell was asking. The neighborhood felt fled from, ghostly. Not much was here.

"Since 1952," Mr. Cobb said. His one-room storefront featured utili-tarian tables with scratched Formica tops, flanked by blue-vinyl booths against the wall.

His wife, Sue, was behind the counter. The specialties were smoked-beef-and-ham sandwiches, turkey, chicken, ribs, hot links, barbecue beans, cole slaw. The band had somehow found this place within min-utes of hitting town.

Mr. and Mrs. Cobb not only brought us our meals, they slid some chairs over, sat with us and asked where we were from.

When I said I lived in Chicago, Mr. Cobb said:

"How many people live there?"

I told him the population. He smiled and said:

"That's too many."

Mr. and Mrs. Cobb didn't eat, but they stayed at the table, telling us about the generations of Bossier City residents who had come through this old room. David Logeman said: "So you do all your barbecuing right here?"

Mr. Cobb stood, motioned for us to leave our meals on the table for a minute, and led us behind the counter and then out back.

"This answer your question?" he said.

We stood next to his barbecue pit, and he showed us how he worked it—how he had always worked it, how, step by detailed step, his food became so addictively delicious. Then, a newly born summer beckoning us once again, a summer of singing and shared memories and many, many sandwiches in each others' company, we ate the first batch of those sandwiches together, and we sat with Mr. and Mrs. Cobb in the restaurant that meant the world to them—that was the world to them—and we all knew, without having to say a word, that we were exactly where we were supposed to be.

"These places even sound like carnivals," Gary said.

"I think that's the point," I said.

We were walking through the casino. There was that high-pitched, bubbling, quasi-musical casino-floor sound, a backdrop of juiced-up electronic noise that came from the slot machines, or at least seemed to. It was a proselytizingly happy sound, something that would be in place on any carnival midway.

It was no coincidence, I thought, that we were being booked into so many casinos. They were the new places of colored lights that never went dim, of willing crowds that never stopped moving, of come-hither music that never fell silent. Once, a person had to travel to Las Vegas to experience this wash of sensations; now the sensory wash was franchised as efficiently as McDonald's. What had brought us to Bossier City? The casino—this casino. Maybe the people jamming its aisles might once have been at a county fair. But they, and we, were here.

"At least at the end of the night the county fairs close until morning," Gary said.

Whatever, in addition to gambling, the old Las Vegas had once exclusively offered—a bequeathed sense of sophistication-for-rent, the freedom of being far from hometown faces and hometown concerns, the chance, for a few nights, to fool yourself into thinking you could be someone different from the person who greets you in the bathroom mirror every morning back home—that was not part of the promise here. At the proliferating local casinos around the country, the patrons tended to be from nearby; most of the gamblers here tonight were from Bossier City, and Shreveport, and this immediate part of Louisiana. They were likely to see their neighbors at the next craps table. If the casino was an escape, that escape came with severe limits, as cloistering as a backyard fence.

It was the new county fair, all right—a county fair that didn't need to wait for summer, a county fair that ran all year, a county fair with a bottomless appetite for workers who would run the tables, staff the restaurants, sweep the floors. And for workers who would entertain the gamblers.

Which is where we came in. Dean was thankful.

"The more casinos they build, the better for us," he said. "Every one of them has a stage that they need to fill every night of the year."

We walked onto this one. During our second show of the night I saw two people stroll in, sit at a table, and watch us sing.

Joe and Sue Cobb. Their barbecue place was closed for the evening. We had seen them do their work; now they saw us do ours.

The thirteen-year cicadas had made their return to Nashville, which of course coincided exactly with our visit to town, and to the Nashville Arena.

We were ripping our shirts off backstage. We were trying not to let out screams, but it was difficult to feign being blasé. You would feel it first inside your shirt—something unpleasant going on. You would hope you were imagining it. But then the creeping, crawling sensation would intensify, and you would open a button or two and take a look. . . .

To find the ugliest, darkest, jumbo-sized, double-winged, six-legged, red-eyed insect that could ever star in your worst three-o'clock-in-the-morning nightmare, except you were wide awake, and the thing was real and scratching its way across your chest.

So we shouted and squealed and threw our shirts to the ground, batted the burrowing bugs off our chests, and counted the hours until we could play and go to the airport and get out of town.

This was something about which I would have liked to joke with Phil Bardowell. Phil, with his musefully mordant views of life, views he invariably expressed with not-a-consonant-wasted economy, could always make me laugh, even during moments that by all rights should make us shudder. But he had left Jan and Dean.

He had been invited to join the Beach Boys, and he had said yes. It wasn't really much of a decision, I surmised. The money was much better.

Phil may have been younger than anyone else in the Jan and Dean band—at soundcheck some afternoons I would catch him playing "Purple Haze" instead of "The Little Old Lady from Pasadena," as a kind of reminder that he wasn't madly in love with the surf hits that had topped the charts before he was born—but when showtime came he sang and played the surf/cars/girls songs with as much passion as he would presumably put into music that he actually cared for. He was a pro.

Mostly, though, he was wonderful company. Once we were playing at the Mall of America in Bloomington, Minnesota, the preposterously gargantuan shopping complex out on the plains. There were more than five hundred twenty stores in the Mall of America, a full-service amusement park under its roof, more than fifty restaurants. The mall covered 4.2 million square feet; forty million people entered its doors each year, which is eight times as many people as live in the entire state of Minnesota.

We had played right out in the mall itself—in one of the retail corridors, facing a bank of escalators. It was a little ridiculous: standing there in our stage shirts, singing "409" and "Honolulu Lulu" while staring at an endless parade of men, women and children riding down the multiple banks of escalators, with shopping bags drooping from their hands. Seven Yankee Stadiums could fit inside the mall—that's what the executives who were escorting us said—and it was hard to concentrate on the show and not just look around slack-jawed.

What had made the night a winning one for me, though, was the presence of Jack Roth, who had been my best friend since we were five years old in kindergarten. He and his wife and daughter had moved away from our old hometown in Ohio, and were living in a Minneapolis suburb; he'd come to the mall to watch us sing.

So much of what I was finding with Jan and Dean was an echo of the summers I'd cherished with Jack and my other best friends back when we were sixteen and seventeen; that's what I was getting back, against all expectations: an approximation, later in life, of what those long nights of fun and friendship had once given me. It's what had struck me that muggy midnight with the band at the Peachtree City Waffle House—how close all of this felt to that.

So, on this evening at the Mall of America, to find elements of both those worlds—the lost world of Jack and my old friends, the new world of Jan and Dean and my new friends. . . .

To find myself in the midst of that gave me a feeling of contentment and humble gratitude.

After the show at the mall the rest of the band went back to our hotel, and Jack and I hung around the empty stage talking. Phil hadn't left. Jack asked if we were hungry, and Phil said he could stand to eat. He and Jack and I went up to the top level of the mall.

The restaurant, as I recall, had some tie-in to the country singer Garth Brooks. Just about every franchised food operation in the United States attempted to get a foothold in the Mall of America, and that year, it seemed, Garth Brooks and his business associates were giving it a try. (Whenever Dean happened upon an operation like that one, trading upon a famous singer's name, I could see something behind his eyes: Why not us?)

But Dean wasn't with us at the Garth Brooks restaurant; it was just

Jack and Phil and me. The two of them talked effortlessly; they hit it off right away, neither felt awkward, and I was loving it, the way the two worlds of mine were intersecting. We stayed late, taking our time, talking until the waiters had to ease us out at closing time.

And the best part, at least in my memory, was this:

We walked to Jack's car in the parking garage of the Mall of America, and we all piled in, and Jack said, "I'll take you home."

Home, for Phil and me on this night, was a hotel on the highway near the mall. Jack knew that; that's what he meant. But as he drove us to the hotel, I thought:

After all the years: buddies in a car while most of the city around us sleeps, and Jack at the wheel, dropping us off before going home himself. He'd done just this hundreds of times when he and I were young—dropped me, and our other friends, off at the end of a good night. Those nights were supposed to be gone forever. But they weren't. Jack drove Phil and me to the front door of our hotel, and the two of them shook hands, and then he drove away toward his house, and his family, while Phil and I walked in and went to the elevator.

"What a good guy," Phil said.

And I knew Jack was thinking the same thing.

So Phil was gone, off playing with the Beach Boys, and to take his place in the band Dean had hired Don Raymond, a beyond-solid rock-and-roll journeyman whose vocals were as tone-true as church chimes, and whose guitar work appeared to be as automatic an activity for him as tying his shoes.

Everyone in the band knew him; they traveled in the same musical circles in California (he had once been a member of the Ventures), and he had the steady personal manner, and straight-down-the-field looks and bearing, of a varsity halfback grown older—maybe not an All-American, but a ball carrier who could be counted upon to pick up four yards any time it was needed. Another sports analogy might have been just as apt: Don carried himself like a well-traveled utility infielder who took pride in being able to fit in with any new team on an hour's notice. The kind of

Bob Greene

player who could be traded at six o'clock one night, and be on a diamond halfway across the country the next evening, in a different uniform with different teammates, at the plate and knocking a single into the gap to score a runner he'd just met for the first time in the clubhouse that dusk.

"*Look* at those things," he said, as a cicada crawled across the floor in our Nashville dressing room, and from out in the arena we could hear the crowd starting to arrive.

In Lynchburg, Virginia, the booking seemed to be a mistake. Here in the home of the Reverend Jerry Falwell's Liberty University, we found ourselves in a airplane-hangar-sized country-and-western bar: a sprawling honkytonk of the kind featured in the movie *Urban Cowboy*, with shades of the tumbledown *Blues Brothers* roadhouse in which Jake and Elwood trepeditiously performed behind a barrier of chicken wire. This promised to be a disaster.

But what was on my mind, as we arrived at the bar to set up, was the opposite of disaster. *Triumph* wouldn't have been too strong a word for it.

"Jan?" I said.

This was the first I'd seen him since I arrived in Lynchburg from Chicago.

"I got your package," I said.

It had come in the mail: small, square, padded.

Inside was a CD. A new musical release.

Second Wave, the album was called. The recording artist was Jan Berry.

He'd done it. Somehow, he'd done it. The tape he had played for me up in his hotel room that years-ago night in Florida, the long-distance calls he'd tried to make via the puzzled motel telephone operator in Oklahoma City, seeking a connection with the off-the-beaten-path-named One-Way Records in Albany, New York. . . .

It had all seemed, at the time, like flailing—it had seemed poignant and not quite attached to reality. Like a fevered dream Jan was having.

But here it was. Fourteen songs, cover art showing a rocky shore at sundown . . . and, on the back, in the left-hand corner beneath the song list, the name of the record company.

One-Way Records. Albany, New York.

He'd done it.

A handwritten note was enclosed with the CD, attached with a strip of adhesive tape to the hard-plastic cover:

> Bob—
> I really hope you like my new album.
> Your friend, Jan

The liner notes indicated that he had worked on it with a friend named Rob Kuropatwa. He had spent eight years—*eight years*—writing, arranging and recording the fourteen songs. He had paid for it himself.

I put the disc into a CD player, not knowing what to expect.

The songs were . . .

Well, they were very pretty. The words, and the melodies, and, especially, Jan's voice.

His voice was softer, less strained, than I was accustomed to hearing it onstage. During concerts, there was a kind of fearful combat in his voice, as if somewhere inside he was swinging at an unseen enemy. Onstage, his voice seemed always trying to countermand something: what he saw in the faces of the audience, his uncertainty about how he was being received, his distrust of the local sound technicians' ability or willingness to pump up his vocals loud enough in the speakers. And of course onstage, he was competing with Dean.

On his album, I thought I could hear in his voice a sense of trust. He didn't have to push his vocals to the limit—he could sing more delicately. There was an evident effort on his part to enunciate clearly, to make each word bright and understandable—an achievement, because of the obstacles and encumbrances that Jan constantly battled, that must have required many, many takes, over months and years. And although I was unfamiliar with the technicalities of modern recording-studio mixing boards, I got the feeling that Jan had received a little digital electronic help—it just sounded as if something had been done to smooth some verses out, to keep his voice on keel.

What mattered—what moved me so—was the unadorned fact that he had accomplished this. Somewhere within him, there was still that all-pervading ambition, that drive to prevail, that had made him a national star when he was a very young man. His body may have been broken, his mind sometimes enshrouded in a fog he could not find his way out of—but wherever inside of Jan that fire burned, on his album you could almost feel the heat from the flames. For eight years, when he had gone home to California after each leg of a tour, this had consumed him. He was going to make a record again—and if no one else would support him, then he would support himself.

The themes of many of the songs were a boy's themes: spring break, and parties, and falling in love.

He sang of hopes for long, happy days:

I can feel spring is coming soon,
I can't wait anymore. . . .

He sang of yearned-for affection:

Walk you home for the first time,
with nothing left to say. . . .

The song that made me sit in silence for a long time was called "Get That Girl." On the surface, it was about starting a new romance.

But there was this:

Better ask her now if you want to dance,
It's getting pretty late, it's your only chance

That was it, right there. He knew that his chances in life were running out. He wasn't going to let the end arrive without giving it everything he had.

I had no illusions that *Second Wave* was going to be a hit; One-Way

Records was hardly a major power in the contemporary music business. I had a hunch that Jan, and not the record company, was the one taking the financial plunge with the release of the CD. The recording industry itself had changed so drastically in recent years that it was unlikely that Jan's songs would receive much, if any, radio airplay, or be given the kind of retail distribution that might lead to significant sales.

But he had tried his hardest, and, fueled by sheer will, he had made this happen. I held the CD in my hand on the day it arrived. So often, on the road, we asked ourselves what was going on within Jan, in the places we couldn't see. This was the answer.

At the Lynchburg bar a country group opened for us—tight and high-volumed and sure of themselves, with a female lead singer who strutted the stage with the absolute self-confidence of an undefeated middleweight boxing champion, knowing how good she was, knowing that her vocals were landing like punches on the people in the audience, people who were staring at her as if they intuited that to look away would be to disobey her command and risk punishment.

She and her band were going to be tough to follow. When we did, though, we found the audience reassuringly welcoming—if we considered the country bar to be a strange booking, so did they, but they clearly liked the eccentricity of it. It was a break in the bar's standard repertoire. Men in cowboy hats and women in leather boots drank beer straight from longneck bottles, and I looked at Jan more often than I usually did during our shows. *It's getting pretty late, it's your only chance. . . .*

When we landed in Erie, Pennsylvania, and got off the plane, it was as if we were setting foot in the world capital of musical happiness.

All because of *That Thing You Do!*

The movie, directed by Tom Hanks, had not just become a favorite of everyone in the band; it had affected the way we talked to each other. The subject matter—a fictional one-hit-wonder rock band from Erie that had its only big record in the summer of 1964—was naturally one that would appeal to this particular group of musicians (although Dean seemed slightly less smitten with the film than the rest of us; this may have been because, unlike us, he actually had been a chart-topping rock star in 1964, and no one-hit wonder at that).

But it was the feel of the movie—the utter rightness of its tone—that enchanted us. So when we at last found ourselves in Erie, an odd little geographic thumb in Pennsylvania's northwest corner (drive thirty minutes to the west and you're in Ohio, drive thirty minutes to the east and you're in New York State), we felt the way that other men might feel if they were walking up the Clark Gable-Vivien Leigh staircase from *Gone With the Wind*, or if they were skipping along the yellow brick road from *The Wizard of Oz*.

And, because we couldn't help ourselves, we did what we had intermittently been doing in the years since *That Thing You Do!* came out: We talked to each other using dialogue from the movie. But now we were in Erie, hallowed Erie, and we couldn't seem to stop.

No explanation was necessary. Out of nowhere, one of us would say:

"Open on Sunday, from twelve to six. You know, I don't believe I want to live in a country where you have to stay open on Sunday to do business."

And everyone would know the reference: Mr. Patterson, owner of Patterson's Appliances in the movie and the father of Wonders drummer Guy Patterson, reading aloud from a newspaper ad for a bigger, rival store.

Or—quoting Lenny Haise, the lead guitarist in the Wonders—one of us would suddenly say: "Are you crazy? A man in a really nice camper wants to put our song on the radio. Give me a pen—I'm signing, you're signing, we're all signing."

The sheer Erie-ness of being here was making us giddy. In the van on the way to our motel, someone—echoing the words of Tom Hanks himself, who played the record-company executive in the movie—said: "You will go on tour with other stars of the Play-Tone galaxy."

Gary—channeling Faye, the betrayed girlfriend of Wonders lead singer James Mattingly II—said: "From now on, you stay away from me. I have wasted thousands and thousands of kisses on you. . . . Shame on me for kissing you with my eyes closed so tight."

The van driver shot us a wary look. Hard to blame him.

We were staying at a Microtel, where the rooms were microscopic, and because we were going stir-crazy we decided to head down the street and have some ribs. We knew we were unlikely to find anything in Erie as good as Joe Cobb's, but Dean said that there was a local outpost of the Damon's barbecue chain.

(Gary did try to dissuade us by saying, "We should go to Villapiano's, the spaghetti place out by the airport." There was no Villapiano's by the Erie airport. It was just another much-esteemed line from *That Thing You Do!*)

At Damon's there were big TV screens all around the restaurant, almost all of them tuned to sporting events. One of them, though, had a network newscast on. The sound was muted; we could see the anchor's mouth move, but could not hear his words.

On the screen some old footage from more than ten years before came up: Al Campanis, then the general manager of the Los Angeles Dodgers, was being interviewed by Ted Koppel. It was the notorious *Nightline* broadcast in which Campanis had made the blunder of saying that black athletes "might not have some of the necessities" to be managers. The remarks had cost Campanis his career.

The old Koppel tape was faded, the colors bleached out; Campanis's face disappeared and then the current-day news anchor was back on the screen, segueing to another story.

"So Al Campanis died today," I said.

"How do you know?" Dean said.

"That's the only reason they would be showing that old *Nightline* clip," I said.

"It could have been something else," Randell said.

"Not on the evening news," I said. "If that clip's on there, he's dead."

Which he was.

You can live seventy or eighty full and varied years, and in the end you'll be summed up by ten or twelve seconds of videotape, maybe of your worst moments. And that's if you happen to be famous. If you're not, your passing will go unnoted. The news anchor's lips moved on one screen, a tennis match progressed on the one next to it. We finished our dinner. We were due onstage at the Erie Seafood Festival.

We couldn't tell if the name of the event was meant as a joke, and it would have been ungallant to ask.

If the Erie Seafood Festival was named for the lake, Lake Erie was nowhere within sight of where we were supposed to sing. We were at the back end of the parking lot of a mall—the only view was of blacktop and the rear walls of buildings.

As for seafood, there had to have been some around, because we couldn't miss the pungent scent of rotting fish. It was coming from a row of garbage cans set up just to the right of the stage. Multiple people at the event must have gotten sick to their stomachs from the fish, because it was impossible to ignore the aroma of the end result of that stomach-sickness.

The crowd, what there was of it, sat complacently on folding chairs that had been set up on the parking lot's surface. Many of the people in the seats were wearing T-shirts printed up for the evening, featuring a cartoon drawing of a smiling lobster under a panoramic "Erie Seafood Festival" logo.

It should have been deflating.

But it wasn't.

We were together on yet another gorgeous night in summer, the instruments were lined up and waiting on the stage, we were going to be singing the songs we loved for people who had built their evenings around their desire to come out and hear us. . . .

And we were in Erie.

We climbed the stairs and took our places under the lights, the way we always did in the minute or so before Jan and Dean themselves made their entrance.

There is a scene near the end of *That Thing You Do!* when the Wonders take the stage of a network television program called *The Hollywood Showcase*. Their big moment is just ahead: they will be telecast coast-to-coast singing their hit. They know that their families back home in Erie are gathered in front of their TV sets to watch.

The Hollywood Showcase is in a commercial break, so the Wonders are standing in place, waiting. This performance will be the apex of their entire lives; nothing that came before or that will come after will ever match it.

Lenny, the guitar player, turns to Guy, the drummer, and asks him a simple question.

Tonight, in Erie, with a smattering of people staring at us from the seats, and the smell of dead fish and vomit wafting toward us, I turned to Gary and asked the same question, in the same words:

"How did we *get* here?"

He smiled. He knew I wasn't kidding, that I wasn't being at all sarcastic. One more wondrous summer night. He pressed his fingers against his keyboard and David Logeman hit his drums, and the show began.

Sixteen

There undoubtedly were myriad cultural opportunities available in the many cities we passed through: art galleries, symphonies, crafts fairs, operas. We didn't take advantage of any of them.

The reason, I suppose, is that we were there to do our own shows, and that didn't leave much time for anything else.

But in Seymour, Wisconsin, we made an exception. We all congregated for a late-afternoon visit to a museum. We showed up at the front door right on time, our hands clasped in front of us. Even out there on the street, we spoke in hushed museum-visitor tones. We might as well have been stepping into a church.

The museum was, after all, the Hamburger Hall of Fame.

"Thank you for making a special trip," Randell said to the curator, who had driven over from his house to unlock the place for us.

It wasn't much of a museum—just a few rooms—and it wasn't open most days. But we'd eaten so many burgers on the road in so many places, there was no way we were going to leave Seymour without setting foot in this shrine.

Seymour, it turned out, claimed to be the town where the hamburger was invented. More precisely, where the hamburger *sandwich* was invented.

As the story had it, a boy named Charlie Nagreen—"Hamburger Charlie," as he was still known in Seymour—came to the Outagamie County Fair in the year of 1885.

(Which is why we had come to Seymour, too—we would be playing at the fair after the sun went down.)

Charlie was just fifteen years old; a hardworking youth, he allegedly arrived at the fair in an ox-drawn wagon and set up a food stand. His goal was to sell meatballs to hungry fairgoers.

He found out soon enough that his business plan had a serious flaw. How were Outagamie County residents, in the sweltering summer of 1885, supposed to go around to the various livestock barns and agricultural exhibits while holding large, hot, juice-dripping meatballs in their bare hands?

Young Charlie—according to Seymour lore—came up with an answer that would make history. He flattened his meatballs and stuck them between slices of bread.

(The story, I found out later, is not without its naysayers. Some people believe that a German-American named Frank Menches first served hamburger sandwiches at the Summit County Fair in New York; others bestow the honor upon one Louis Lassen of New Haven, Connecticut.)

But we weren't in Summit County or New Haven. We were in Seymour, where Hamburger Charlie was hailed—revered—as the bona fide item. He was said to have returned to the fair where it began every year until his death in 1951.

"This is good," Gary said as we stood and looked at various hamburger doodads: hamburger teapots, hamburger candles, hamburger cookie jars, hamburger coasters. There was a framed color portrait of Hamburger Charlie himself, wearing a white apron and holding a burger in his left hand, his likeness superimposed over the skyline, as it were, of Seymour, with Seymour's water tower amended to resemble a hamburger.

On display out back of the museum was a prodigious grill, constructed from raw metal one year by the people of Seymour for a town festival. Upon this grill, it was said, was cooked what was claimed to be the world's largest hamburger—5,520 pounds. Pieces of it were reported to have been "enjoyed by over 13,000 visitors."

A 5,520-pound hamburger would not seem to be wholly logical—

Hamburger Charlie's entire concept of a hamburger sandwich was predicated on its portability—but all of this was making us famished.

"So, how do we order some burgers?" Dean said.

"Oh, we don't serve them here," the curator said.

The rest of the band was willing to wait until showtime to eat whatever backstage food the promoters had provided, but the Hamburger Hall of Fame had exerted its potent sway over Randell and me. We found a bowling alley—Wally's Seymour Bowl, it was called—on Lake Road, a block or so north of the Outagamie County Fairgrounds. There were no other customers and the lights were for some reason dim to the point of blackness, but there was a bartender who had a grill in the middle of his work area, and we sat down.

"Two cheeseburgers, two beers," Randell said.

The bartender took two pieces of cheese and laid them flat on the surface of a side counter that did not appear to be as clean as, say, a surgical instrument tray—think of what the bottom of a highway worker's boot looks like at the end of a long shift; that's what the counter looked like. He left the cheese there while he waited for the burgers to fry.

"The heat will kill any dirt on the cheese, right?" I said very quietly to Randell.

"Do *you* want to complain to this guy?" he said just as quietly to me.

I did not. The bartender seemed like a man best not trifled with even when he was in the most blissful of spirits, and from his countenance his spirits at the moment seemed not blissful at all.

Our beers appeared, and I walked over to the jukebox. I saw that it had country singer Alan Jackson's great twang-and-power-chord remake of "Mercury Blues," the old ode to a '49 sedan. I punched it in five times.

We'd be singing ourselves in an hour or two. For now we sat in the lightless bowling alley, drinking our beers, eating our burgers, listening to Alan Jackson selling those words from long ago:

If I had money, tell you what I'd do,
I'd go downtown and buy a Mercury or two. . . .

"Why does this day seem so great?" Randell said.

"Because it is," I said.

"They all are, aren't they?" he said, and the bartender asked if we wanted more cheeseburgers, and we said yes. He put two more slices of cheese on the same dicey patch of counter, but we didn't care. The grill would burn off anything bad.

Alan Jackson's name was up on the fairgrounds marquee; he and his band would be coming to town after Jan and Dean.

We were singing "Little Deuce Coupe" onstage, and the people were literally hopping up and down as they sang along, and I thought: It doesn't change. Alan Jackson might sing about old Mercurys and we might sing about deuce coupes and somewhere tonight the Beach Boys and who knew how many cover bands were probably singing about 409s, but car songs, and nights like this, and people made jubilant just to be out in the summer air and hearing the music. . . .

It doesn't change, and if we're smiled upon by fortune, I thought, it never will.

I didn't know if this was the same fairgrounds where Charlie Nagreen had arrived in that oxcart in 1885—I figured it had to be, Seymour didn't seem like a town where things got rearranged too often—and I didn't know if he veraciously was the first person (at age fifteen, at that) to come up with the idea of putting hamburger meat between pieces of bread. Tonight, though, I was more than willing to give him the benefit of the doubt; tonight I was pleased to silently thank him for all the cheeseburgers over all the years.

We sang:

She's my little deuce coupe. . . .

This one's for you, Hamburger Charlie. That's what I was thinking. Bet you never knew just how many American nights you made a little better.

"I'm in Babe Ruth's room," Dean said. "What about you?"

"John Wayne's," I said. "The bathtub has these claw feet."

"I think I'm in Cecil B. DeMille's," Gary said.

We were in Deadwood, South Dakota, in a remote pocket of the Black Hills, and had just checked into the Franklin Hotel. All we knew as we arrived was that we'd be playing outdoors on the town's main street.

The Franklin had opened for business in 1903. The lobby, with its ceramic mosaic tile floors and its walls wainscoted in golden oak, looked much like what it must have on that first day. The mining town's past had been drenched in lawlessness and violence; Wild Bill Hickock's life came to a bloody end during a poker game in the No. 10 Saloon when he was shot in the back of the head by Jack McCall. The cards Hickock was holding—a pair of aces and a pair of eights—are still referred to around the world as a "dead man's hand."

At the Franklin—whose 1911-model Otis elevator was manually operated by a hotel employee—many of the eighty-one rooms were named for noted persons who had once spent the night. As Dean walked out the door of the chamber where Babe Ruth had slumbered, and encountered Gary and me as we walked out of bedrooms where Mr. DeMille (in Deadwood while working on *The Plainsman*) and the Duke (in the Black Hills to film scenes for *Stagecoach*) had slept, we decided to forgo the ancient elevator and instead use the grand staircase.

"Look at this," David Logeman said. He was standing at the entrance of an anteroom.

There was a sign:

THE FAINTING ROOM

The explanatory text read:

"In the 1800s, women wore tight corsets to obtain the ideal 18-inch waistlines fashionable at that time. When the discomfort of the corsets became unbearable, the ladies retired to a private parlor to rest on the fainting couches."

Inside the room was an actual fainting couch—green in color.

"The world could use more places to faint," Randell said.

"Faint later," David said. "We're late."

There weren't many moments when I had to remind myself that I was still, in certain ways that counted, an outsider. When those moments arrived, though, they were unmistakable.

Just before the Deadwood show began, Gary, David, Randell, Don Raymond and I huddled at the rear of the stage. Jan and Dean were talking with each other a few feet away.

"What do you want to add to the dance segment?" Gary said.

The show was scheduled to be longer than usual. The place where we lengthened the performances on nights like this was the "Let's Dance"/"Do You Wanna Dance"/"Dance, Dance, Dance" part of the concert.

"I can sing 'Runaround Sue,'" Don said. As Phil's replacement, he was still new enough that he was feeling his way.

"We can always do 'Wooly Bully,'" Randell said.

I held up one palm with all the fingers and the thumb extended, and the other with three fingers showing.

"All right," Gary said, understanding the eight fingers. "You can do 'Eight Days a Week.'"

It was one of the songs, back at that pool-deck show in Huntington Beach, that I had suggested when the rest of us did our opening set without Jan and Dean. I'd thought it had sounded terrific that night; there was something about the old Beatles song that was just right for live performance (although I don't think the Beatles ever sang it in concert; they stopped touring not long after they recorded that song).

So in Deadwood we did our show on the town's main drag, with people packed in the entire length of the dusty street. The women near the front of the stage were particularly demonstrative, in short shorts and skimpy halters; their glad brazenness as they danced seemed millennia removed from the demure shrinking violets who once must have sought out the Fainting Room when it came time to crumple and swoon.

From our vantage point the people in the street appeared, as the music boomed and the sun dipped, to become one living, writhing organism, a fat snake convulsing as it stretched to the horizon. During the dance segment Randell and I sang "Eight Days a Week" together, and by the end of the performance everyone, band and audience, was soaked with sweat and happily exhausted.

We were all feeling pretty good about the concert. We were relaxing behind the stage when Dean, clearly annoyed about something—although for him, the annoyance needle did not usually move past sardonic pique, which was about where it was tonight—approached us.

"Why are we singing 'Eight Days a Week'?" he said.

There was a silence.

Dean waited for an answer.

"He said we should," Randell said, nodding ever so slightly in my direction.

"*Who* said we should?" Dean said.

Gary pointed at me.

Dean looked at me. He didn't have to say a word. His expression said it all. Which was:

Why is *he*—meaning me—determining what's on our set list? How exactly did this happen?

He shook his head in that clearing-out-the-cobwebs way he always did when he was particularly consternated with Jan. But right now I, not Jan, was the consternator.

"We're not a Beatles tribute band," Dean said. "This isn't some British Invasion show."

Not knowing what else to say, I said:

"Did you see the rocking chairs?"

There were six of them, and seven of us, so we had to take turns.

They were red—red rocking chairs on the front porch of the Franklin Hotel.

It was something you seldom encountered anymore: hotels with broad front porches, let alone rocking chairs. But these were holdovers from the days when the Franklin was the one outpost of strived-for gentility in Deadwood. Guests back then were invited to rock their cares away as they looked out upon Main Street.

"So how does a town have gunfights and Wild Bill Hickock and pros-
titutes, and also have rocking chairs and fainting rooms?" Dean said,
rocking.

"I already asked someone at the front desk about that," I said, rocking.

Main Street, in the early days of Deadwood, was divided with an invisible line. The part of Main Street where our stage had been located used to
be known as "lower Main"—also, locally, as the badlands. Lower Main was
a place of crime and mayhem. Upper Main—where the Franklin sat—was
where what passed for well-heeled society in Deadwood congregated.

"It just doesn't seem like the kind of town where people would go to a
special room to faint, and rock in chairs on a front porch," Don said,
rocking.

"I agree," David said, rocking. "You think that people shot bullets at
each other and fought over gold nuggets, and then fainted and rocked?
That doesn't make any sense."

"Yes it does," I said, rocking. "What were they supposed to do when
they were upset in Deadwood back then? Make an appointment with
their psychiatrist?"

Our chairs creaked away on the big porch. We must have been quite
a sight.

Gary, in his red chair, curled his lip, sneered, and swiveled. He was
imitating Elvis Presley. Rocking.

Sometimes on the road I asked myself whether Elvis, at the very end,
was even tangentially aware of just what he was giving up.

That was one beneficial part of being an outsider at this: having an
outsider's appreciation of the things those who had lived their whole lives
inside this world inevitably came to take for granted.

We were outdoors at the Silverton Hotel and Casino in Las Vegas,
playing the first evening of a two-night stand. Visible behind us—I
turned several times during the show to take in the sight—was the Silverton's soaring main sign, designed to be read clearly from the nearby
highway. And on the brilliantly illuminated electronic marquee, in letters as tall as houses, were the words "Jan and Dean."

Which was how things were done in Las Vegas—when you headline, you get the bigger-than-life, name-in-a-million-lights treatment. No one ever got that treatment on the scale that Elvis got it—his first name, on the monumental sign in front of the Hilton whose showroom he filled for years (as well as on billboards all around town), dominated the Las Vegas landscape, commandeered the senses. What a boost to the ego, to the sense of self-regard and accomplishment, to see one's name displayed like that. At least you would think so.

But I suppose you can get used to anything. By the end, Elvis by all accounts was experiencing only distress; by the end, being that name on the marquee was something from which he felt the necessity to escape, using any means available.

You can never quantify another person's pain. But as we sang in Las Vegas, I contemplated Jan and I thought: however hard life might have been for Presley, it couldn't have been any harder than it was for Jan Berry. The outdoor stage at the Silverton was a good distance from the main hotel building, so Jan had needed assistance coming over. He'd made it, though, like he always made it, and now he was enthusiastically singing his songs, with his name blazing on that hulking hotel sign that loomed above the desert.

There was nothing that could have kept Jan away from his microphone. And I found myself wondering: Was this—the vaunted pressure of performing, the much-lamented price of musical fame—really so terrible, so unbearable, that Elvis had to die at forty-two to get away from it? Was seeing his name in lights, literally and figuratively, for all those years truly such a burden that he had to obliterate his senses to blot it out?

The casino was holding a bikini contest each night in conjunction with our weekend shows—the contests had little to do with the bikinis, and everything to do with the women inside the bikinis—and as the entrants paraded across the stage inches in front of us, Don Raymond, his guitar strap around his neck, looked at me and raised his eyebrows.

I knew the translation. As a matter of fact, I had once heard Elvis Presley, in Las Vegas, say the words that summed up the translation perfectly.

A woman had run up to the stage at the Hilton and had thrown her arms around Elvis and had kissed him full on the mouth. He had turned to his backup band and, grinning, had said to them:

"Tough way to make a livin', boys. Tough way to make a livin'."

That's what Don was indicating, with his arched eyebrows as the bikini contestants sashayed past us on the stage. Tough way to make a livin'. Meaning: What a great way to make a living.

I was singing in Las Vegas tonight and Elvis wasn't and never would be again, which seemed so wrong on so many levels that it was almost too much to absorb. So I just kept doing it, while thinking of him, and wishing he had somehow been able to figure out a way to better love his life.

One thing about all these casino dates:

We each were gaining about seven pounds a day.

At least it felt like that. At non-casino shows around the country we were accustomed to the promoters furnishing catered dinners, or arranging for us to sign for our meals at the hotels. But casinos, generically, were known—lampooned—for their inexpensive all-you-can-eat buffets. So the casino bosses just gave us passes that allowed us to wander at will through the buffet lines for the length of our stays.

"How great is this," Randell—the chief buffet aficionado—would say, like an explorer taking his first tentative steps into a lush and fertile forest, as he set eye upon yet another enormous room whose walls were lined with long tables bearing hundreds of platters of food. With those buffet passes in our hands, the temptation—a temptation never resisted—was to have the pot roast *and* the roasted chicken, the pasta bolognese *and* the skirt steak, the Caesar salad *and* the spinach salad, the chocolate cake *and* the raspberry cheesecake *and* the make-your-own sundae *and* the apple pie alamode. . . .

Bloated and ashamed, we would leave the buffets to go to our rooms to rest. Only to hear the phone ring a few hours later, and hear the voice of one of the others:

"We still have some time before the show. You want to hit that buffet again?"

Plus, the buffets were open all night. The food never ran out.

Ring, ring, at two o'clock in the morning.

"You asleep? You feel like going down and checking out some of those fried clams?"

The mirrors in our rooms in casino hotels might as well have been imported from carnival funhouses. We looked like Humpty Dumpty by the time we checked out.

"Good career move."

That was the cynical response John Lennon reportedly had uttered when he heard that Elvis was dead.

Had he really believed it? There was no way to know, just as there was no way for Lennon to have known that, within four years after Presley died, he himself would be dead.

Good career move? Perhaps, in the context of legend-making, there was a terrible case to be made in support of that proposition. If there is any way to be even bigger than Elvis Presley or the Beatles, it's to be Elvis or a Beatle once you're gone.

In Las Vegas on the second of our two nights of concerts, Randell and I sang "Eight Days a Week."

(Dean had relented. He found it impossible to be an inflexible taskmaster. "Yeah, I guess 'Eight Days a Week' does sound pretty good onstage," he'd said. So it was back in the show. It had really never left.)

Randell and I were doing something the Beatles had never done—they had never stood on a stage in front of people and sung this fine and rollicking song that they had written. The reality of their fame—their cold understanding of the fact that their popularity had escalated so far out of control that touring was no longer necessary, or advisable, or safe—had largely confined them, right up until the breakup, to making their records in the studio and letting their voices coming out of the vinyl do their only public performing for them.

Good career move, perhaps. But the idea that Elvis had made certain decisions that ultimately meant he would never be here again on a night like this, the idea that Lennon and his bandmates had made certain decisions that meant they would never even once give themselves the pleasure—the fun—of singing "Eight Days a Week" on a stage for the very fans for whom they'd written it. . . .

Good career moves? It was difficult to accept that. In Elvis's Las Vegas Randell and I harmonized on Lennon's and McCartney's words:

Eight days a week,
is not enough to show I care. . . .

Why, given a choice, would a man ever deprive himself of this?

Unless the man's life has taken such unexpected and disorienting turns, turns he never could have imagined as a boy in Tupelo or in Liverpool, that he comes to believe the choice is no longer his.

David Logeman feinted to his right, than pivoted left and shot an imaginary jump shot at a basket that wasn't there.

"This is about where it should be, right?" he said.

"Almost exactly," I said.

I'd been to games here, back when the arena was called the Summit. By now the name of the place had been changed to the Compaq Center, but it was still the home of the Houston Rockets of the National Basketball Association. The Rockets weren't here tonight; they hadn't been on the premises for months, even though their NBA exhibition season was supposed to be in full swing.

We were still touring well into autumn. We walked the floor of the Compaq Center in the hours before the doors opened to the public. This was the year the NBA and its players were engaging in a protracted labor dispute that would delay the season until the next February. No basketball in Houston; no basketball in any of the league's cities.

We went to one of the locker rooms and changed into our stage clothes. By the time we came back into the main arena the seats had filled. Cheers reverberated off the walls, vendors sold hot sandwiches and cold beer, the 16,285 seats reached toward the ceiling where the Rockets' world championship banners hung and the giant TV screens were poised to display instant replays of dunks and blocked shots.

As we sang "Surf City" in the cones of the Compaq Center's powerful spotlights I turned to Gary during an instrumental break and saw that he was looking at the banners too. I had to shout to make myself heard: "I hope these guys know what it is that they're throwing away."

It was a permutation of Elvis not being in Las Vegas, of the Beatles never having sung "Eight Days a Week" to a live audience. I didn't know which side in the NBA dispute was right and which side was wrong; probably there was more than enough blame to go around. There existed dumptrucks full of money that the owners and the players just couldn't figure out how to divide. As we sang in the basketball arena where there was no basketball, I couldn't help but think:

Someday, when the current squads of NBA players are no longer young men, they may realize that there are some things in this life you can never get back.

The cash that was at stake? The agents and attorneys would work that out.

But nights like this one—nights on which people have come to the arena to see you, when there is tingling electricity in the air, when you are doing what you love the most in a vast indoor stadium and thousands upon thousands of people are shouting their pleasure, are honoring you by their spellbound presence . . .

These nights—the number of them you have available to you in your life—are finite. If, for whatever reason, you choose to let some of these nights sit empty, you are giving away something far more precious than money.

Ben E. King was back on the bill with us tonight, and Ronnie Spector; they had first been gladdened by the sounds of cheers in the 1950s and 1960s. Some bands who had come to prominence in the 1970s were playing tonight, as well: America, who'd had million-selling hits with "A Horse With No Name" and "Sister Golden Hair," and Three Dog Night, whose "Joy to the World" had, for a time, been a song that spurred people behind the wheel in every city and small town in the nation to drive a little faster each time the first words came out of the dashboard radio.

When you are young, you think it will never end. What the basketball stars would find out, I knew, was that it always does end—it always goes away. The people who own the arenas will always be able to find new entertainment to draw customers into the seats. To those owners, the names of the entertainers, the names of the athletes, don't matter.

There's not much that any entertainer or any athlete can do about that. But I looked at the men singing next to me on the stage, and I looked toward the wings, at the other bands as they waited their turn to perform, and what I saw was the no-longer-young faces of people who, thirty years later, were finally fully valuing just how lucky they had been to be a part of all this—and how lucky they still were to be keeping it alive.

I glanced up at the Rockets' championship banners one more time as we sang. I hoped that the NBA players who weren't playing stopped at least occasionally to contemplate:

There's no guarantee that this kind of chance will come along twice in a lifetime. Nights in the arena, once they are gone, are usually gone forever. You can't put a price on what that means—or on how much you will miss those nights when, sooner than you realize, they are no longer yours for the asking.

We sang "Surfin' U.S.A." and departed. The crowd screamed for an encore and we returned to the stage, to the arena, gladly.

At our hotel, the Crowne Plaza, the concert's promoter had invited sponsors and business associates to a small after-party.

There weren't all that many people in attendance: maybe fifty or sixty. Gary and I were having some hors d'oeuvres when a man approached and said:

"You sang with Jan and Dean tonight, right?"

When we said yes, the man—he talked with the friendly and endearingly innocent semi-rural Texas drawl of Hank Hill, the propane-salesman/dad in the animated television series *King of the Hill*—said:

"May I ask you a question?"

We waited.

The man looked directly at me and said:

"Do you think Dean would sign my daughter's ass?"

I thought I was hallucinating.

I waited a few seconds, and the man repeated:

"Do you think Dean would sign my daughter's ass?"

He nodded at a woman in her early twenties—she looked like a college student—who was standing a few feet away. She was quite pretty, was wearing a pair of very tight jeans, and by all indications this man was her father.

The man's tone of voice implied that he hoped he wasn't intruding by asking for such a favor. He looked at me, waiting for some guidance.

"Sir," I said, "I think that's something your daughter would have to take up with Dean himself."

I gestured across the room, to where Dean was standing talking with some concert sponsors.

"Can my daughter just ask him?" the man said.

"I think he'd be honored," I said.

The man walked over to his daughter, said something to her—she brightened—and we watched as she walked across the room to Dean.

She said something to him.

If a man's face can turn vivid red and go absolutely pale at the same time, that's what Dean's face did.

The young woman handed him a pen.

No matter how long the winter ahead might last, the memory of this would get us through until the spring.

SEVENTEEN

The winter didn't last that long after all—at least on our alternate-universe calendar that defined de facto summer as any time and any place "Help Me, Rhonda" was sung on a live stage—because on a cold and slushy February night in Connecticut we found ourselves sitting in a high-end steakhouse inside a behemoth of a gambling-and-entertainment complex known as the Foxwoods Casino.

This is where, and when, the new Jan and Dean season would commence. There were five of us at the table: Dean, myself, Mike Love and Bruce Johnston of the Beach Boys . . . and Phil Bardowell. Of the Beach Boys.

Phil slipped me something under the table. I felt several very small disks in the palm of my hand. They were hard yet slightly flexible.

"Just put them in your pocket," Phil said quietly. "Look at them later." He seemed a little embarrassed.

We all were here because Foxwoods was swimming in money. Owned by the Mashantucket Pequot Tribal Nation, it advertised itself as the largest casino in the world. Its proportions were like one of those Bruce McCall illustrations of humongous, fanciful vintage oceanliners or triple-deck airliners-that-never-were, except the Foxwoods Casino was no artist's joking pipe dream. The place felt like what would happen if the Mall of America figured out a way to make even bigger profits than it already did, without the pesky problem of needing to sell merchandise.

The Foxwoods complex covered 4.7 million square feet. There were six separate casinos that contained more than seven thousand slot machines and four hundred gambling tables upon which seventeen different kinds of games of chance were played (there were one hundred tables just for poker). Foxwoods claimed also to have the world's largest Bingo hall; its three luxury hotels, including the Grand Pequot Tower where we were sleeping, had 1,416 guest rooms.

The casino's owners seemingly could afford just about anything. Which explained why, on this weekend in February, they had hired not only the Beach Boys to perform in their 1,400-seat main theater, but also, as a kind of musical dessert, Jan and Dean to sing in the casino's nightclub immediately after the Beach Boys show was over.

Under some circumstances this pecking order might have chafed Dean a little, but Mike Love had invited him to perform with the Beach Boys as a guest vocalist before our nightclub show. The five of us dined in the steakhouse on the night we arrived; this was the first I had seen Phil since he had switched bands.

"How are you going to tell Jan that you're singing with us?" Mike Love asked Dean.

"Can I wait until tomorrow to worry about that?" Dean said, cutting into his meat.

"You need a map to walk around inside this place," Phil said. I didn't know if he was kidding, but I handed him one.

"I picked up an extra," I said. The Mashantucket Pequots may have been able to traverse this land in total darkness when it was all wilderness, but even under billions of watts of bright lights we didn't stand a chance without some help.

In my room I reached into my pocket and pulled out what Phil had slipped me.

It was three guitar picks. Each bore the Beach Boys' logo, and, beneath it, Phil's name.

Apparently that was part of moving up to the Beach Boys: the guitarists were provided with personalized picks, the equivalent of a Fortune 500 company executive's engraved heavy-vellum business cards. No wonder Phil hadn't wanted me to look at them in front of Dean; Jan and

Dean's guitarists used standard-issue picks they bought for a quarter apiece out of the glass bins on the front counters at music stores, just like any other customers off the street.

My phone rang.

"Did you see that Paul Anka thing on the TV?" Gary's voice said, aghast.

Indeed I had.

"I'm speechless," he said.

What he was referring to was a videotape that ran continuously on one of the casino's in-house channels. The first time you saw it, when Anka appeared, you assumed he was singing "My Way." Anka had written the song; Frank Sinatra had made it his own.

But if you listened carefully, you found that Anka had altered the words. The tune was the same—but now "My Way" was not about the vagaries of a prolonged and bittersweet life, but about the Foxwoods Casino, and, more specifically, about its president and chief executive officer, Floyd M. Celey.

"Here it comes," Gary said.

"I know," I said. "I'm watching. I've been watching it over and over."

Anka, with complete evident sincerity, sang:

With ease, each guest you please, such amenities, the finest really
Your CEO, is all aglow, that's my friend Bud Celey

"Beyond belief," Gary said. We hung up.

The phone rang again.

"Did you see Paul Anka?" Randell's voice said.

"You mean Bud Celey's friend?" I said.

As for friendship, that part of this never seemed to stop.

The next day—the day of our show—Gary said to me: "Let's go down and watch the Beach Boys soundcheck."

"I don't know," I said. "We're going to their show tonight. I don't need to see them rehearse."

"Come on," Gary said. "Come with me. I don't want to go alone."

He was adamant, which seemed odd. But he and I went down to the big theater, and watched the Beach Boys test out their instruments. About thirty minutes into it I saw Randell and Don Raymond come into the theater, and I thought I saw them exchange nods and conspiratorial smiles with Gary.

"All right," Gary said. "Enough of this. Let's go shower and get ready for dinner."

I rode the elevator to my room—wondering why all of a sudden Gary had grown tired of the Beach Boys' rehearsal—opened my door, and almost jumped when I saw what was on my bed.

It was a giant movie-theater-lobby standup display for *That Thing You Do!* There were lifesize die-cut likenesses of Tom Hanks, of the four actors who played the Wonders, and of Liv Tyler, who played Faye, the girlfriend.

Over Faye's black sweater, in gold marker, was written a paraphrase of her much-revered (among us) line from the movie:

Bob—
I would NEVER waste my kisses on you.
Liv

The band had found the lobby display at some secondhand store in California, had bought it, scrawled the fake autograph, taken the display's pieces apart, packed it up and carried it with them across the country, gotten me out of my room to go to the Beach Boys' soundcheck. . . .

And, while I was away, had talked a housekeeper into letting them in, where they reassembled it and placed it atop my bed.

All for this moment.

The friendship, as always never expressed out loud, was with us every moment. That night we watched the Beach Boys play, then hurried to the nightclub, where we sang. It was a much smaller room than the main theater, and there were no seats, just people standing and drinking and dancing.

About halfway through our show, from my position on the cramped stage, I saw someone near the front of the crowd, standing with a drink in his hand and watching us.

It was Phil.

He wasn't one of us anymore; he was a Beach Boy. I'd never seen him in an audience before. Maybe I was imagining it, but as we looked at each other I thought that I could see in his eyes that he missed this. Designer guitar picks and bigger paydays or not, I thought that maybe he missed the friendship part.

In a barnlike arena on the Indiana State Fairgrounds, with a piercing and frigid wind whipping through a pair of open doorways, we prepared to go to the stage for what was being billed as a winter beach party.

In the dressing room Jan and Dean sat on folding chairs next to each other, not speaking. I looked at them and thought: Give them this. At least they really are Jan and Dean.

They provided a constant dose of truth-in-advertising that was rare on this circuit. Whatever else anyone may have said about the Jan and Dean show, it was authentic. Some of the groups whose paths we crossed on the road had almost nothing in common with the groups that had originally borne their names, save the titles of the songs they sang each night. We had played on a bill with the Temptations—that's how they were promoted, with that legendary Motown name—and there was, at the most, one person in the group who may have been in the original Temptations; I found myself wondering if any of the others in their current lineup had ever even seen the real Temptations perform. At a minor-league ballpark show on which Jan and Dean shared headliner status with the Drifters, I watched as one of the Drifters worked the crowd—making his way past the box seats on both the first- and third-base lines, letting the ticketholders lean forward and touch his hands—and he kept saying into his handheld microphone: "I am Charlie Thomas! I *am* Charlie Thomas! I am *Charlie Thomas!*" Gary explained to me later that Charlie Thomas was the only member of this touring version of the Drifters who had any connection with any of the original configurations of the Drifters. It was as if Charlie Thomas felt he must present a verbal ID card to the people in the Midwestern ballpark: he was Charlie Thomas, he had once been a genuine Drifter. If anyone in the audience even cared.

But Jan and Dean were an exception: an act that was just what it claimed to be. Some of the early rock and rhythm-and-blues groups were represented on the road by two or three competing acts, crisscrossing the country at the same time, each using a slight variation of the original name. Even when there wasn't an intent to confuse or deceive, it was unusual, because of deaths or of disputes over the decades, for a famous band to feature all of the same stars who had recorded the chart-topping hits. The Rolling Stones themselves had toured for years with one member of their front line—Ron Wood—who hadn't been a Rolling Stone when the band first formed. Jan Berry and Dean Torrence were the same fellows who had been Jan and Dean from the beginning. They played by a set of rules that few others adhered to.

Not that it was always easy. One night in Daytona Beach, backstage at the Ocean Center where we were preparing to play at a convention of Amway distributors, Jan asked Dean to go over with him the list of songs for the evening.

Dean didn't respond. So Jan, aloud, tried to come up with the names of the songs from memory.

"Aruba, Slippy John B . . ." Jan said.

We knew what he was referring to: "Aruba" meant the song "Kokomo," which begins: *Aruba, Jamaica, oooh I want to take you. . . .* "Slippy John B" was his way—on this night—of saying "Sloop John B".

Dean, preoccupied and thinking about the show, continued to ignore him. Dean had told us that he hoped to impress the Amway dealers with a crisp, high-energy performance; his desire was for Jan and Dean to become a regular attraction at Amway events, and pick up fifteen or twenty extra paychecks a year.

"Aruba," Jan said again, "Slippy John B . . ."

"The songs are the same as always," Dean said, a little sharply. "I'll let you know."

"I want to know now," Jan said.

"Jan, we haven't sung 'Sloop John B' for years," Dean said. "Just watch me on the stage."

"Dean, you don't give a fuck!" Jan shouted at him. "You always treat me this way, my whole life! You don't give a fuck!"

It was one of those moments when the rest of us wished we could evaporate, or magically transport ourselves to somewhere else, preferably in a different ZIP code. It was excruciating, like watching a long-married couple argue at a dinner party they are hosting.

But there was nowhere for us to go. We were all in the dressing room.

Dean did that biting-the-heel-of-his-hand thing he always did when he was upset with Jan. He walked into an adjacent shower room and stayed there by himself for a full minute, trying to calm down. When he came out, he said to Jan:

"Do you ever wonder why sometimes I talk onstage between songs, and I look at my watch?"

Jan just stared at him.

"It's to bring the show in right on time, every night," Dean said. "Sometimes I have to stretch the show. Sometimes I have to shorten it. I give the buyers the show they booked, right to the minute. Maybe you don't notice it. But it's part of my job. I will always let you know on the stage what songs we're singing. Have I ever not?"

It wasn't an uncomplicated matter for the two of them, being the real Jan and the real Dean. On another night in Florida—this was in Pompano Beach—I had seen Dean, in the dressing room, on his knees. There was chicken cordon bleu in a serving tray, and roast beef in another tray, part of the pre-show buffet provided by the promoter. But Dean, kneeling on the floor, wasn't eating.

He was rolling up the bottoms of Jan's pants legs, one at a time, so that Jan wouldn't trip when we were called to the stage. Jan lacked the dexterity to lean down and do this himself. There was something paternal in the way Dean did it for him, something close to kind, although he would have bristled if I had said anything to that effect. Jan was silent and the two did not make eye contact as Dean folded his cuffs.

To break the moment, to defuse its quiet poignancy, Dean, still on his knees on the concrete, said to me: "After the concert, let's pound back about a hundred beers."

He was kidding—he seldom drank, and never to excess. He had developed an aversion to it early in his life.

"When I was a kid, about fourteen years old, I worked as a liquor delivery boy," he said.

His hands remained on the cloth of Jan's trousers.

"I'd deliver to some pretty famous people's houses," he said. "Gene Kelly, Peter Lorre. . . ."

The southern California of his growing up was very different from the central Ohio of mine. Sometimes I forgot that.

"I got in a fight in an alley once when I was making deliveries," he said. "I fought Tommy Rettig, the kid who played Timmy on *Lassie*."

"Why did the two of you fight?" I said.

"Because he was a star on *Lassie*, and I was a liquor delivery boy," Dean said. "I had a fight with another kid, too. He was on a show about a horse."

"*My Friend Flicka?*" I said.

"No," he said. "Another show with a kid and a horse."

He finished with Jan's cuffs. He looked at me and said:

"Just let me win the lottery. Just once."

On the night in Daytona Beach—the "Aruba, Slippy John B" night—the Amway executives in charge of the event had arranged for a photo session as a reward for their Diamond Level distributors. The entire weekend in Daytona Beach was Amway's method of both holding a corporate pep rally, and singling out the men and women who had performed best for them during the last year: the high performers and their spouses, or so we were told, had been flown down to Florida as a gesture of thanks and appreciation.

There were some six thousand of them in the arena. But the Diamond Level winners—the most successful Amway distributors—were seated on the main floor, at dinner tables with white cloths. The others sat in the arena bleachers for our show.

And before the concert, the Diamond Level Amway winners, as an extra prize, got to have their pictures taken with Jan and Dean.

Canvas walls had been erected in a corner backstage to form a makeshift photo studio. Jan and Dean, in their stage clothes, had been brought into the improvised studio.

One-by-one, each Diamond Level winner, along with his or her spouse, was led into the little room. Two-by-two the husbands and wives, in tuxedos and beaded gowns, were escorted up to Jan and Dean, where they stood facing the professional photographer.

Just a few minutes earlier, Dean had been biting his hand back in the shower room, and Jan had been screaming at him. Now the two of them stood, smiling, as two-by-two-by-two-by-two Amway's most valued salespeople approached them, said hello, made sure their own smiles were in place, and peered at the camera.

Flash. Flash. Flash. Flash. Jan and Dean looked like cardboard cutouts, not moving, not changing expressions, just standing together as the men and women were ushered steadily and efficiently in and out of the temporary studio. *Flash. Flash. Flash.* They were the real Jan and Dean. No one could take that away from them. I tried to read something in their faces that night, but I could not.

And now, on the Indiana State Fairgrounds, we prepared to go onstage for the indoor beach party on a February night.

The rest of us took our positions first. I could see, out in the crowd, that some people had kept their overcoats on. The surface of the arena was sloppy from where they had tracked in snow and ice.

But the promoters had provided beach balls and Hawaiian leis, and I thought I could see that there was sand poured on portions of the floor.

"Ladies and gentlemen . . ." the announcer cried out.

Gary and Randell and Don hit the opening chords of "Ride the Wild Surf."

The crowd began to cheer.

The announcer escalated the volume of his voice:

"Jan . . . and Dean!"

They came onstage as they always did. The real deal, as ever.

"You wonder what the decision process is when they get up in the morning," Don Raymond said. "When they make the call: do they come here, or do they stay home?"

Summer—real summer, not beach-parties-in-winter summer—had finally arrived. We were in New Richmond, Ohio, looking out at a huge crowd that was still gathering before an afternoon outdoor show.

"Boy, a lot easier for people not to come, with so much traffic to fight," David Logeman, standing with us, said.

But here they were—tens of thousands of them, with more entering the area by the minute. They'd had to battle clogged highways on the way to the concert site, they'd had to stake out patches of grass still wet and muddy from a rain shower the night before, they would have to sit in the heat for hours to see the entire show, with Little Richard closing the program after dark. Inertia, you might expect, would rule—the music promised to be fine, but there would be much less potential aggravation for people if they chose not to be a part of this mob.

"Just be appreciative they always do decide to come," Dean said.

Whatever it was that we were providing, they were happy to be buying it. Maybe the product we lugged from town to town—the songs, the guitar licks, the energy—was, in the scheme of things, not all that important, or essential. The songs weren't medicine; the songs weren't oxygen; the songs weren't nutritional building blocks. This was an elective purchase—no one absolutely needed what we were selling. Their lives would go on without it.

"Remember that Snaxpo convention?" I said.

It had been in California—Newport Beach. I had never heard of Snaxpo, before we arrived. Snaxpo, it had turned out, was the annual national gathering of the Snack Food Association. The association was exactly what it sounded like: the trade group representing all the things you pop into your mouth even though you know you probably shouldn't. Potato chips, cookies, salted peanuts, Snickers bars . . . talk about the antithesis of those nutritional building blocks. No one truly couldn't do without any of the snacks being promoted at Snaxpo. They were the ultimate in discretionary buys.

Which had made us just about the ideal entertainment for the Snaxpo convention (whose theme, the year we played, was "Snacking: A Global Vision"). We—this kind of music, this kind of show—could probably be considered as the leisure-time equivalent of empty-caloried snacks. What we did made people feel good, even if the satisfaction was transitory, even if their time might have been more productively spent elsewhere. We were, I supposed, a bag of popcorn, a fistful of gumdrops.

But everyone can't go out and sell the leather-bound works of William Shakespeare; everyone can't sell gallery-quality oil paintings or classical violin lessons or guided tours of the sites that inspired Mozart. Some people sell Popsicles.

Jan and Dean and the other bands we saw regularly on the road had been doing their version of that for many decades. And the people—people like the ones even now filling the big field in New Richmond—were still getting up in the morning and choosing to come.

"This feels like it's going to be a good one," Gary said.

For us on the stage, no matter how many people were in the audience, it just about always was. Soon enough we'd be playing, and for that one hour, for us, everything would feel speeded up and loud and in Cinerama.

And for the people watching and listening?

Maybe, in the end, we were in fact nothing more than a snack to gobble. An impulsive pleasure. But impulsive pleasures are a part of life, too, not to be belittled.

"Come on," Dean said to us, as showtime approached. "Let's go get 'em."

I'd heard of *The T.A.M.I Show*, but had never seen it.

People who had viewed it told me that if I wanted to get a fuller understanding of the torment that must constantly go on inside of Jan Berry, then I should find a way to get a copy.

The T.A.M.I Show was a concert film, although "film" is something of a misnomer. In the autumn of 1964 some promoters in Hollywood teamed up with a low-end movie distribution company to put together a performance at the Santa Monica Civic Auditorium. The idea was to cash in on the national fever over rock music—to record a concert, with no plot or storyline, and get it into theaters as quickly as possible. To facilitate this, *The T.A.M.I. Show* was recorded not on conventional movie film, but on something breathlessly billboarded as "Electronovision." Electronovision, it becomes clear upon viewing *The T.A.M.I Show* now, was an early version of black-and-white videotape.

On October 28 and 29, 1964, segments of the concert were recorded before live audiences at the Santa Monica venue. Performers included the Rolling Stones, Chuck Berry, the Beach Boys, James Brown, the Supremes, Marvin Gaye, Lesley Gore, Gerry and the Pacemakers, Smokey Robinson and the Miracles, and Billy J. Kramer and the Dakotas. None of the acts were imbued with even a hint of nostalgia or tepidity; everything was right-this-minute, impelling-as-a-news-bulletin, crackling with power. *The T.A.M.I. Show*—the acronym stood either for "Teenage Awards Music International" or "Teen Age Music International"; the full title appeared variously in different publications, and no one seemed overly concerned with what it meant, anyway—was not presented as something for which the nation's parents would necessarily grant approval (if they even knew the movie existed), was not supposed to be cute or cuddly or safe. Female dancers, gyrating and humping with a sexual ardor that is startling to see even now, were positioned behind the bands; the ceaseless, desperate wall of shrieks from the California girls in the audience were cries of open longing, an impression amplified by frequent close-ups of the girls' overwrought and contorted faces.

The film of *The T.A.M.I. Show* had a brief run in American movie theaters, mostly drive-ins, and then disappeared from sight. When home video systems came into wide usage, the show, because of legal disputes over musical rights, was not widely available. If you hadn't seen it the first time around, you probably were never going to.

I was able to locate a copy. The masters of ceremonies of *The T.A.M.I. Show*—hosts as well as singers—were Jan and Dean. And the first time I viewed the tape, the first time I caught sight of Jan, it was almost painful.

He was so handsome—tall, rangy, athletic, self-confident in the manner of a championship quarterback—that his presence blasted everyone else in the show right off the screen. The rest of them were rock stars; Jan was a movie star. The Rolling Stones, in particular, were brilliant in the concert; they were young and brand-new, just starting to make their way in the business (Keith Richards looked like an optimistic and beseechingly-eager-to-please boy), and I don't think I have ever seen a Rolling Stones performance quite as riveting and raw.

But of all the performers at *The T.A.M.I. Show*, Jan Berry was the person who stood out, a dweller on a separate stratum from the rest. I'd noted the movie star analogy before, based on old photographs of Jan and Dean. But to watch him move or shoot a glance at the audience or simply stand still seemingly doing nothing during *The T.A.M.I. Show*—to observe the unselfconscious grace, the to-the-manor-born cockiness, the Clark Gable teasing flirtation with the camera lens, the James Dean eyes . . .

It required nearly a suspension of disbelief to equate the man on the screen with the man with whom I'd been spending my summers. Somewhere inside Jan, I knew, the young man on the movie screen still had to reside; sometimes even now, when he closed his eyes, there must have been moments when he was that young man, dazzling and strong and unscarred and whole.

I didn't know if Jan owned a copy of *The T.A.M.I. Show*, and, if he did, whether he ever went into a room by himself and watched it. And I knew I would never ask him. There are some echelons of anguish, even for a man who makes his living in public, that best remain private.

Once, in San Diego, he waited in a dressing trailer for the opening act to finish.

David Logeman had driven him down from Los Angeles; because the show was so close to where the band lived, they were going to commute and not spend the night.

I sat with Jan in the trailer. He kept getting up to look out the door. He couldn't sit still. It wasn't the act on stage that he was interested in— as I recall, it was either Tommy James without the Shondells, or Gary Puckett without the Union Gap. Whoever it was, the act wasn't what was on Jan's mind.

After he had looked outside for perhaps the fifth time, he said excitedly to me:

"My wife is coming today."

I had never met Gertie Berry. The band saw her regularly in Los Angeles, when she would drop Jan off at the airport or pick him up at the end of a trip. Most of them had been present on the night in Canada when Jan had first met her. But because she didn't travel with Jan, I didn't know her.

He and I sat and talked—he was distracted, nervous—and he walked to the door one more time and said to me: "There she is!"

I got up to stand beside him. I could see that a car had pulled up to the area behind the outdoor stage, and that two women had gotten out.

"In the white!" Jan said.

He was so proud.

Gertie Berry and the other woman—a friend from Los Angeles, I found out later—looked up at the stage where the opening act was finishing its set. Jan seemed almost ready to burst, so happy was he.

"Do you think she's pretty?" he said to me.

"She's very pretty," I said, and she was.

She and her friend appeared to be in no hurry to come over to the trailer. They watched the singer. Jan waited in the doorway.

Gertie saw him and walked to where we were.

"We got caught in traffic," she said to Jan.

He introduced me to her, saying my name.

I extended my hand to shake hers. As I did, Jan said, shyly:

"This is my wife."

She smiled, and we all talked for a few minutes, and then it was time to perform. She watched the show from the side of the stage, and Jan looked over toward her after every one of his solos to see if she had been paying attention, and if she approved. He seemed to be trying especially hard that day.

She and he returned to Los Angeles after the concert, and it was the one and only time I saw her at a show.

Eighteen

On Highway 61, on the way south from Memphis into the northernmost part of Mississippi, it was impossible not to think of Bob Dylan.

Dylan was a young man back in 1965, when he wrote "Highway 61 Revisited." He couldn't have known.

Yet there are the words, right in the song:

Now, the roving gambler, he was very bored. . . .

In 1965, there were no casinos in Tunica County, Mississippi. Tunica, for many years, was called the poorest county in the poorest state in the country. It was mostly cotton fields and catfish ponds—old plantation country with little cash (except for the cash that belonged to the few families who owned the fields), a scarce supply of energy, wretched poverty and empty spaces and desolate miles.

And Highway 61, cutting through.

But then, in the early 1990s, a law was passed. Casino gambling would be permitted to come to Tunica.

The particular law did not apply to all of Mississippi, or to other counties near Tunica. Just Tunica itself. The key to the law was that there were no limitations written in. In most parts of the United States that allow casinos, there are stringent rules about how many can set up business. Not in Tunica County. The new law said that any casino that wanted to open its doors could; there were no table limits, no downtime, just twenty-four hours a day of gambling, with no ceiling on how much an individual gambler could bet. This was purposely set up to be Casino America at its most unbridled—Casino America with all the barriers gone.

Dylan, in 1965, wrote that it could be very easily done.

We'll just put some bleachers out in the sun,
And have it on Highway 61

On Highway 61 we approached a Tunica County that in the span of a handful of years had been wholly transformed. In financial terms, it had become America's third-largest gambling destination, behind only Las Vegas and Atlantic City. Its nine casinos were closing in on a billion dollars a year in revenue. This was in a county that had only 8,500 residents. The number of men and women working in the casinos was 13,000.

Before the casino law passed, the number of hotel rooms in all of Tunica County was six. As we arrived to play, the number of hotel rooms was six thousand. The year before the casinos came, the county collected $3.5 million in taxes. Now the figure was $35.8 million.

We could see that in Tunica County there was no city, in the sense most people think of a city. Just the nine casinos. This resembled the Las Vegas cityscape not at all. The casinos (including the tallest building in Mississippi) rose out of the land near the cotton fields, but you could not walk from one casino to another; most of them were a car's drive away from the others. There appeared to be practically nothing to do, unless you were in the casinos.

The Mississippi River—stolid, unchanging, the river that once defined the heart of America—rolled by the gambling palaces. More than a million people a month arrived. Which was the plan: Bring them down Highway 61, get them into the casinos, and start the meter running.

Now, the roving gambler, he was very bored . . . .

"I want you to memorize these," Dean said. "It will make you a better person."

There was a series of signs on the private access road leading from Highway 61 to the casino where we would be singing. They were like the Burma Shave signs of yore, placed on sticks, intended to be read in sequence. Except that these signs were the creation—the credo, apparently—of the casino itself.

The first read:

SMILES . . . INSTEAD OF BLANK LOOKS.

The second:

WARMTH . . . INSTEAD OF INSINCERITY.

We weren't in Las Vegas, all right. You can bring Casino America to rural Mississippi, but . . .

COURTESY . . . INSTEAD OF BEING IMPOLITE.

It was the second phrase of each slogan—the redundant "instead of " phrase—that was so beguiling. In a United States that has placed such value in the pursuit of the cutting-edge—of the snide and smirking—the literal, when you encounter it, can come as a shock.

UNDERSTANDING . . . INSTEAD OF CLOSED MIND.

FRIENDLINESS . . . INSTEAD OF RUDENESS.

PATIENCE . . . INSTEAD OF ARGUMENTS.

"Why is it that the straightforward all of a sudden seems radical?" I said.

"See what you learn in the places you go with us?" Dean said.

The signs kept flashing by.

HELPFULNESS . . . INSTEAD OF NOT CARING.

RESPECT . . . INSTEAD OF INDIFFERENCE.

It was the Southern hospitality of old—with slot machines. And as slogans went, I supposed these were better than "What Happens in Tunica Stays in Tunica."

ATTENTION . . . INSTEAD OF NEGLECT.

APPRECIATION . . . INSTEAD OF THANKLESSNESS.

"Are we going to a Billy Graham Crusade or to a gambling casino?" Randell said.

Billy Graham, as far as I knew, never performed behind a working bar.

This was a first for us. The stage was directly in the middle of the casino floor proper—not in a theater or a showroom or even a lounge. It was set up behind the bartender—we looked down into the eyes of people who were wandering up and ordering their cocktails and beers. Where the mirror behind the bar should have been, was Jan and Dean.

"Humiliation . . . instead of grandeur," I said to Dean, but he didn't appear to hear me over our guitar chords and the jangling of the nearby slot machines. We had to keep moving around on the stage, or run the risk of someone asking us for a Smirnoff and cranberry juice.

We were maybe five feet from the people sitting on the barstools. I half-expected some of them to start confiding their woes to us.

Between songs, Gary, off-microphone, began to croon:

Well, set 'em up Joe,
I've got a little story I think you should know. . . .

And the inspirational Burma Shave signs, or the shallow stage behind the bar, weren't even the most unusual things about this casino booking. That distinction belonged to the Southern United States Ballroom Scholarship Championships.

The dancing championships were being conducted in a conference room that we passed on our way to and from the casino floor. Most of the contestants competing for dance scholarships (whatever those were) were women who appeared to be in their sixties or seventies; some, we were told (we ducked in to watch this; how could we not?) were in their eighties, and one was in her nineties. They had been accompanied to Tunica County from around the country by their dancing instructors, most of them men who were thirty or forty years younger than the students. The women wore ball gowns, even in the daytime; the men wore costumes that all but cried out "bolero."

There were different divisions in the competition: the International Preliminary Bronze Tango, the Silver Waltz, the Two-Dance Samba/Mambo, the Merged Peabody (the mere thought of that one made me blush). It was teeth-chattering cold in the conference room, and the official program explained why: "Contrary to popular belief, there is no Arctic life in the ballroom. The ballroom temperature will be modified for the comfort of the dancers, not the spectators. If you are a spectator, we suggest you bring a wrap for comfort."

I watched the Basic Social Ease Cha-Cha bracket play out, but left before the winners of the Miss Elegance and Mr. Gentleman Awards were announced. We performed two nights behind the bar; at a few minutes after three-thirty in the morning after our first night, the phone on my bedside table rang.

I reached for it in the darkness, held the receiver in the vicinity of where I thought my ear must be, and was greeted by the sound of Jan's voice.

"Do you know where the ice machine is?" he said.

His tone betrayed no recognition of the hour, or of the inadvisability of the phone call. Things like this were happening more and more often.

A daily ritual I enjoyed without fail was watching the show be built from scratch.

Because the product Jan and Dean sold was ephemeral, a concert that was here and gone in sixty or ninety minutes, the temptation was to think of it as something separate from hard goods, from the conventional concept of manufactured merchandise. Yet the show was, in fact, manufactured from an invisible Square One each day, and I would get to the venues early to observe every step.

The local sound companies, hired by the promoters in each town, would pull up to the grandstand or the auditorium or the ballpark early in the afternoon of the show. I'd watch them back their trucks up to the stage, carefully maneuvering as close to the side lip as they could. Then the hometown employees—usually proud-to-be-grizzled men who appeared to be permanently sleep-deprived, wearing T-shirts and cutoffs and knee pads and looking like, if they weren't here, they would be doing this kind of muscle-intensive work at a meatpacking plant or a cold-storage warehouse or maybe a rodeo—would throw open the metal rear doors of the trucks and begin to wrestle the equipment onto the surface where we would play.

There was so much of it—steel microphone stands, wedge amplifiers to be placed in front of each musician, spools of worn black electrical cables, sound-engineering boards both for the side of the stage (where a man would regulate what came through our monitors during the show) and out in the audience (where another man would do the same for the music coming through the house speakers). The drum kit, as arcane-and-complicated-looking as a kid's old-time model airplane at the instant the disparate pieces were first removed from the Revell box, would be laid out and then assembled element-by-element, each needing to be unerringly placed and, when called for, tightly fastened. Guitar stands, each of them with little U-shaped devices facing straight out on its main pole for the necks of the instruments to rest against before we came onstage, were retrieved from the truck and put into position; the microphone heads, one for each singer, several for the drums, were clicked onto the stems and wired to their power sources.

The local lighting men would be doing their own hoisting and adjusting at the same time; all of this would look as if someone had suddenly emptied everything that had for generations been crammed into a dark and musty attic, and aired it out in the light of day. But the seeming effluvia—all the snaking cords, the colored bulbs, the iron-and-cloth audio apparatus, the tool boxes and electricians' gear and metal stepladders and oversized rolls of heavy silver duct tape and battered headsets and, always, the crates upon crates upon crates, each of them on rollers, each labeled with pithy descriptions (written on strips of that duct tape) of what belonged inside—all of this was unpacked and then repacked by the sound-and-light companies every working day, for every band that came to their towns. The men straining as they climbed and knelt and stretched and crawled to lay everything into its proper place would be tearing it all down again by the time the last member of the audience was out the door.

But that would be later, as midnight approached. Now the sun was still in the sky, and we would straggle onto the stage, even as the men were continuing to set it up, to do our own pre-show work.

The band wasn't in concert clothing yet; that was back at the hotel, or hanging in the dressing rooms. David would invariably start first, striking his drums so forcefully, and so repeatedly, that it was enough to give anyone

in the vicinity a headache. It seemed like the sound of a schoolboy banging around on his first set of drums in his bedroom, just to marvel at the
racket he can make, until you stopped to consider that David had indeed
been doing this since he was a boy—and that the last thing he needed to
hear, for the fun of it, was a drum being smacked. He did this because he
had to—he tested out the snare, the kick drum, the toms, the hi-hat, the
crash cymbal, the ride cymbal, the cowbell, the wood block—everything
had to be right and had to feed into the amplifiers just so. Sometimes
this—the walloping of the drums with no additional music—would go
on for fifteen minutes or more.

Gary would begin to work with his keyboard; Don and Randell would
listen to how their guitars sounded through the monitors. It seemed pure
cacophony for half an hour or so: different tunes, different keys, each man
apparently oblivious to the noise being made by the instrument of the
bandmate next to him. Each of them would speak with the audio technicians supplied by the promoter, asking for equilibrations, explaining
where something sounded wrong. They might as well have been auto mechanics checking under a hood—at this point, the process had more in
common with tuning an engine than with making music.

Then would come the vocal checks. One at a time, we would step up
to our microphones and say ten or twenty words, as the sound men twisted
dials and slid levers. When they were satisfied with the levels, the band
would sing a song—ordinarily "The Little Old Lady from Pasadena"—a
cappella. The purpose was to allow the sound engineers to listen to the
vocals without the distraction of the electrified instruments. But, hearing the coalesced, exposed voices of the band, I always stopped to think
once more, after all these years with them, about just how lovely and
remarkable those voices were. There could be no possible hiding of
flaws in pitch, not with the absence of the guitars and the drums and
the keyboard; if these singers were sour even a little bit, it would be out
there for anyone to hear now. It never was. They sounded like a surfing
chorale.

Finally, when everyone was satisfied with the local audio setup,
we would perform a complete song or two—"I Get Around" was usually
one of them—with everyone singing and playing their instruments and

the power pumped up full-bore in the house speakers. For the first time of the day, the band would sound like a band. All of this had come together in the interval since the trucks had arrived at the stage. By the time the audience would be let in, and would set eyes on that stage, it would look like it was ready for a rock-and-roll show.

We would be backstage, waiting, hearing the rising hum of the voices of the people in the seats as those seats filled. The show itself when it eventually started would almost always be fun for us. For me, though, the building of the show—being there for all the tiny, accumulating moments of its construction in the long hours before the master of ceremonies called out Jan and Dean's names—was a progression, a pleasure, that was close to addictive. A bare stage in the afternoon, with no one on it. And minute by minute, in one town after another, it became something else, until it was poised to provide happiness to strangers.

By the time we were back in our beds at the hotel, the stage would be barren again. But next show, in the next city, the manufacture of this would begin all over. I did my best never to miss a moment of it. I loved it anew each time.

Sometimes at odd moments I found myself wondering what these guys would do if this was suddenly taken away from them.

"A few minutes ago that was us," Gary said.

The two of us were sitting in the audience at a big outdoor show; we had finished performing, and had decided to watch the next act from the seats.

What Gary was looking at was not the band, but the immense live video screen behind them.

"Pretty impressive," he said.

And it was. Looming in full electronically enhanced color, the guitarists looked like heroes from a luridly hued comic book, the lead singer looked like the commander of the universe—their images on the screen were so huge that, to the people in the far reaches of the crowd, they might as well have been an alien master race.

"We probably looked just as big," I said.

"Yeah," Gary said. "And look at us now."

We were a couple of regular-sized middle-aged men sitting in an audience. No one had said a word to us since we had sat down; all eyes were focused on the stage, and on the screen behind it. On the screen, during close-ups, you could just about count every pore on the singer's face.

If an audience can forget you—us—in the time it takes for another act to walk onto a stage and onto a giant screen, then what chance do singers in a band have once they are no longer a touring attraction? It could probably go away just that fast.

"Now, there's something you don't see very often," Gary said, gesturing to an area to the side of the seats.

It was a Jack Daniel's booth. We always saw soft-drink booths at the shows, and usually beer booths, but not this: hard liquor being sold like cotton candy or peanuts.

"And you know we'll hear the obligatory 'Drive safely on the way home' announcement," I said.

On the streets of the cities of their own homes, back in California, my guess was that the men in the band found themselves being faces in the crowd. Out here on the road, they drew admiring looks every time they stepped behind their microphones. Back home they went to the grocery store.

"Look what he's doing," Gary said. "Dork."

The singer, dozens of feet tall on the screen, was hoisting his microphone stand and pointing it skyward, base end up, a stance surely stolen from an old photo of Rod Stewart.

The crowd didn't think he was a dork. He was massive, on that screen. The crowd was screaming.

"Come on," Gary said. "Jan's probably done selling his merchandise. Let's go backstage to the vans so we don't hold the others up."

As we made our way, a woman looked over, did a double take, and said:

"Hey! Weren't you guys just up there playing?"

Apparently the big screen provided a little longer half-life than we had thought. But probably not by much.

"We've got a five-thirty A.M. lobby call tomorrow," Gary said to me.

They had an early flight back to California. By the time they landed, they would be life-sized, at best.

Dean yelled in my direction:

"Bobbo!"

From time to time he used the word to address me; it had a playground sound to it, somehow appropriate for the places in which we found ourselves.

I looked over toward him. We were nearing the end of an afternoon show on an outdoor stage at the tip of a skinny isthmus on the West Coast.

He made a motion like a man taking his shirt off. But it wasn't my shirt he wanted me to remove.

He pointed to the wings, where his friend Skunk Baxter, guitarist for the Doobie Brothers, had been watching us play.

Dean made the take-your-shirt-off motion again.

I lifted my guitar over my neck; that's what Dean was requesting.

"We've got a special guest today. . . ." Dean said into his microphone.

Skunk half-sprinted onstage and toward me. I handed him my guitar. He hadn't brought one.

Back in Chicago between shows over the years, I had worked diligently—if sporadically—on trying to get better at my guitar playing. I knew that I'd never be proficient enough to really crank up during the concerts—same as Dean himself, which made me feel somewhat better about my lack of skill—but at least during soundchecks, I wanted to sound as little cringe-worthy as I could. Still, my guitar—cool as it looked, its black-and-white face glistening under the stage lights, or, on a day like today, under the summer sun—felt, to me, like a sturdy and stodgy old family car kept carefully in a garage and only taken out for prudent five-miles-an-hour-below-the-speed-limit Sunday spins around town. Because of my limitations, that guitar of mine was a stick-in-the-mud.

Skunk Baxter took the guitar from me and quickly, as if by second nature, tied a hard knot in the black cloth strap, making the strap shorter. He was like a Boy Scout doing a rope maneuver for which he'd received a merit badge years before; his hands made the knot as if he had done this so many times he could accomplish it in his sleep. Which he undoubtedly could.

He liked his guitars to ride higher up his chest than I did; the knot in the strap accomplished this. He held the guitar close to one of his ears, made a few tuning adjustments, and . . .

Wow.

My guitar began to squeal and moan, to sing and soar. Skunk was strutting across the front of the stage, squeezing notes out of it, pushing it to its limits. The old slow-Sunday-drive sedan was now going ninety miles an hour, being rudely shifted into high gears it had never hit before. He made it scream; he made it tremble. It seemed to be having a great time.

I was sharing a microphone with Randell, singing backup vocals, watching my guitar as Skunk ran it through its suddenly volatile paces. There seemed to be nothing it couldn't do; whatever Skunk asked of it—long, high, stuttering runs; low, rumbling, guttural growls—it gave him. I thought of my long hours with it back home, working cautiously with it as I tried to commit my clunky four chords to finger memory. Now Skunk was making it screech and yelp, and it was doing so without vacillation.

He played three songs as the audience roared its appreciation, and at the end he sauntered over to me, lifted the strap over his head, handed me the guitar, and said: "Sorry."

I didn't know what he was sorry for, and then I saw: one of the steel strings, torn at and wrenched and yanked by Skunk, had snapped, and was hanging loosely, drooping toward the stage floor.

He waved to the crowd, and I stared at the guitar. *Didn't know you had it in you.* That's what I felt like saying to it. *Uh . . . good show.* I was a little jealous of it.

The night Jan fell, I wasn't there.

The band was playing at a casino near Kansas City, on an outdoor stage behind the casino's hotel. I was traveling elsewhere in the country, doing reporting for a book I was working on about World War II. I talked to Gary on the phone right before their concert began; everything sounded routine.

The next day they called to tell me what had happened.

Midway through the show, they said, Jan had collapsed to the stage.

He went down hard and once he hit he did not move.

"I could tell that something was wrong just before it happened," Gary said. "Jan knew, too. He moved behind my keyboards right before he went down, like he hoped the audience wouldn't see it. But there was no way to hide it. I mean, you could hear him hit."

From the seats, apparently, it looked like Jan was dead.

The music stopped; someone summoned an ambulance.

"And all the time he's just there flat on the stage," Gary said.

It would turn out that Jan had had some kind of seizure, either as a result of the lingering effects of the old injuries, or of a combination of all the prescription medication he took each day to manage his pain and to keep in check the catalogue of things that were amiss inside his body. Jan had shown me his daily admixture of pills once; it was sobering to see how much medicine was required just to keep him going.

So there was Jan, motionless on the surface of the stage; there was the band, gathered around him, looking straight down; there was the audience, confused and, almost certainly, frightened.

"There's nothing that says surf music and good times like a singer flat on the floor and the sound of ambulances pulling up to the stage," Randell said.

Jan was carried to the ambulance; Bill Hollingshead, who was traveling with the band on that leg of the tour, accompanied him to the hospital. With the blaring tone of sirens in the ears of the band and of the audience, now came the decision: What to do?

"Don made the announcement," Gary said. "He was very good, very calm."

Don Raymond—the newest member of the band, the steady halfback, the guy you instinctively knew you could count on—took it upon himself to go to his microphone and explain to the crowd that, as they probably knew, Jan continually and courageously had to battle the aftereffects of the "Dead Man's Curve" accident. He apologized for the

disruption in the show; he said—although he really didn't know this—
that Jan was going to be fine. And he told them that Dean and the rest
of the band would now continue with the remainder of the night's
show.

"Real festive atmosphere, as you can imagine," Gary told me.

They limped through "Sidewalk Surfin'" and "Surfin' U.S.A." and
the other songs that always closed the set; some members of the audience
stayed to watch, some left. The doctors at the hospital stabilized Jan and
said he was all right to travel. The next day they all left for New Orleans,
where they had another show scheduled. Jan was embarrassed but determined to go on.

"I guess it made a lot of things we already knew pretty clear," Gary
said.

He didn't have to elaborate. It was some variation of that question I
had been asking myself:

What would happen to these men if, someday, this was taken from
them? If the music, and the travels, suddenly ceased?

There would be times, on the day of a show, when something would
transpire about which we took no immediate note. It wouldn't be until
later that I would think about how quietly extraordinary it was.

It was this:

We would be sitting in a dressing trailer or a dressing room before
soundcheck, or before the concert itself. We'd all be talking and laughing. Dean would be recounting some old story about when he and Jan
were first touring—Dean's narratives tended to interminable, so we
would be getting every detail, every vaguely recalled nuance. Or Randell
would be rhapsodizing animatedly and with great passion about food—
giving his critique of the latest buffet, its high points and low. Or Gary
would be doing a dead-on vocal impression of someone, getting every
syllable, every inflection, just right.

That wasn't the extraordinary part—guys sit around and pass the hours
with each other in ways similar to that all the time.

The thing that would strike me later, the thing that would make me shake my head in gratitude for all this, was what would happen when there was a knock on the door.

The promoter or one of his assistants would say: "It's time."

Time to sing. Time to perform.

And we would have forgotten about it.

Not really, of course. Everyone in the band knew why they were there: to do the concert.

But we would have pushed it out of our minds. The hanging out together—just the being there with each other, the sharing of the company and of the laughter, the relishing of the night—was enough for us. We could have done this forever—we could have let it go on and on.

The knock would remind us:

Oh. Right. Time to do the show.

It was almost an intrusion.

The show would just be gravy.

The night had already been a fine one, before the first guitar chord was sounded. Because we were here, again—even in places we had never visited before, we were *here*, with each other, again.

Which is probably why Jan's fall on the stage carried the significance it did. He was already reasonably recovered by the time of that next show in New Orleans; he tried to pretend it never happened.

We all understood, however, what it portended. No one could put a timetable on it; no one could predict the specifics of what lay ahead, or how many years of uncertainty would be involved.

Yet the message was there, even if we didn't want to think about it too deeply.

On its most basic level, it was something everyone everywhere knows from the time they are children:

Summers always end.

Nineteen

"You still hearing it?"

Randell called toward the stage from several hundred feet out on an expanse of lawn.

The man working the sound board waved to him, meaning: the signal's still strong.

Randell swept his pick over his guitar strings; simultaneously, a musical chord boomed out of the banks of loudspeakers.

"So I can go this far out?" Randell yelled.

"Farther, if you want," the sound man yelled back.

This was hours before the gates would open to customers; Randell was testing the signal of the wireless transmitter on his guitar. He was going to be roaming out into the audience tonight, and he was making certain that he could play his guitar at a far remove from the stage, and still have it be heard.

There was a reason for this.

To say that after Jan's fall the band began to feel it was living on borrowed time would not be quite accurate. Borrowed time had for so long been the central, if seldom explicitly expressed, aspect of the touring life — just taking this music on the road year after year spoke to an abiding faith in the power of borrowed time — that Jan's new level of potential physical distress was not so much a revelation as a confirmation. This was the Lost Boys syndrome, writ large: the band was still out in the country, pinballing from state to state, not knowing how long it all could last but comforted as always by the company of each other.

Borrowed time, in the context of these men's shared traveling existence, had long felt not like a threat, but a bequest. Borrowed time was in a way the entire point—borrowed time was the foundation of this, its baseline definition.

Still, modifications needed to be made, which is why Randell was out on the grass, verifying that his guitar's signal would carry. The century had turned, and although that fact by itself did not require a change in the show—"The New Girl in School" and "Little GTO" and "Drag City" seemed to light up audiences every bit as effectively in the Twenty-first Century as they had in the Twentieth—the passing of the years, in the framework of Jan's new level of tenuous physicality, meant that certain alterations to the structure, if not the substance, of what went on during the course of a concert might be called for.

So as another summer began Randell would leap into the audience at an ordained point in each show, luring people to form a conga line behind him as he led them through the grass or over the sand. On most nights he would also climb up on top of one of the stacks of speakers on the stage, tilting precariously ten feet or more above the rest of us, drawing the audience's attention. Dean and Don Raymond would, increasingly, move back and forth across the breadth of the stage as they sang, bringing more seemingly spontaneous motion to the performances than before. That was the plan.

No one knew, on a given evening, how well Jan would or would not hold up. There was now always a chair placed in the wings for him, out of sight of the audience but ready should he become winded and need to rest. The running around during the show—Randell's snake dances, the guitarists' crisscrossing, the bringing of fans up onto the stage to dance behind us during "Let's Dance" and "Do You Wanna Dance" and "Dance, Dance, Dance"—had, in varying degrees, been part of the performances for years. Now, though, there was new emphasis placed on them; now they served a purpose of which the audience was supposed to be unaware. They were meant to entice the eye aggressively away from Jan, if necessary; they were like a magician's fluttering of one palm so the audience wouldn't see him slip the card up his sleeve with the other hand, they were like an army's diversionary maneuver. Randell, in the new summer, would teeter atop the speakers, grinning winningly and playing the middle guitar run in "Help Me, Rhonda" and delighting the crowd, and the idea was that as long as they were looking at him, they wouldn't be looking too fixedly at Jan.

That was the intention.

It never quite worked, because Jan early and easily figured it out. It made him more stubborn to be center stage, literally and figuratively, for every minute of every show. His sense of borrowed time was more acute than anyone's, and for good reason. He knew it, and, we could tell, he was determined to take advantage of every minute of it.

He wasn't alone.

The best moments of these years were like a series of snapshots in my memory. And one that always made me stop and smile—a sight that in a single, nonmusical image summed up the enduring pull of these good times—was of David shooting baskets.

It was before another outdoor concert, this one in Pennsylvania; there was an opening act, and from our dressing area we could hear the muffled sounds of them singing, and the filtered-through-slush chord progressions from their guitars. They were out on the stage, their music being amplified in the direction of the audience; we were in back, the opposite direction of the speaker cones.

For some reason, in the backstage parking lot, there was a basket, with a net, set up. David had seen a scuffed basketball resting against the bottom of the pole.

That is where I found him, in his surf shirt, ready to go out and drum. And in the minutes before we were called to the stage, he was shooting away.

"Come on," he said to me. "We've got some time."

I joined him. Soon enough, we'd be performing—playing. But now, in the short time we had before that? What to do now?

Play.

Play basketball, play music—play upon play upon play, every moment you're given. The TODAY WE: PLAY notation from the tour schedule sheets, still the constant resolute goal, the subject of all staunch aspiration, on this night, and on all nights.

The men in Jan and Dean's band were never going to become prosperous on these tours—the $500-a-night paycheck for each of them had not changed over the years. I seldom heard them complain about it. What brought them out here, season after season, had to be something other than money.

David and I shot. We heard applause drift over from somewhere removed yet reachable. The opening act was ending its set.

"A few more," David said.

He carried the basketball to where the three-point line might be on a regulation court.

He shot.

Missed.

"All right," he said. "One more. I'm getting my range."

Playing, ever playing. On borrowed time or not.

Snapshots:

In small-town Indiana one weekend, after the band had headed back to California, I went to an Amtrak station to wait for a train to Chicago.

The stationhouse was tiny: wood-framed, one room. There was a ticket window inside. I walked over and could see that no one was in the agent's office.

Only two other people were in the waiting room: a young woman who appeared to be in her late teens or early twenties, and a man who must have been her father, or maybe her grandfather. They sat together and did not speak.

She had two large suitcases and a cardboard box at her feet. He looked sadder than she did.

The train was coming from the East Coast; it was due to stop here for just two or three minutes, and then continue on to Chicago.

I went back to the ticket window. Still no one. I saw that the stationmaster, if that's who worked back there, had a desk, a phone, a fax machine with a dirty cover, and, on the wall above the desk, a train-themed calendar. He must have been around, somewhere—there was a cup of coffee on the desk, with steam rising.

The man sitting with the young woman—father or grandfather—said to her: "How long will it take you to get to Arizona?" She was leaving town; he wasn't.

"I don't know," she said.

Their silence resumed.

The door that faced the tracks opened. The stationmaster came in. I looked out the door and could see what he had been doing: driving a little cart up a gradual hill to the tracks, probably for any bags that any arriving passengers might have checked, assuming any passengers would get off in this town.

He went into his office and I asked him, from my side of the ticket window, if the train was on time. He said no, but close enough.

The grandfather, if that's who he was, said to the young woman:

"What are you going to do for a car out there?"

"I'll work," she said.

Each stared straight ahead.

The train arrived. No one got off.

The young woman stood, and so did the grandfather.

"Don't forget we love you," he said.

She smiled as weakly as a person can smile, accepted a kiss on her cheek, and carried her bags to the train. Her grandfather followed with the box, handing it to her as she boarded.

I took a seat next to a man in an Army uniform. From the train window I could see the stationmaster driving the little cart—empty—back to the side of the stationhouse.

The soldier and I had an amiable conversation; he said he was going home to Chicago on leave.

After a few minutes he put some earphones on and started to listen to music. It was loud enough that I could hear the song. It was a rap tune, full of especially obscene lyrics and violent imagery and startling remarks about women. The tune was followed by another just like it, and another after that, all of this efficiently being fed into his head. The soldier had seemed like a very pleasant young man, and after he tired of the music he took the earphones off and we talked about baseball and food.

By my estimation, the band, on a jet, was about halfway to Los Angeles by now. We moved slowly through the Indiana countryside. I thought of the stationmaster in that lonely building, and of the little enclosed space of his behind the ticket window, with the phone and the calendar and the coffee. For some reason I wondered if he had a son, and if so, if he ever brought the son to work with him. To see dad's office.

Dean seemed always pensive now, which was not difficult to understand.

His livelihood was at stake. And there was little he could do about it.

It wasn't the fact of Jan's having fallen—it was that it had happened in full view of an audience.

Dean had been Jan's default on-the-road caretaker for so many years, he was resigned to any mishap, as long as it occurred in private. He could deal with that.

Once, when we were in the mid-South, Dean had told me backstage before a late-evening show that Jan had fallen in his hotel room.

"I'm in my room around eight o'clock," Dean had said. "And the phone rings, and it's Jan. He says, 'I fell down. I can't get up.'

"So I ask him his room number. He says, 'I'm on the carpet. I don't know my room number.' I say I have to know his room number, or I can't help him. He says, 'You never try to help me.'

"So I call down to the front desk. I say that Mr. Berry needs a wheelchair. They say OK. I tell them to send it up to Jan's room, and I'll meet them there. And I ask them for the room number, so I can meet them.

"They tell me that they're not permitted to give out that information. I say that I'm Dean—this is Jan and Dean, and he's Jan, and I'm Dean. They say they still won't tell me.

"I say, fine. Send the wheelchair up, and I'll follow it. I know his room is on the seventh floor. So I go stand in the hallway next to the elevator, and someone from the hotel gets off with the wheelchair, and I follow it down to his room.

"Jan's already on his bed. He's gotten up. He asks me, 'Where's the band?' I tell him that everyone has gone over to the show, and that he and I are going to go separately. He says, 'I guess I'll take a nap.' I tell him we're supposed to leave for the show in an hour. And I apologize to the hotel person with the wheelchair, and say that the emergency is over."

Those kinds of incidents, Dean was accustomed to. They almost always happened away from public view. Now, though, he seemed edgy all the time. On the stage, he was looking at Jan more than in the past, trying to sense if things were going to be all right. As if you can ever tell.

"Excuse me . . . Marilyn?"

Randell was addressing a waitress in a hotel coffee shop. He always asked the name of every waitress, every waiter, every van driver . . . if he could get into the cockpits of the airplanes we took from city to city, he would have asked the names of the pilots.

And he generally asked if they had children, and, if so, how old the children were, and what *their* names were.

And ages.

And eye color.

So in this coffee shop he had known Marilyn's name from the moment she had handed us our menus. That had been about ten minutes ago; now it was time to order.

Specifically, it was time for Randell to order. The rest of us already had. As always, he was the last, studying the menu as if he had never before seen such a remarkable artifact: a laminated piece of cardboard with the names of food items on it.

He peered.

The seconds passed.

And passed.

"Yes?" Marilyn said, still waiting for him to speak further.

"What is . . ." Randell said.

The slow passage of more seconds.

"... a *Reuben* sandwich?" he said.

Gary let out a breath.

David dropped his silverware to the surface of the table.

Dean shook his head.

"You've never heard of a Reuben sandwich?" Marilyn said.

Of course he had. Randell had been a rock-and-roll guitarist on the road for decades. He'd eaten in thousands of restaurants. He just liked the back-and-forth.

"Hold on," he said, serious as could be. He was never making fun of anyone at junctures like these. He was just, for whatever reason, forever totally involved in the mundane moment.

His eyes moved down the menu.

"Marilyn," he said, "on this hamburger sandwich . . ."

Don put his hands on top of his head and stared ruefully at the tabletop.

"Yes?" Marilyn said.

". . . is your beef for the hamburger fresh, or frozen?" Randell said.

"It's a hamburger," Gary muttered. "It's just a hamburger."

"Do you want me to go to the kitchen and check?" Marilyn said.

"No!" the other voices at the table said, all at once.

"Are you guys in a hurry?" Randell said, looking up from the menu, laughing.

He held dear the fact of being out here—held dear every tick of the clock while we were on the road. So did we all, in our own ways. For him, this—the drawn-out massaging of the smallest occurrences, the prolonged narration of the commonplace—was part of it. Always.

Low drama, high drama, melodrama . . . whatever you wanted to call the vicissitudes that visited the touring life, we were constantly reminded that none of this was limited to us. Every band that was out here—especially every band that had a history behind it—had its own tribulations.

One night Jay Black of Jay and the Americans ("This Magic Moment," "Come a Little Bit Closer," "Only in America") was on the bill with Jan and Dean, and we could tell that something was wrong. Laryngitis, or maybe worse—whatever it was, he went through the evening's performance in a visibly agitated state.

Gary and Randell and I were watching from the wings when, suddenly, he stopped in midsong and strode offstage.

This seemed to catch the rest of his group by surprise. He hadn't said a thing to them—he just departed.

One of his backup musicians began to sing a song of his own—What else was he supposed to do? The outdoor arena was full of fans—and meanwhile Jay was now standing right next to the three of us, behind the edge of a curtain and out of sight of the audience. He was a big, burly, broad-browed man with a hint of Joe Namath in his face.

He held his hands up imploringly and stared at us. None of us had ever met him.

"I have *no* . . . *fucking* . . . *voice!*" he said. "I cannot . . . sing . . . 'Cara . . . *Fucking* . . . Mia'!"

We didn't know how to respond. His group, a few feet away, was struggling on.

So here was Jay—Jay, of the Jay and the Americans of our boyhoods—his hands still extended, his eyes still riveted on ours, as if somehow we had the answer.

"Drop two octaves," Gary said.

Not a bad suggestion, in a pinch, I thought.

Jay considered it for a few beats, then said:

"Nah. That won't work."

At which point he returned to the spotlight (to great applause) and proceeded to nail "Cara Mia."

Low drama . . . there was the night when one of the more famous female soul groups of the 1960s showed up for a concert lacking several essential backup musicians.

(For reasons that will soon become obvious, I will identify the group no further than that. In the words of drummer Guy Patterson in *That Thing You Do!*, "It would be ungentlemanly for me to elaborate.")

The leader of the female group asked our band if she could hire a guitarist and a bass player for her set. She would pay each of them $200, she said. This was when Chris Farmer was still with Jan and Dean; he and Randell said they would do it.

So the two of them joined the soul group's musicians for their set, doing creditably enough on such short notice. As we were all getting ready to leave the concert site after the show, Chris approached the famous singer. He asked about the money.

"How are you!" she said, smiling and very friendly, as if she hadn't heard his question.

"I'm fine," Chris said. "I don't see you reaching into your pocket."

"No, I'm not," she said. She told him that her business manager would mail him and Randell the money; she asked Chris to write down their addresses.

She was trying to bluff the wrong guy. Chris, had he so chosen, could have done very well as a hedge fund manager. There was no way he was leaving without the money.

"I don't think it's right that I should have to pay you cash out of my own pocket," she said to him.

"I just don't want to have to chase the money later," Chris said.

The candlepower of his smile easily matched the candlepower of hers. They were beaming at each other in the summer night, in a cold showdown.

"I hope you can play with us again sometime, when you can rehearse first," she said, trying to change the subject, beaming.

"Right," Chris said, not biting, beaming.

Finally she said to him: "I have the money stashed."

It was a stiflingly humid, almost tropical, night.

"That's all right," Chris said. "I'll wait."

At which point she said: "I put the money down my pants for safe-keeping."

And she stuck her hand into her underwear, and came out with a wad of cash she had hidden by her crotch.

She peeled off the bills for Chris and Randell.

They accepted the cash from her gingerly, with the tips of their fingers.

It was hard to say who won that battle.

The melodramas took varying forms, some more soggy than others.

Jan's desire and resolution to be out here singing grew only fiercer.

If his tumble to the stage had changed the dynamic of touring for everyone in the band, he was the one who of course took the ramifications most personally. Not that he ever spoke about it directly. To do so would be to acknowledge his fear.

But he was getting to soundchecks earlier, becoming more demanding and obdurate when he bickered about microphone and amplifier levels with local crews, talking to the audiences more volubly from the stage during the performances. His way of showing how much the concerts meant to him was to ignore—or pretend to ignore—the fact that he had collapsed. To act as if it simply had never happened.

It wasn't a new posture for him to take. It was a variation on what he had been doing for years.

No one was more aware of how the Dead Man's Curve accident had changed his life than Jan himself. Every time he looked in a mirror, the reminder was there.

He dealt with it by willing the thoughts to go away. Even while knowing that they never would.

Late one night, in the early years of when I was traveling with him and the band, we all went out to an Applebee's/Bennigan's type restaurant. The NBA playoffs, as I recall, were under way; we were in the Eastern time zone, somewhere in central Florida, and we wanted to watch a West Coast game while we ate.

So we did, all of us, and when the game was over and we had finished our meals we decided to walk back to the hotel. It was two or three blocks away, and it was easier to walk than to wait for a cab or call for the hotel van.

"Easier to walk," though, is a relative term. It was never easy for Jan Berry to walk.

Still, he assured us that he wanted to do it, that the trip on foot would be no burden to him.

He moved slowly, dragging that one leg behind him, pulling the dead side of his body forward with each stride. And when we were about halfway to our hotel, a car filled with teenage boys drove past us, and one of them, seeing Jan, leaned out the window and yelled at him:

"Hey, Igor!"

It happened just that fast and then they were gone. It was such a casually cruel thing to do, and because Jan showed no indication that he had heard—or, if he had heard, that he had understood what the taunt had meant—we said nothing. We continued to the hotel and we all went to bed.

I still, to this day, don't know if Jan apprehended what the boy had yelled at him. I do know for certain that the boy had no idea that the man at whom he yelled was once one of the lustrous and graceful luminaries of America's youth-cherishing culture, was once a flawless face on the covers of countless magazines, dreamed over by young girls from one coast to the other. To the boy in the car late at night, showing off for his buddies, Jan, hauling himself down the street, was a monster. *Hey, Igor!*

Jan may or may not have heard the boy that specific night, but he knew. He had been the leading man of *The T.A.M.I. Show*, and then he had become something else, and he knew quite well every aspect of what that signified. He knew it every day. Which is why, now, his need to be on-stage, his dependence on the cheers, was even stronger than before. As long as he was on the stage, he was still, in some secret place within him, the man on the magazine covers. He was still one half of Jan and Dean.

"If you could know everything about one historical event, which event would you pick?"

The questioner was Randell. It was so early in the morning. We were waiting in an airport boarding area; we had been up since well before dawn.

David Logeman had his eyes closed.

"Which event?" Randell said. "You only get to choose one."

"I don't know, Randell," David said, not bothering to open his eyes. "Why does it matter?"

A few seconds went by.

Randell then said:

"How many times between the day you were born and right now do you think you have hit the drums?"

"Don't," David said, eyes still shut. "It's way too early for this."

But Randell was wide awake. Not wanting to miss a moment of this itinerant musical life.

Each of us, in varying degrees and on varying days, sought the same thing Randell did: to keep this ever alive. Even—and especially—on borrowed time.

"I don't think I can even name all of them—there are so many," Gary said.

He was on the phone from California. We would talk most days when the band was back there and I was in Chicago.

Our conversations were not always on the loftiest of subjects. This one was about the word "well."

That's what Gary couldn't name, without sitting down and thinking about it for a while: all the Beach Boys songs that started with "well."

When I had mentioned it—the "well" theory of Beach Boys lyrics— he said it had never occurred to him; he had been singing this music for his entire adult life, yet had not, until I asked him, stopped to think that so many of the songs began with that particular word.

"There's 'Little Deuce Coupe,'" he said. "'Well, I'm not braggin', babe, so don't put me down. . . .'"

"'California Girls,'" I said. "'Well, East Coast girls are hip, I really dig those styles they wear. . . .'"

"'Don't Worry, Baby,'" he said. "'Well, it's been building up inside of me for, oh, I don't know how long. . . .'"

"'Fun, Fun, Fun,'" I said. "'Well, she got her daddy's car and she cruised through the hamburger stand now. . . .'"

"'Help Me, Rhonda,'" he said. "'Well, since she put me down I've been out doin' in my head. . . .'"

What could be the reason for this—why had all those songs begun with that same four-letter word? The colloquy in which we were engaged may not have been on the exalted philosophical level of Hegel or Kierkegaard. But then, how many Top Ten hits did they ever have?

So I pressed the point: What specific narrative function did he think "well" served in starting out a lyric?

Gary paused to ponder.

"It immediately sets a tone of informality," he said. "It's as if the singer is saying, 'Well, sit down. I have a little story to tell you.' It's almost as if, when you begin a line with 'Well,' you're indicating that it's a continuation of a conversation you've been having with your listener."

So that little word carried a weight far beyond its size?

"It conveys a sense of intimacy, right away," Gary said. "With that one word, the people in the audience get the sense that they know a lot about the singer. He's letting them in on something, like an old friend who's telling them an old familiar story. 'Well' says: 'As I was saying to you . . .' It establishes a connection between the person who's listening to the song, and the person who's singing it."

There was, I submitted, a concurrent possibility: that Brian Wilson and Mike Love had not been aware they were using "well" to begin all those two-minute-thirty-second musical novels. That it had just been a verbal tic of theirs.

Gary went momentarily silent as he let that sink in.

"Maybe they started so many songs with 'well' without even knowing they were doing it," he said, hesitation in his voice as he considered the question.

This, and discussions much like it, was what passed for deep reflection between us. It got us through until the next time the house lights would go down and the stage lights would go up. At which moment, happily, there would be no need to talk about anything, at least until the encore ended.

TWENTY

Because an undeniable selling point of the music was the memories it brought back to the audiences, it took a while for something occur to me: I had now been traveling with this band for long enough that the memories the music brought to me were not just of the boyhood places I'd been when I had first heard the songs, but of my time with Jan and Dean.

We were scheduled to return to Daytona Beach for a concert, and I arrived from Chicago before the band's plane got in from California. I didn't know anyone in town, and I didn't want to sit around the hotel room watching television, so I thought: I'll just walk over to Hog Heaven.

Hog Heaven was a barbecue place on a heavily trafficked commercial strip. The clientele was a little biker-heavy, but the atmosphere was loose and agreeable: picnic tables inside instead of regular dining tables, big rolls of paper towels instead of napkins, six kinds of sauces for the ribs and sandwiches. It wasn't until I got there and placed my order that I realized I was treating this place like an old reliable hole-in-the-wall from my hometown, when in fact the only time I'd been here before was with the band.

I knew what to order without looking at the menu, I recognized some of the waitresses, I knew where the restroom was—this place was a pleasant part of my past. Except the past it was part of was my Jan and Dean past; what had seemed so novel, almost incomprehensible, when it began—the idea of traveling the country with these men, singing the songs I loved—by now had fashioned itself into a history of its own. My reference points had become people and places from the tours; now when

267

we sang "Shut Down" or "California Girls" or "Honolulu Lulu," as I stood onstage the flashbacks the songs sparked were less about the friends of my growing-up years and the streets of Ohio, and more about the towns the band and I had passed through as we had sung these songs together on tour.

It was a change that was at the same time welcome, and a little melancholy; these times, based in large part on the hand-delivery of shared memories to audiences across the United States, were developing their own layers of memories. We'd sing "Little Deuce Coupe" and I'd get yearnful twinges not only about the cars in which my friends and I had ridden when the song had been a radio hit in 1963, but also about specific summer nights, and specific faces in the audiences, in towns the band and I had visited during the decade just past. It felt like missing something that wasn't over yet.

I finished my meal and went back to the hotel, and three or four hours later the band checked in. David Logeman called my room and said, "Hey, Daytona Beach! Want to go over to Hog Heaven?"

I told him I already had.

We went there together anyway.

The seeking of memories—using the music as a backdrop in the search for new experiences, for minutes and hours that will be recalled with fondness later on—was not limited to those of us on the stage.

One night we were playing farther down the east coast of Florida. Jan and Dean had opened a multi-act show. This never sat all that well with Dean—he wasn't happy being anything but a headliner, he thought that for him and Jan to do anything but close a show was something of an affront—and he always encouraged the band to try especially hard when Jan and Dean were the opening act. That way, if the set was a big hit, leaving people on their feet and shouting for more, he could turn to us and say: "Opening act, huh? Good luck to the rest of 'em, trying to follow this!"

On that night in Florida Jan started autographing his merchandise as soon as we finished our set, and Gary and I went into the audience to find some seats and watch the remainder of the concert. A group of women who had come to the show together were sitting next to us.

One, who said she was a schoolteacher, began to talk to us over the sound of the band that was now performing. She said she felt like going up to the front of the audience and dancing.

"You should," Gary said.

We knew there was an area right in front of the stage where people were encouraged to dance around—we had seen it as we'd sung a few minutes before. Some of the people danced as couples, some danced alone—it was a place for the more uninhibited among the audience members.

She turned to her friends and asked if any of them wanted to go up and dance along with her.

They reacted as if she had suggested that they dance naked.

"No!" one of them said. "What if some of the kids' parents are here? We can't have them see that."

Apparently they all were schoolteachers, too—they must have worked together.

"Come on," the would-be dancer said. "It'll be fun."

"Really, don't," another of her fellow teachers said. "It's not worth it. Stay here with us."

The teacher who wanted to dance sat there for a moment, then said to Gary and me: "My friends can't leave me alone to do something I want to for even one night."

At which point she stood up, stepped past us and into the aisle, and started to walk, then run, to the front of the outdoor arena.

Her friends seemed that they might call after her, but none did. It was an exquisite evening near the ocean; Gary said to me, "This is a good part of not closing the show." Nights like this, when we finished early, were the only times we could sit among the ticketholders and listen to music.

We couldn't see the teacher—she was too far toward the front of the house, and the aisle sloped downward—but after two or three songs she came walking back, a little out of breath, a layer of perspiration on her face.

"That was so great!" she said to her friends.

She reclaimed her seat. She was still breathing unevenly, but seemed elated.

"I'm really very conservative," she said to us, as if she needed to explain.

"You need a night like this once in a while," Gary said to her.

"I need it more than once in a while," she said in the darkness, her new memory only a few moments old.

"Ken, are you married?"

Randell was talking, and not quietly. It was very early in the morning. All of us were in a van on the way to an airport. It was going to be a long ride; we'd played the night before in a small Western town far from major transportation hubs.

Everyone else was either asleep, or trying to be.

"I am married," Ken, the van driver, said.

"Cool!" Randell said.

There was no need for this; we had all agreed as we checked out of the hotel that we wanted to snooze.

Those of us who were still awake thought—hoped—that this might be the end of Randell's inquisition.

"Just you and your wife, or do you have kids?" Randell asked.

Dean opened his eyes, then shook his head. Randell's voice was like the second alarm clock of the day.

"We have kids," Ken said.

The sun wasn't even all the way up yet. Was there a chance that Randell was finished?

Come on.

"You do?" Randell said with much enthusiasm. "That is so great!"

Now everyone was waking up. Gary, not knowing where he was for a second, looked around the van, then at Randell, and muttered: "Ahhhh-hhhh."

A second or two passed. Eyes closed again.

"Boys or girls, Ken?" Randell said.

"You know, Randell," someone in the back of the van said to him, "the chances are pretty good that it's going to be some combination of the two."

But he was doing what he always did: filling his invisible scrapbook with bits and pieces of the trip, loading up on the details of another day on the road. He was a collector of moments; if they'd been tangible, he would have had warehouses overflowing with them by now.

And some of the moments needed no elaboration. As we got closer to the airport and the van filled with sunlight and everyone was awake, the driver asked if we wanted to hear some music.

Someone said sure, and Ken turned to a local oldies station.

A few songs played, and then the early Beatles hit "Do You Want to Know a Secret" came on.

We listened in silence. Sometimes it was easy to forget that when songs like that one were on the radio for the first time, they were sharing the air with the first Jan and Dean hits.

Midway through the song, Randell said to me: "Here it comes."

I knew exactly what he was referring to, although the two of us had never discussed the song.

George Harrison's voice sang:

. . . I've known a secret for the week or two. . . .

"Do you think they didn't catch the mistake until the record was already out?" I said.

That's what Randell had been alerting me to: the line where Harrison transposed the words. Almost certainly, his intention had been to sing: "I've known *the* secret for *a* week or two."

"They must not have," Randell said. "It makes no sense the way it is. They've already established that they have a secret, earlier in the song. By that line, the right way should have been: '. . . for a week or two.'"

"Nobody says they've known something for 'the week or two,'" I said. "It has to have been a mistake they didn't notice."

It was like finding a typo in the Declaration of Independence (if calligraphy could have typos). A small error that's destined to be there forever, for every new generation to notice. Or not.

"That's the thing about hit records," Randell said. "You know every millisecond of them. Harrison sang that line in the early 1960s, and we're still aware of the transposed words."

And Randell had assumed—correctly—that because he knew, I knew. When he'd said "Here it comes," he didn't have to ask himself whether I'd be aware of the blown line about "the week or two." Asking me if I knew about it would have been like asking if I knew that May followed April.

All those young men, recording all those songs in those studios all those years ago. And every beat of every drum, every turn of every guitar line, every choice of every vocal cadence—still with us.

Two of those young men, young no longer, looked out the window of the van. Somewhere this morning—many somewheres, no doubt—people were hearing Jan and Dean's records on oldies stations in their own towns. Knowing, two seconds into the intros, exactly what would come next.

"You checking anything curbside?" Ken said as we approached the terminal. By nightfall, in a new city, a new audience would be gathered to hear the music.

The day I sang lead with the Beach Boys, I was half-convinced I would wake up and find out it hadn't happened at all.

Still am.

On a Saturday afternoon I got a call from Phil Bardowell. He was somewhere in Kentucky with the Beach Boys; they had two shows in two different cities that day—their summer was packed—and they were on a bus, on the way to the second concert.

"We're going to be in Chicago tomorrow," he said. "Will you be in town?"

I said I would. He said they were going to be playing at Navy Pier, the big entertainment complex on Lake Michigan just east of Chicago's downtown. Did I want to come?

"Should I start rehearsing now?" I said.

He laughed. "'Honda'?" he said.

The last time I had run into the Beach Boys, Mike Love had asked me what songs I was singing with Jan and Dean. When I told him one of them was "Little Honda," he said, "You'll have to sing it with us some day." I couldn't tell if he was kidding.

But now, with Phil on the phone. . . .

"I'd do it if I had the chance," I said.

"Let me ask Love," Phil said.

And little more than twenty-four hours later, there we were, back-stage at Navy Pier.

"You know, we don't use stage monitors," Love said. We were in their dressing room; the Beach Boys traveled with their own support personnel—they had wardrobe trunks and road managers and stage backdrops . . . quite a bit more elaborate, and expensive, than the Jan and Dean routine.

"We'll set you up with ear monitors," Love said. "I'm going to move 'Honda' to the encore. We usually do it higher in the show. Be listening. I'll introduce you."

I stood in the wings, clutching the neck of my Buddy Holly guitar like it was a security blanket, and watched them perform in front of a full house. I had a few beers; this was going to require some artificial courage. It was beyond anything that, as a boy, I ever could have imagined. Back then, the only thing that would have seemed more impossible than this would have been singing with the Beatles.

From where I was standing, I noticed something right away: I couldn't hear their voices. All of them were wearing the ear monitors—a power pack clipped to the back of their pants, a wire snaking up their shirts, a plug in each ear. A Beach Boys employee working a backstage sound console provided every musician his own mix through the ear monitors. Each man chose what to hear—whose guitars, how much of the drums, how much of the backing vocals. Each singer could hear his own voice as the dominant sound in his ears, against the personalized musical backdrop he had asked for.

Because this did away with the need for wedge monitors on the stage, there were no vocals being directed back at the band. Everything was going out toward the audience, through the house P.A. So here, behind the lip of the stage, I could only hear traces of anyone singing, although I saw clearly that they were. The guitars were faint, too. Only the drums were as loud as on a Jan and Dean stage.

It was more than a little sterile. I could look out and see that the audience was loving the show—a show that, from where I stood, was more like a silent movie.

"Let's get you hooked up," the man at the sound board said about forty minutes into the concert.

He gave me my own ear monitors, showed me what to do with the wires, and—when the plugs were in my ears—mixed some guitars in and asked me to tell him when it sounded right. It was distinct, loud, personal—the music was being played that moment by the band that was a few feet away from me, but the sensation was like walking down the street listening to a song through a headset.

The Beach Boys finished their main set, waved to the ecstatic audience, walked to the wings to towel off—they knew they'd be called back for the encore, they always were—and then, less than a minute later, returned to their microphones, waving again. They did a song—it may have been "Surfin' Safari," I was too nervous to really be paying proper attention—and then Mike Love said that someone was going to join them, and called me out.

I barely remember walking to the microphone, which a stagehand had placed directly at the front, next to Love. I could see all the faces in the audience, but could hear only what was in my earplugs.

Which was the insistent opening chords of "Little Honda."

With Jan and Dean I always let the *dah, dah, dah, dah dah-dah / dah, dah, dah, dah, dah-dah* of the guitars repeat four times. I hadn't asked Love if that's the way the Beach Boys did it, but I supposed it made no difference. The song, it dawned on me, wasn't going to be sung until and unless I sang it.

I looked to my left and behind me. There was Chris Farmer on bass, that not-necessarily-merry grin across his face, unchanged since the first day I had met him with Jan and Dean. He was looking straight at me, and I imagined he was thinking, with much-less-than-complete approval: How in the world did this ever happen?

I looked to my right. Bruce Johnston was gesturing for me to move closer to the microphone.

I looked a foot or two to my left. Mike Love was meeting my gaze.

My goodness.

My mouth was dry.

I saw the audience clapping along to the guitar opening; some of them were already on their feet.

I began:

I'm gonna wake you up early 'cause I'm gonna take a ride with you. . . .

I understood immediately why the Beach Boys used the ear monitors: they helped to make a singer's voice as good as it possibly could be. Which in my case was many miles from perfection—but I could tell that this was the best I could ever sing. It was like singing in the shower; with everything else shut out of your head except your own voice, and, on a softer level, the guitars-and-keyboards-and-drums mix that you had customized with the sound engineer, you could promptly correct yourself if you started to go off-key, you could emphasize just the right words. . . . it was, for want of a better term, *private*. It was as if you were singing only for yourself, your voice going straight from the microphone into your ears.

With the onstage monitors in the Jan and Dean shows, it was never like that. On the Jan and Dean stage, you could hear everything—the other guys singing, the sometimes muddy mix of instruments, the audience shouting . . . and many times you couldn't really hear yourself. It was like being at a rambunctious party. Your wedge monitor was aimed up toward you, but how well it worked depended on the guy setting the levels at the side of the stage, and how loudly the guitarists were playing and David was drumming . . . on the Jan and Dean stage the pervading sonance wasn't much different than if you had been standing out in the audience. And a person in the audience singing has an imprecise idea of how he sounds.

Here on the Beach Boys' stage, I heard nothing but me. I knew I was doing all right. But there was something unsettling, distancing, about it.

. . . put on a ragged sweatshirt, I'll take you anywhere you want me to. . . .

I sang the words, and if the good part of it was that it was like singing in the shower, the bad part was that it was like singing underwater. I saw the people in the audience, up and dancing, and they seemed a thousand miles away; their noise was blocked out entirely. I saw Mike Love next to me, singing backup—that should have been a life moment never to forget, and of course, it was, but it was like Love was there and not there: he was singing backup to my lead, I saw his mouth moving, but he just as well could have been on a different stage, in a different town. The sound in my ears was as if a goldfish bowl had been lowered upside down over my head.

It all went by so fast and I wanted it never to stop and it was so boxed-off, and when I finished the song I stepped to the back of the stage where the percussionists and keyboard players were, and sharing a microphone with one of them, I sang backup on "Fun, Fun, Fun" to end the show. Then it was over and we walked off and I didn't know what to do.

I saw everyone removing their earplugs so I removed mine.

"Thanks," I said to Love.

"Any time," he said, then added: "Don't take that literally."

Phil and Chris came over, and I said to Chris: "You don't have to say it. I know—you're thinking you could have stopped this years ago."

He laughed, and we talked about getting something to eat before they left town. There was something going on in the back of my mind, and it took me a second to realize what it was:

I felt a little guilty. I felt that, by having done this, I was cheating on Jan and Dean. Was being disloyal.

Stupid, I know, but there it was. I thought I should be careful about how I told them about this—or even if I should.

Mostly, though, I couldn't begin to conceive of what had just happened. Short of watching *Casablanca* on a movie screen after having watched it dozens of times over the course of my lifetime, and somehow, this time around, seeing myself in it, nothing could be much more unfathomable than this.

I knew there was only one person who would really understand, and so I called him.

Jack Roth, my oldest and best friend, had bought those first Beach Boys records with me, had cruised around central Ohio during those summers, listening to the radio as, day and night, their then-new songs had made the rounds of our young lives with us. Jack had been with me the first time I ever saw the Beach Boys in person, at Euclid Beach amusement park in Cleveland the August before our senior year in high school. He was the one person in the world who would know just how much this meant.

So I called him in Ohio—he and his family had moved back from Minneapolis to our old hometown—and I told him, minute by minute, what had taken place at Navy Pier. He didn't interrupt; he knew me well enough not to ask if I was kidding.

When I was finished telling the story, and there was silence on the line, I said to him:

"Serious question, Jack: What would you have said if in 1964 I had told you that I could look into the future, and that one day one of us would sing lead with the Beach Boys?"

He paused, and then, to my serious question, he gave a serious answer:

"I would have believed you more if you had said one of us was going to be president of the United States."

President wouldn't have been as good. Not back then. Given a choice between the two, neither of us would have picked being president.

Not now, either.

The September county fairs were the ones that usually won my heart.

The night air in September was always a tossup—we knew going in that we might get an evening to fool us into thinking it was still July, we might get one that was a preview of late October. The skies seemed blacker than summer skies; the multicolored lights from the midway rides contrasted against a September sky more starkly than at fairs in June. The fair sounds and the glow from the rides in September tried to convince us that summer survived, but it was the sky, leaning toward chill, that told us the truth: summer's heading out the door, and there's nothing anyone can do about it.

We arrived at the Delaware County Fair in Ohio to find lawn chairs chained to the exterior of the fence surrounding the horse track. We were playing a few days before the running of the Little Brown Jug harness race, and this, we were told, was part of the tradition: residents of the county lashing their chairs to the fence, staking out places for the race. The sun, as we soundchecked on an infield stage facing the grandstand, felt diffused through an unseen filter of ice. Families roamed the grounds; September fairs seldom drew the crowds that midsummer fairs did—there was more competition for people's time, in the afternoons the children were still in school, at night there was homework and bedtimes, on weekends high school football games and dances—but still the families came out. We knew that for some of the families in every county—the families without much extra income—the fair was the year's one entertainment extravaganza. Walt Disney World might not be a fiscal option, but the county fair, for a week or two, was the next best thing.

At the Delaware County Fair an announcer directed visitors to the dog obedience competition, to the rabbit skill-a-thon. As we walked to the stage for our show—Jan appearing to have a harder time of it than usual—we could see the sure signs of September fairs: jackets and sweaters in the audience instead of tank tops, hot chocolate and warm cider instead of ice cream and soda pop. By the time we sang our last song of the night, people in the seats were hugging their sides with crossed arms to ward off the falling temperatures.

We went back to the Delaware Hotel on South Sandusky Street. More than a few of the fairgoers had come to the hotel bar; the kitchen was closed, but a woman went out and brought pizzas back. Gary sat at the bar's piano and started to play "It Hurts to Be in Love," the old Gene Pitney hit. Soon enough everyone in the bar, including Jan, was singing, and the free concert-after-the-concert went on until closing time. September fairs: always gamely saying hello when logic says it's time to say goodbye.

"Let's go see where you grew up."

Gary's words surprised me. The Delaware County Fair was north of Columbus; he had rented a car the next day so he could drive down to Cincinnati to visit his parents.

He was offering to drop me in my hometown, and saying he'd like to spend a little time there before continuing south.

With few exceptions, our touring worlds and our lives outside the tours did not often intersect. That's what had caught me unawares about Gary's offer: usually the way stations of our shared universe were limited to hotel lobbies and arena dressing rooms, airport boarding lounges and late-night diners. And always, the endless succession of concert stages.

On this September Saturday morning, though, he drove to Bexley's Main Street. I showed him the public library, and Rubino's pizza place, and the old drugstore that's now a furniture store. That, I supposed, was what felt a little foreign about this: driving down these streets that were filled with memories of old friends, and realizing, because there had now been so many years with Jan and Dean, that Gary by this point qualified as an old friend, too.

We drove to the town football stadium, and to Johnson's ice cream stand where I'd passed so many summer nights, and then he said he'd take me out to my mother's house before continuing on his way.

My parents, many years before, had moved to a community about fifteen minutes east of Bexley. My father had died in 1998, so my mother had been living alone in the house since then.

When we pulled up and she answered the doorbell, I could see that she was frazzled about something.

"I've been trying to call the city water department all morning," she said. "I can't get anyone to answer on the weekend."

She had turned on her kitchen faucet, she said, and the water had come out black.

"I don't know what it is," she said. "There's a number for the water department in the phone book, but all I get is a recorded announcement."

"Well," Gary said to her, "luckily your son's here to take care of everything."

She and he both laughed.

"Right," she said. "When he was a boy and the pilot light would go out on the stove, he would run out the front door and down the block while we tried to relight it."

"What was he, about four?" Gary said.

"Eighteen," my mother said.

"Let me have a look," Gary said.

We went into the kitchen and he turned on the faucet; the water did, indeed, come out grimy black.

"Do you have a wrench, or a pair of pliers?" Gary said.

My mother told him where in the house to find the tools.

He took the faucet apart and fooled around with the spigot, and after a minute or two fished out a circular black rubber washer, hollow in the center.

"You're water's fine," he said to my mother. "It's just this rubber washer—it's gotten old and corroded. That's why the water looks black—it's from the washer. Put a new one in, and you're ready to go."

He turned on the water, which came out clear and fresh.

"Thank you," she said to him. "You're a lifesaver."

"I would have dealt with it even if Gary wasn't here," I said to her.

"How?" she said.

"When I saw the black water I would have told you to sell the house," I said.

She offered him some lunch, but he had picked up sandwiches from a shop in Bexley to take down to Cincinnati with him. He left in the rental car, and it wasn't that it had felt bad, this momentary melding of the two worlds, just a little confusing, the friendship outside the context of music and manic motion.

TWENTY-ONE

One Fourth of July we played on a multi-act bill in a Midwestern high school football stadium — the culmination of the community's Independence Day celebration.

We sang and then left as the fireworks were beginning. The van picked us up behind the stage and drove us around the track while, above our heads, the Roman candles, aerial salutes, peacock comets and whistling rockets exploded in the night. Jan and Dean may have headlined the show, but on July 4 in the United States no band, regardless of how renowned, is the closing act. The fireworks are.

So the driver proceeded cautiously in the darkened stadium, making certain there weren't any children dashing out of the seats to run onto the football field, and thus, inadvertently, in front of our van. No eyes were on us; every eye was on the sky.

There was little traffic at this hour of this night because just about everyone in town was at the stadium, so we made good time back to our hotel. Before going to our rooms we ducked into the bar, where some of the groups that had preceded us were having drinks. They'd been back for a while; they'd left the stadium as soon as they finished their sets.

Sitting on a stool at the bar itself was Frankie Avalon. He waved me over.

I did my best not to reveal what a welcome, even terrific, moment I thought this was. We'd run into Avalon several times on the road over the years; he and I had talked on occasion. He knew that I was an outsider, although by now a pretty permanent one.

Tonight he had opened the Fourth of July show with a few songs of his own, and then had acted as master of ceremonies for the rest of the concert. He still had the melt-the-ladies'-hearts looks that had made him one of the original teenage idols on *American Bandstand*; he was, as I had come to understand, a very bright man with a keen business sense, and he had figured out how to make Frankie Avalon a brand that would never go out of style. He was not only his own product, he was his own package, and there was no discernible expiration date.

My first memories of him predated the *Beach Blanket Bingo* days; if most people might recall him from that enormously profitable string of fun-in-the-sun movies he made with Annette Funicello, my recollections went back far enough to know that the movies had merely been his Act 2. Act 1 was the series of appearances with Dick Clark, not just on *Bandstand*, but on Clark's Saturday night Beechmint Spearmint gum show. In those early days, the Avalon brand wasn't quite as safe and staid as it would become later, in the movies; when the new-on-the-scene Avalon, his young face all hard jags, sang "DeDe Dinah" live on national television, the screams were electrifyingly urgent and the screamers didn't think of him as anything approaching innocent.

So on the Fourth of July in the middle of the country I tried to act as if this was the most old-hat thing in the world: being gestured over to the bar by Frankie Avalon. He offered to buy me a drink and we sat there watching the television set above the bartender's head, and then Avalon said to me, more as a statement of fact than as a question:

"Do you have any idea what kind of an experience you're having?"

I said I thought so; I said I thought I understood, but that there were times when some of this seemed beyond understanding. We sat together and talked of summers past and summers yet to come.

I was spending as much time alone with Jan as I could.

He was fearful.

There had been other times over the years when I had sensed that his lapses were frightening him. One in particular had been painful to witness: We had been booked into a county fair in a rural community, and a local construction and real estate big shot had arranged for us to stay not at a hotel, but in his home.

It was a nice enough place, out on farmland, with a man-made lake in the backyard. But there weren't enough bedrooms—Gary, Randell and David slept in the basement rec room, with a pool table in the middle, and it was a little ridiculous, like three grown men having a slumber party.

Jan, as I recall it, had been given his own bedroom, but there was something about this—the lack of privacy inherent in staying in someone's house, the idea that the real estate man and his family were walking around the place—that was making Jan feel skittish and unfocused. In the pool-table room there were sixteen guns mounted on the walls, fifteen with their barrels pointing up toward the ceiling, one with its barrel pointing down.

Whether it was his unease about this whole setup or some other reason entirely, Jan was out of sorts onstage that night, an oppressively torpid one rife with mosquitoes swarming in the spotlights' warm shafts. He walked over to Dean in the middle of the show and said: "Let's do 'Honolulu Lulu.'"

Dean informed him that they had just sung "Honolulu Lulu"—that Jan had sung lead on it. The audience could not hear Jan's request, or Dean's rebuff, but Jan didn't know that, and he was deeply embarrassed. After the show he came up to me.

"What did I say?" he asked, sadness in his voice. "I said 'Honolulu Lulu.'"

"That's OK, Jan," I said to him. "You were asking to do it a second time as an encore."

My attempt to persuade him to treat it lightly, as a meaningless slip, didn't work.

"I have to think more," he said to me.

But that was becoming a more difficult task for him, and it was making him scared, and by now no one, Dean included, was blaming him.

If Jan loved being famous, if he lived his days for the one-hour feel of the spotlight that would come after darkness descended, then Dean seemed not to care about those things at all.

It wasn't that Dean disliked his celebrity, or that he liked it; it wasn't even that he could take it or leave it. The truth was, he couldn't leave it—it had been part of his life for so long that he just put it on each morning without thinking about it, like a pair of socks. His face might not have been instantly identifiable by every single stranger he passed in an airport concourse or a hotel parking lot (although he was continually getting quizzical, haven't-I-seen-that-guy-somewhere-before glances), but his name, especially in combination with Jan's, would always mean something to tens of millions of Americans who grew up at a certain time. He was the jelly in peanut butter and jelly, the pepper in salt and pepper. Being the Dean of Jan and Dean was the defining element of his existence, something he did not have to pursue, and could not abandon.

Like the stage shirts he ironed in his hotel rooms each sundown, the fact of his fame was something to which he gave routine maintenance, simply because he felt it was his responsibility. He conscientiously kept on doing pre-concert interviews with local disc jockeys, knowing that was the most efficient way to draw more people to the shows; he did not lust after the airtime, airtime being another fact of his life that had been constant for forty years. He expressed no desire to write and record new music. As he had said to us many times, his singing voice continued to be on the radio as often as the voices of newly famous music stars, because every oldies station in the country had Jan and Dean's hits placed permanently on their playlists. He was singing every day in cities he'd never see, and he had seen a lot of cities.

His pleasures were private ones. On a trip early one fall to sing at Central Missouri State University, we arrived in Kansas City, where we were going to sleep before driving down to Warrensburg for the show the next day. At nightfall Gary and Randell and I were heading out to a restaurant for dinner, and we looked for Dean to ask him to join us. He was nowhere to be found.

We waited, and then went out to eat without him, and when we came back he still wasn't around. This was a little unusual. The next morning, though, he was in high spirits.

"I had the greatest time last night," he said.

He told us that he had walked down the street to a Dairy Queen. It was a Friday night; the place was full of people who were on their way to a high school football game.

"I ordered a Blizzard and a barbecue beef sandwich," he said, "and I could see all the people outside on their way to the stadium. They were all walking in the same direction, gathering for the game.

"So on the spur of the moment I walked with them. I took my Blizzard and my sandwich with me—you can't always get a barbecue beef sandwich at a Dairy Queen—and I walked toward the stadium lights, and there was this hill overlooking the field. Most people went into the stadium, but some people were sitting on the hill—right on the grass— and I sat down in the middle of them and had my dinner.

"That's what I did last night—watched the football game from the hill. It was such a nice evening, I stayed for pretty much the whole game, and then I walked back to the motel."

"Did you talk to people?" I asked.

"Only when there was a good play or something," he said.

"Do you think they knew who you were?" I said.

He scrunched his face up. "I doubt it," he said. "It was dark, anyway."

If the touring life were to stop, this—nights on a little patch of America he'd never visited before, sights he'd found just by wandering down a sidewalk—was what he would miss more than the adulation. At least that's what I sensed. The applause was like the paycheck—it came with the job. Nothing more than that, nothing less.

For the band—all of the backup guys—the changed set of circumstances with Jan meant that they went from grousing very little to grousing not at all.

As big-name acts went, Jan and Dean were not notably demanding in the amenities they asked local promoters to provide. All the stories of touring bands that insisted on masseuses in the dressing rooms, and specific brands of bottled water, and macrobiotic food prepared by private chefs . . . Jan and Dean tended to shake their heads in derision at that. In the contract rider that was sent to every promoter, they even poked fun at the syndrome of prima donna rock groups making unreasonable stipulations. In a paragraph of the rider devoted to what the band would like to have in the dressing room upon arrival at a venue, there was this: "Candy dish (M & Ms—no 'M's on candy, only 'W's.)"

Mostly, as far as food, drink and physical surroundings went, they took whatever the local promoter gave them. Some pre-show meals were better than others; some dressing trailers were grungier than the band would have preferred. But, having been on the road for so many years, they knew that the town in which they found themselves tonight would be a memory by this time tomorrow; it was less stressful just to accept what was in front of them, and not throw tantrums when certain things were not as lavish as they could be.

Sometimes a promoter would surprise the band in a good way. That construction/real estate executive with the lake in his yard and the guns in his rec room had arranged, without being asked, for personalized towels to be placed just offstage at the concert. "Jan and Dean," the monograms read; when we walked to the wings between songs to mop ourselves off, the towels were handed to us by local stage workers wearing T-shirts that read "Jan and Dean Crew," also provided by the real estate man. I think it had as much to do with his self-esteem as with the band's; he knew he was overdoing things, and he seemed to like being known in town as a man with the means to overdo.

Generally, though, the surprises were on the other end of the spectrum, and in my earlier years on the road someone's temper would occasionally flare. I remember one night when the band had flown all day from California to a small town on the East Coast; David Logeman and I were having dinner at a picnic table behind the stage, and he was clearly on the edge of exhaustion.

"We had to be at the fairgrounds at three o'clock yesterday afternoon in California," he said. "We were supposed to do a soundcheck, and then two full shows. We have this tiny—I mean, *tiny*—trailer to dress in, with no air conditioning . . . and no toilet. We're going to be there maybe eight hours. No toilet.

"Bill Hollingshead was there, and when I told him that this was really not acceptable, he said that if we were too demanding, if we pushed things too far, we might not get hired at some places. He said the word got around about bands who demanded too many luxuries.

"Luxuries! Come on! We're not demanding! We would just like the basics! We're going to be there from three in the afternoon until late at night, and we would like a toilet! And that's asking too much. That's being difficult."

Even that kind of sporadic griping, justified as it might have been, now came to a halt as Jan's situation became more shaky. Everyone seemed to realize that the best amenity of all—the grandest luxury—was in jeopardy: the being out here. The chance to travel the country together.

That was what could no longer necessarily be taken on faith. If these men liked hanging out on the road, and having long, laughter-filled dinners, and playing their music next to each other on stages in town after town after town . . . if they liked that, which they did, then they knew, without having to check with each other, that the time for complaining about anything had ended. The quality of dressing rooms and meal selections and hotel accommodations had become not just secondary, but almost irrelevant. All that mattered was keeping this alive.

And anyway, the amenities that meant something—the ones that reside in the memory even now—were not provided by any third party, and were never spelled out in a written contract.

On one of our trips to St. Louis—we seemed to play there more often than just about anyplace else—we finished the show in mid-evening (it had been an after-work concert for people employed in downtown offices), and were hungry.

Bob Costas, who made his home in St. Louis and who had been a friend of mine for many years, had told me, before we arrived in town, that he would try to come to the show and introduce the band from the stage. But family obligations delayed him; he called me as soon as our performance ended to apologize for not being there, and to ask us if we wanted to meet him and get something to eat.

"Do you want to come here?" I said. There were plenty of restaurants downtown.

"No," he said. "I want to show you a place called O'Connell's. It's mainly a bar, but it has the best cheeseburgers in the world."

"How far is it from where we are?" I said.

"About twenty minutes," Costas said.

That sounded like a long way to go for a cheeseburger.

"It's well worth it," Costas said. "These are the greatest cheeseburgers you'll ever taste."

It still seemed too far, but he promised me we wouldn't regret it. I talked to the guys in the band, and we got into two cabs and asked the drivers to take us to O'Connell's.

We made it there in the twenty minutes, maybe a few minutes more than that, and Costas had saved us a big round table. We sat and ordered beers, and after we'd had a few the waitress asked us if we were ready to order dinner.

I said I'd have a cheeseburger. American cheese, medium.

"What would you like on it?" she asked.

"Onion, pickle, tomato," I said.

"We don't have tomatoes," she said.

"You're out of tomatoes?" I said.

"No," she said. "We don't carry tomatoes."

I wasn't sure quite what to say. The place with the best cheeseburgers in the world—and they didn't have tomatoes?

"No," she said.

It wasn't that they had run out, or that tomatoes were out of season (which they most certainly weren't, in the middle of the summer). It was a matter of policy, she said. No tomatoes at O'Connell's.

The manager of the restaurant confirmed this for me. "Our customers know not to ask," he said. And what was the reason for this edict? "It's our tradition," he said. "You can't be sure that tomatoes are good all year 'round, so we don't serve them at all."

This made no sense to me. But we all ordered our cheeseburgers, and we were discussing the indisputable oddity of the no-tomatoes policy, and the door to O'Connell's opened and in walked Randell.

He said he was sorry for being late—he had run into a friend, he said, and the friend had given him a ride to the restaurant.

We started to tell him about the lack of tomatoes at O'Connell's, and without missing a single beat he said:

"That's no problem. I have one."

He reached into a bag he was carrying and came out with a plump red tomato.

Costas's jaw literally dropped.

"This is a setup, right?" he said. "You called this guy and told him that there were no tomatoes."

"You don't know Randell," Dean said to Costas. "It's hard to explain."

"He travels with his own condiments," I said to Costas. "It's usually pepper or mustard or something. We just lucked out that tonight it's a tomato."

Randell put the tomato on the table and said, "Let me have a knife. How many slices for how many cheeseburgers do we need?"

Air conditioning and bathroom facilities, the band didn't always get. But the perquisites that mattered—the symbolic side dishes to last a lifetime—kept coming around. We put Randell's tomato slices on our sandwiches, making them, in fact, just about the best-tasting cheese-burgers in the world.

When we finished dinner that night Costas told us that we shouldn't order dessert.

He wanted to show us another of his favorite St. Louis places; there, he said, and not at O'Connell's, was where our dessert should be eaten.

He had his car; Randell's friend had another car. So we split into two groups, and headed for the Ted Drewes Frozen Custard stand.

"Between the cheeseburgers at O'Connell's and the custard at Ted Drewes's, you're having just about a perfect meal tonight," Costas said.

Ted Drewes's proved to be every bit as good as Costas promised; the stand offered shakes, malts and sundaes, but the specialty was something called a Concrete. It got its name from the thickness of the mix; it was a concoction made of frozen custard and other ingredients, and its defining characteristic was this: it was handed to you in a paper cup, and you could turn the cup upside down and hold it over the ground and the dessert would not fall out. It was just that firm—like concrete.

But for me, the key moment of the trip to Ted Drewes's with Costas came just as we were arriving there, and he was pulling off the street and into the parking lot.

Dean and I were in Costas's car. The radio was tuned to KLOU, a St. Louis oldies station.

One song ended and another began; the second song was "Dead Man's Curve."

"All right, now this is amazing," Costas said.

He sounded more astounded than when Randell had produced the tomato.

Dean, in the back seat, said nothing.

"I mean, how cool is this?" Costas said.

Silence from Dean. He seemed eager to get out of the car and walk over to the order window at the custard stand.

Costas turned around and said to Dean:

"I'm with Dean Torrence—and 'Dead Man's Curve' by Jan and Dean comes on. You've got to admit, that's quite a moment."

"I guess," Dean said.

"How many times is that going to happen?" Costas, still full of enthusiasm, said.

"It happens," Dean said.

It had been happening to him since he was a very young man. For him, to hear a Jan and Dean record come onto the radio without warning was no more noteworthy than for Costas to zap through the channels on a television set and come upon a tape of a sporting event or a talk show he had broadcast.

"Sure, it happens, but how often?" Costas said to Dean.

"More often than you'd think," Dean said.

"Well, I still think it's cool," Costas said.

"Maybe," Dean said.

The Concretes were superb. So good that Randell had nothing in his bag that could possibly improve them even a scintilla.

There is a sound I have been encountering all my life.

It starts out half-heard.

You'll be somewhere at night—the first times I heard the sound, I was a child in my family's home—and you'll think you hear it, although you can't be sure.

If the sound was more distinct, it wouldn't be as seductive. If it was right in the room with you—if you could see its source—then you might shrug it off. There would be no mystery to it.

But, half-heard, it is in its own way as powerful a sound as exists in this world.

The first piece of the sound that you hear is the bass guitar—low, rumbling, almost a rumor. The bass line, coming from a distance, subjugates, by the time it reaches you, what must logically be the dominant lines of the lead guitar. But the tenor notes of a lead guitar apparently don't travel as efficiently.

So it's the bass that you hear—muffled, far-away, making you listen hard to be certain it's really there. And, beneath that, drums. And, always, the mere intimation of vocals—there are voices singing, that much you can tell, but there is no way you can make out the individual words.

You can't even really discern from which direction the sound is coming. It sort of floats, as if emanating from somewhere beyond a stand of trees, even when you hear it in a neighborhood where there are no appreciable groupings of trees. You sense that the sound is near enough that if you went looking for it you could find it—but at the same time it feels far enough away to be just out of reach.

It's the sound of a party—that's what it was when I first heard it, as a boy in my parents' house on summer evenings. Someone in the town was having a party, and they had hired a band, and that band was playing. Somewhere, someone was having fun—good times were just around the next corner, if only you could find that corner, and make your way to it.

The sound is one that always catches you unaware. Which is part of its magic—you will be doing some work or watching television or taking a walk, and you'll be hearing it—half-hearing it—for twenty or thirty seconds before you process what it is. That is the potency of its allure; it is a reminder that those good times are out there—*tonight*—and that you hadn't even known they were available. The rumble—the bass guitar line from somewhere in town, the fainter chorus of voices harmonizing on an up-tempo rock song you can't quite make out . . .

Not that you go out looking for it, at least not usually. When you're a kid, looking for the music would be out of the question—you're not even allowed to leave the house by yourself at night. When you're older, and you perceive that the sound is coming from a party, you tell yourself that you're not invited.

But there are times in your life—traveling on business, alone in some downtown—when you hear the sound from your hotel room, and you go out to search for it, and you navigate by moving toward the escalating volume. You walk in the direction of the noise, and when you get there—when you find the music, at some city festival or on a public-building plaza or a blocked-off street—it's like the end of a treasure hunt. There's the band—local, uncelebrated, playing cover versions of other, famous, bands' music—and the local band is always good, or good enough, and you're always glad you followed the sound, and you always stay awhile.

Yet the sound, when you reach it, is somehow never quite as tantalizing as it was when you could barely make it out. The sound you half-hear at first—an echo of what you first heard from your parents' house, the teasing promise that somewhere reachable, people are having a good time, a good night, a good summer . . .

That's the sound that is unequaled, a sound better than all others. Precisely because of the promise—when a promise is still a promise, it can never disappoint.

All my life I have heard that sound, and there were times, on the road with Jan and Dean, when I understood that the greatest of the gifts inherent in my travels with them was that as long as we were on tour we carried that sound with us. We were the ones bringing the sound to the neighborhood, whatever neighborhood in which we might set down. And once we arrived, and the show began, there were people—people beyond the tree line—who would be in the midst of doing something else, maybe something tedious, and then, as if swimming through a dream, they would sense that something in the air had shifted, that the very atmosphere had been enriched. And they would pause, and they would hear, from somewhere not quite close enough to touch, that bass, and those drums, and the unseen voices.

With Jan and with Dean, for all the years, I never had to strain to hear the sound because the sound was right there, where we could hold it. The promise of good times on the other side of the trees was a promise we brought with us. That's what would be so difficult to lose. That's what we all, without needing to say to each other just how important it was, wanted not to disappear, not to die.

TWENTY-TWO

"You going to finish all of those French fries?"

Randell was talking. He was sprawled on one bed of Dean's hotel room; Dean was on the other, eating a room-service cheeseburger.

"Yes, I'm going to eat all the French fries," Dean said. "If you want French fries, why don't you just order some?"

"I'm not that hungry," Randell said.

"Then why are you asking?" Dean said.

"Because I'm hungry enough for some of yours," Randell said.

There was something about this—all of us, late at night, in Dean's room watching TV—that had come to feel like an approximation of home. Some of us on the beds, some of us on the floor, Randell trying to cadge a free snack . . . we'd been here before, many times. Not in this room, not in this hotel—but we'd been here, it was how we ended so many evenings, and there was a real and winsome rightness to it.

On the television set a newscast was on; the anchor, over video of a politician waving to a large and zealous crowd, said: ". . . and he was greeted like a rock star. . . ."

"Yeah," Dean said, deadpan. "Right. Hope he enjoyed it." He hit the zapper and found a basketball game.

He didn't have to say anything else. "Like a rock star"? It was one of the most overused phrases in American life—people dragged it out any time they wanted to indicate that someone was being treated like royalty, only better. "Like a rock star" meant: there's nothing higher.

Dean Torrence, who by now had been a rock star for well over half his years on earth, understood all too well the absurdity of the notion. If being treated like a rock star meant being denied a toilet by a parsimonious promoter, if it meant standing tireless sentry over your French fries so your lead guitarist doesn't grab any . . .

Once, in Iowa, we had been playing an outdoor show where Fabian was on the bill. Jan and Dean were headlining; Fabian had sung earlier in the evening. He and Frankie Avalon came from the same Dick Clark era, and it is hard to explain, to people who weren't around then, just how immense a national presence Fabian was. Impossibly handsome, coached to work the front of the stage and make young girls weaken and quiver, featured on posters and in fan magazines and smiling his sultry smile off the ubiquitous four-color 45 rpm record sleeves . . . Fabian, for an instant or two, had been the living definition of a rock-and-roll star.

Fabian, back then, was not someone whom mortals ever believed they might actually meet. So in Iowa, just before we went onstage, I told Gary I wanted him to go with me to Fabian's trailer and knock on the door, and I asked if he thought Fabian would be amenable to greeting us.

"I flew out here from California on the plane with him," Gary said. "He couldn't have been nicer."

We walked to the trailer.

"What should I expect?" I said to Gary.

"From Fabian?" Gary said. "He's an old, cool guy."

But when we got there, he was gone—he had sung his songs and departed the grandstand. His evening's work was completed. The young, cool guy had turned into the old, cool guy—the Fabulous Fabian, as Dick Clark had regularly introduced him, had returned to the hotel to call it a night. There are up arrows and down arrows in this life, and none of us can really control when they will flip. When they do, we should probably consider ourselves lucky if, in the end, people we meet on airplanes tell their friends: He's an old, cool guy.

In Dean's room we watched the basketball game. Dean, his eyes remaining fastened to the TV screen, said:

"I see you, Randell."

Randell, who had been reaching for Dean's room service plate, grinned and withdrew his hand. We'd been here so often.

Like a rock star:

One winter we played a show in Florida, and the next night had to fly to Minnesota for another one. When we landed in Minneapolis there was snow and sleet in the darkness outside the windows of the plane.

Jan was in shorts. Maybe no one had thought to tell him in Florida that we would be flying to a much colder climate, maybe — probably — someone had, and it hadn't registered.

But there he was, the only person walking through the Minneapolis airport in shorts. He hadn't thought to put on a coat or a jacket, either; after we retrieved our bags and went outside to wait for the promoter's van, he stood in the nighttime snow shower, shivering.

The van pulled up and Dean helped Jan into the front passenger seat. The driver, a genial enough young man, decided to make conversation with Jan.

"So," the driver said, "you're . . . ?"

He let the question mark hang in the air.

"Jan Berry," Jan said to him.

"I know you guys are famous," the van driver said. "But I wasn't born until 1971. What were your hits?"

Dean, had the question been directed at him, might have sat there wordlessly. But Jan, having to make a decision, elected to answer.

"'The Little Old Lady from Pasadena,'" he said. "'Surf City.' 'Dead Man's Curve' . . ."

If Jan considered having to list his hits for the driver to be an indignity, it was probably a necessary one — when you make your living by trading on your lingering presence in the haze of the cultural ozone, there will come times when you realize you have to refresh that haze. When those times arrive, you might as well attend to the refreshing with as much grace as you can muster.

"You must be cold," the driver said, looking at Jan's bare legs.

"I'll be all right," Jan said, and the driver turned the heater up a click.

I kept in touch with Phil Bardowell as frequently as I could. I missed his play-it-as-it-lays company, his flinty-eyed on-the-run observations of the world as we passed through it.

One night he called from Washington, D.C.; the Beach Boys were about to perform at some sort of celebration honoring President George W. Bush.

"We're waiting in the van outside the hall," he said. "The Secret Service is going through all our equipment, and we're waiting until they've finished before we go in."

The music's power could be a fickle thing. Yes, there might be occasions, away from the arena, when, as with Jan on that airport access road, you had to explain to someone who you, and your songs, were. That always went away, though, once the show commenced, and those songs began to speak for themselves. I thought once more of all the places the music could take a person. For Phil, it had taken him to a room in which the president of the United States would be watching him play and sing.

I told him I would call him after the show, to see how it had gone. When I did, he was just leaving the stage.

"What did you open and close with?" I asked.

"You know," he said, the sound of the party audible behind him. "Same as always. First song 'California Girls,' last song 'Surfin' U.S.A.' "

The republic endures.

The crowds kept coming. Jan's deepening travails did not deter them — there were nights when it seemed they didn't even notice how bad things had gotten. They knew about the aftereffects of the 1966 accident, of course — the announcement before each show prepared them for that. Maybe that was it — maybe, having been told what Jan's obstacles had been, they became conditioned in advance to accept anything.

So the audiences did not react much differently than they had been during all the years I'd been traveling. There were nights with overflow crowds, and there were nights when the turnout was dismal. But that had been the case for a long time.

There had always been evenings that felt ominous just, it seemed, by the luck of the draw, by the position of the moon in the sky. Once we played on the biggest stage at Musikfest, a ten-day outdoor gathering in Bethlehem, Pennsylvania. Everything about the town the night we were there seemed grim and portentous—the sullen-faced, aimless kids wandering Main Street, looking openly for fights; the young desk clerk at the Hotel Bethlehem, her eyelids clipped off and disfigured by some sort of surgery that must have gone terribly wrong, as if performed by a sadist in scrubs; the starkly laid out front page of a newspaper from Munich, with not a word of English on it, posted in the hotel's lobby for all to read (at least all who preferred to learn of the day's events in German), the way other hotels feature *USA Today*.

Our night in Bethlehem was an anomaly, I was told later; other bands who were booked into Musikfest over the years said it was a fine and felicitous production, with not a glint of gloom. We must have had a *Twilight Zone* night there, they said; the spooky town we had encountered was nowhere to be found on the days they arrived.

We were used to the pattern—good shows, big crowds, interrupted by evenings that didn't feel so right. In Gaithersburg, Maryland, about four years after I started touring, the desolate view from the stage—row upon row of empty seats, the few people present sitting on their hands, no one responding in a way that could remotely provide a flicker of encouragement to the band—prompted Phil to walk over to me during the guitar break in "I Get Around" and, maintaining his concert smile, nod toward the audience and say quietly to me:

"This is what the end looks like."

Perhaps so. But as we were departing that concert Randell said: "We ought to always keep in mind on a night like this that the people in the audience are the ones who *came*. They deserve the best show we can give them—they shouldn't be penalized for the people who didn't show up. There may only be a few people out there, but they're not the empty seats. They paid money for this."

He was as right as he could be, and what I recall about packing up our equipment after the show that night was that the guitar cords and cases were covered with thick brown dirt, just caked with it. I still don't know how all that grime got onto an elevated stage, but we carried it to the next town, because we had no choice, and it was the opposite of a blithe sand-in-your-shoes feeling, it was just filth, and now it was traveling with us.

Nights like that, though, had always been the exception, and now they still were, which I wouldn't have guessed. If the people had looked closely at Jan, they would have seen how desperate matters were becoming. Perhaps not looking too closely was the conscious choice those audiences had made. In Randell's words, they weren't the empty seats. They were the ones who had come, the ones who had paid for, and expected, carefree fun.

In every one of Jan's hotel rooms, the television sets were perpetually on.

He kept them switched on even when he wasn't looking at them. Sometimes, when I would visit, he would think to turn the volume down, but there were other times when he wouldn't bother. He and I would just talk over the sound of the people talking on his television screen.

I think the purpose of this was to keep him company; I believe that was why the screens were always glowing and filled with motion and noise. With the hotel-room television set on, he was never really alone. I wouldn't be surprised to learn that he slept with the television on, although I do not know.

And I'm not certain how much attention he paid to the programs. When he was relearning his songs each day, with the headphones from his tape machine pressing against his ears, I know that he was concentrating only on that; when he was teaching himself once more the words to the songs he had written so long ago, that's all that was on his mind. The television set, even though it was playing, was just there, like the lamp or the night table.

Often he would choose to watch the news. Sometimes we would discuss it. He offered opinions about the events that were being recounted on a given day, occasionally strong opinions, but they tended not to last.

He seldom seemed emotionally invested in what the newscasters were reporting.

Except for once.

I remember it so vividly because it was so out of character.

In 1997, when Princess Diana died, Jan sobbed, and he couldn't stop.

He was inconsolable, consumed with grief. He appeared heartbroken. He just kept crying.

At first, none of us could figure it out. Jan Berry had never shown any particular interest in Princess Diana; as far as we knew, she was, to him, just another famous woman who was always in the news and on television. Certainly he had not, over the years, expressed any great affection, or even inquisitiveness, about her.

But now he was shaking in his sorrow, and this was so unlike him, and then of course we understood:

A beautiful young person: celebrated, and strong, and full of health, with the world and all its best possibilities stretching endlessly ahead.

And then, the beautiful young person slides onto the seat of an automobile.

He wept and wept, and there was nothing we could do.

Gary had gone to see my mom, and now he asked me if I would come with him to see his.

What she, and he, were dealing with, I found out, was considerably more life-changing than the broken faucet he'd fixed in my mother's kitchen.

Gary and his parents, after consulting with the family's doctors, had reluctantly decided that the time had arrived for his mother to move into a nursing facility. His father had selected the place, and now Mrs. Griffin was moving out of their longtime home and into these unfamiliar surroundings.

We had played in Ohio the night before, and in the morning Gary and I drove down to Cincinnati. He had the directions to the facility where his mother would now be living; we pulled into a parking lot in the back.

We walked together through hallways that smelled of disinfectant. Nurses and attendants in drab uniforms moved from room to room.

I was surprised, and flattered, that Gary had wanted me to come along. This had the potential of being a very private moment; that he would ask me to accompany him said something about what our friendship had become, something that neither of us would ever try to verbalize.

Yet there was something about it, as I glanced over at him while we walked down the nursing home hallway, that felt awry. It was the setting— we had been so many places together since Gary had first read that reference to Jan and Dean in the paperback copy of *Be True to Your School* and had written to me about it; I had seen so many things I otherwise never would have happened upon, I had found myself in the midst of so many experiences that never would have been a part of my life. But this was new—something this personal, in a setting so paradoxically impersonal, was unexplored territory.

After all the music, all the county fair midways, all the Waffle Houses and airports and hotel lobbies, we strode together down the hospital-like corridor and it was like cold water being thrown in our faces, it was like all the unforgiving lights being switched on at once after last call has been announced. If our time on the road was a never-ending effort to escape the world's wearying conventions, to hold at bay the traditional notions of humdrum reality, then this was a reminder that there is never truly a getting away. Not one that you can rely on. But then, I supposed we probably knew that all along.

"Hi, Mom," Gary said as we stepped into the doorway of her room.

She looked up.

"You look good," he said. "You remember my friend Bob Greene, don't you? You and Dad met him at one of our concerts."

We went in and I talked with Mrs. Griffin. Gary's father was there, too, and it was hard to read what was going through his mind, and through his heart; a lifetime of living under the same roof with his wife, and now he would not be. Tom Griffin shook my hand and was as nice and welcoming as could be, as if this was any other day in any other building. Whatever his fears, and his pain, he wasn't showing them, but then, he was used to keeping things inside. A man who was ordered to fly in that B-25 off the deck of the USS *Hornet,* who was told to hit Tokyo and then make it as far away as he could, even though he and his commanders knew the bomber did not have enough fuel . . . a man like Mr. Griffin had lived his life understanding you could not really count on anything. And here he was.

He and Gary and I talked with Mrs. Griffin, and then Gary and I left so the two of them, husband and wife, could have some time alone. Gary drove me to my hotel in downtown Cincinnati—he would be staying with his dad—and friendship, I thought as I rode silently in the passenger seat, is a curious thing. All those nights on all those stages, all the laughter and all the songs, and this, in a way that moved me more than I could say, was the payoff. I was honored that he'd want me here and I knew that for me to tell him that would make him uncomfortable, so I just got out at the hotel and said so long and watched him drive away.

Our reason for being in Ohio was that the show the night before had been in Jet Stadium in Columbus—the old minor-league ballpark to which my father had taken me to my first baseball game.

This was the third or fourth time we had played there since my travels with Jan and Dean had begun. I never really got used to it; the memories in that place, the meaning of stepping onto the field . . . Jet Stadium (I still couldn't bring myself to call it anything but that, even though there had been no Columbus Jets for years, and the Clippers were now its longtime tenants) had a hold on me far beyond its objective size, which was modest, and sumptuousness, which was nonexistent. To me, it would always feel like Buckingham Palace.

The Clippers were playing the Toledo Mud Hens. We would be singing after the ball game ended—the fans, for the price of their tickets to the game, got to see the concert, too. We would be performing on a portable stage that was for the moment parked behind the left-field fence; it would be hauled to the pitcher's mound as soon as the contest was completed.

We were hanging around the stage, out there beyond left field, and from where we stood we could see some of the game, but the vantage point left much to be desired. So Gary and I walked into the stadium itself and found unclaimed seats along the first-base line.

The Clippers' first-base coach had his back to us. I could see that he wore number 40 on his uniform.

That seemed like a blasphemy. In central Ohio, number 40 has almost religious significance. It was the number that Howard "Hopalong" Cassady, the speedy halfback from Columbus's Central High School who led the Ohio State Buckeyes to a national championship in 1954 and who won the 1955 Heisman Trophy, always wore. Hop Cassady's legacy in town endured and held its resonance well beyond his years in Ohio Stadium, as all of us who had loved Woody Hayes knew; Woody had been having a very rough time his first few seasons as head coach at Ohio State—the fans and university boosters were pitilessly critical of him, and were calling for him to be fired. They rewrote the first verses of *Carmen Ohio*, the Ohio State alma mater hymn, and chanted them to him from the stands:

> *Oh come, let's sing Ohio's praise,*
> *and say goodbye to Woody Hayes. . . .*

He was a young coach in trouble. He might not have lasted. And then came the arrival of Hop Cassady, and that national championship, and the real beginning of Woody's remarkable twenty-eight-year career. Hop saved him.

But on this night in Jet Stadium Woody was long dead, and the Clippers' first-base coach was wearing number 40, and it seemed wrong to me. In the ninth inning Gary and I left the seats and returned to the stage behind left field; the game ended, and as the stage was being dragged into position I saw Ken Schnacke, the general manager of the Clippers.

I said to him that I had to ask him something: Who on his coaching staff was wearing number 40?

He said: "Hop."

And it was true. Hop Cassady—sixty-seven years old on this night—

was the first-base coach for the minor-league Clippers. It was his job now; it was how he spent his summers.

Schnacke said he would introduce me, if I liked. So we walked down the steps of the Clippers' dugout, went though a narrow tunnel—and there, in the locker room, was Howard Cassady, half-undressed, getting out of his uniform and into his street clothes. We shook hands, and then Hop said:

"Sorry we couldn't give you a win tonight."

It took a moment before I understood. The Clippers must have lost to the Mud Hens.

For which Hop was apologizing.

Does the world get any more wonderful?

The stage was ready, the evening was warm, the sky was filled with stars. We played a longer set than usual—no one should ever be in a hurry on such a night. As we sang I tried to see if I could find Hop Cassady up in the stands. I hoped he was there. On nights like this one, there's more than one way to get a win.

One blistering afternoon when the sun seemed four times its usual size and the sky was such an unbroken shade of flat blue that it might as well have been a slab of dry paint from a child's old-time five-and-dime-store metal paintbox, Jan turned toward me onstage.

"Look at that!" he said.

In recent months we all had seen that he had been gaining too much weight; he was moving more slowly. There were days when it seemed to deplete him just to climb the six or seven steps to the surface of the stage.

And on this day—a concert that started a few minutes after noon—he was perspiring so heavily that his shirt had turned dark.

But he was grinning as he said the words to me. "Look at that!" He was seeing all the people in front of him—an ocean of people in swim-suits and shorts, kids batting inflated beach balls back and forth, bare-chested men hoisting their girlfriends above their heads so they could better see the show, couples dancing and pumping their arms into the air to meet the rhythms of Randell's and Don's guitars and David's drums.

Bob Greene

Jan, watching them, just seemed so full of contentment. We were nearing the end of the performance, into the final bars of "Surf City," and as Jan took in the churning scene in front of him he appeared to be a man who, at least for a few seconds, might be allowing himself to believe: maybe my life has been a success.

That, at any rate, was what I read into his face; that was what the moment felt like. We sang and I looked at him and I thought about what had brought all of us, audience and band alike, to this place on this day. It had something to do with Surf City itself—that make-believe spot that Jan Berry had come up with all those years ago. Surf City as a state of mind—Surf City as the happy, cloudless place we all want to believe is somehow out there, the place where we all wish we could end up.

All the dreams that do come true, and all the dreams that don't . . .

When we get to Surf City . . .

"Look at that!" Jan said, seeing his audience so in love with the summer day, and I thought to myself that if someone told him right now that for the rest of his life he could stay right here, on this stage, with these guitar chords sounding and these people cheering for him, he would gladly and gratefully say: yes.

TWENTY-THREE

The surprising thing, I suppose, is that even with all we knew, when the day came it caught us by surprise.

There were moments, over the years, when we talked about it without really talking about it.

"Jan just hates it when the summers end," Dean said.

It had been one of those nights in his room—we had gotten in on a late flight from one city, and wouldn't be performing until the next evening, so we had gathered in Dean's hotel room and ordered up some pizzas.

Everyone had worn-out eyes. Autumn had arrived; we knew we wouldn't be seeing each other, at least like this, for many months.

"I won't mind the break," Dean had said. "But Jan just dreads the winters. It's like he believes he's really only Jan Berry when he's out on the road. I've known the guy a long time. It never changes. He *hates* it when he has to accept that summer is over."

The moments:

Sometimes the contracts would call for Jan and Dean to perform the main show, and then for the backup band to play another set or two so people at a party or a convention could dance. The Jan and Dean show was considered the concert; the sets afterward were easygoing.

The contracts specified that Jan and Dean themselves were not required to be present for the sets after the main show. They were free to go back to the hotel—transportation awaited them as they came off the stage. And that was what Jan always did—went back to his room.

There were times, though, when Dean would stay and sing. He would be just another guy in the band. Or that was his intention: the people in the audience knew who he was, of course, they had just seen him and Jan do the main concert.

But Dean seemed to like the sets in which he was not the designated star as much as—if not more than—the shows in which he was. He was so much more relaxed; when Jan wasn't present it was as if Dean was absolved of the responsibility of making the Jan and Dean show live up to some elevated set of expectations. He seemed younger during those end-of-the-night extra sets; the principal show may have been just thirty or forty minutes earlier, but during the late-night sets he looked, and acted, as if he had shed ten years.

During one of those late shows I was singing lead on "I Saw Her Standing There"—no one in the band really cared who sang what during the extra sets, we were just a musical backdrop for the men and women dancing in front of us—and, fearful that I couldn't hit the most extreme tenor notes, I was singing the whole song in a conservatively low register.

Dean put his hand on his hip and watched me, and as I got to the "heart goes boom" part of the chorus his face brightened and he yelled across the stage to me:

"Higher, chicken!"

He was laughing, breaking himself up, and it was contagious—and it was too late in the song for me to change the key in which I was singing. So with everyone else in the band laughing too as they sang the backup parts, I finished the song as best as I could, and I knew that Dean never would have done this during a main concert; the main concert was the meal ticket, the payday, and "Higher, chicken!" would not have left his mouth in that setting.

But this was different. Jan was back at the hotel asleep, or staring at his television set, and Dean, as the hour grew late, became the approximation of someone other than who he customarily was, became unperturbed, a man who didn't have to be in charge.

Moments:

We were all in a Big Boy restaurant once—the van ride from the airport to the concert city was an especially long one, and we voted on whether to stop for lunch, and the vote was unanimous—and we were sitting in two separate booths, three or four of us in one, three or four of us in the other.

Jan, as if he had discovered platinum ore, said excitedly: "Hey!"

He held up a little cardboard promotional thing—one of those tent-like in-house advertisements—from the top of his table.

"Peach Month!" he said.

And it was—it was Peach Month at the Big Boy, either nationwide or in this Big Boy region. The restaurant was offering peach pie, and peach milkshakes, and peach cobblers, and peach ice cream—it was the peak of summertime, and the Big Boy was celebrating with peaches.

We went for it—how could we not? We'd be back on the highway soon, on the final leg of our drive to the new town, and if the Big Boy was offering peach specials we weren't going to pass up such an opportunity. It was a moment that meant nothing and that meant everything, and we didn't have to say a word about it, or about how much we would miss days like this if somehow they were to be taken away.

Moments:

Because the band was usually traveling from California and I was usually traveling from Chicago, there were many times when either they would arrive in a city first, or I would.

On one such day, at a hotel just off the Indiana Toll Road, my cab pulled into the lot and I started to unload my suitcase from the trunk, when I heard someone—actually, multiple someones—calling my name.

I looked up. In four contiguous open windows on the second floor of the hotel, the band—Jan, Dean, everyone—was leaning out. Some were in their own rooms, some were visiting the others' rooms . . . they were passing the afternoon before the show.

A few of them were drinking beer. Gary tossed me a can—cold, unopened—and as I caught it the cabdriver said:

"You know those guys?"

"Yep," I said.

"You work with them?" he said.

"Sort of," I said.

"So this is a business trip?" he said.

"I guess so," I said.

He looked up at the guys in the band—some of them now leaning farther out the windows with their hands on the sills, some of them sitting, one leg in the hotel, one leg dangling out. I paid him, and he said, "I don't know what kind of business you guys are in, but I wouldn't mind a business trip like this."

We knew he was right and we never lost sight of it and sometimes the moments—guys who like each others' company, hanging out the windows of hotel rooms on a summer afternoon—felt like picture postcards even while they were still present tense.

Moments:

When flights were delayed the airport card games were a staple. They required no announcement. Someone—almost always David Logeman— would turn a piece of carry-on luggage on its side in the boarding area, bring out the cards, and deal.

The games were an efficient time-waster. These men had traveled together so constantly for so long that they were past complaining about late flights. All around them other passengers might be grumbling, or phoning ahead to alert loved ones. Not the band. The grumbling, they knew, would be squandered energy—moaning wouldn't make the plane take off a second earlier—and who were these men going to call about being delayed getting into the next town? The only people who needed to know were right here.

So the cards were shuffled and the games were played and David was sometimes in his enthusiasm a little too loud, and there were times, during these games, when I would look at the players—at the men in the band—and I would think that in many ways, after all the years, this summed up in one self-contained frame what it was that they possessed and cherished: the journeys, and the airports, and each other.

David would deal and eventually the gate agent would apologize for the delay and say the airplane was ready for boarding. The other passengers would look at their watches and calculate how much time had been lost. The men in the band seldom dwelled on the clock. They put the cards away until next time, never questioning that next time would always come.

On an afternoon in March of 2004 I was sitting on the end of a lounge chair on a beach in Longboat Key, Florida, looking out at the Gulf of Mexico. I was the only person on the beach who was fully dressed.

I was waiting for a phone call. I had packed; I was waiting to find out where I should go.

Jack Roth—my best friend since I was five—had been diagnosed, out of nowhere, with a kind of cancer from which a person doesn't necessarily get better. I had received the call with the news a few days earlier. Now I was waiting to hear the details of what his treatment would be.

Depending on what his doctors said, I would either be flying straight to Columbus to visit him, or I would be going to Chicago to await further information. Either way, these were going to be gray days.

So I was sitting there, awaiting the call from Jack himself, or from his wife, or from one of our other lifelong friends, and I listened to the sound of the waves and finally the cell phone rang.

I answered, hoping for a miracle.

But it wasn't Jack, or anyone else in Ohio.

It was Gary Griffin.

"Hi," he said. "I didn't know if anyone else had reached you."

"Reached me about what?" I said.

"Jan Berry died last night," Gary said.

He had had a seizure at home in California, and could not be revived. That was the official cause of death.

But really the cause was the car accident in 1966. By rights, Jan should have died that day; the first emergency workers to arrive at the site of the automobile wreck had, indeed, presumed that the driver—Jan—was dead.

The coma, the protracted rehabilitation, the decades-long regimen of medication . . . Jan had overcome so much, for so long, that it always seemed that he had figured out a way to keep death ever at bay.

He had been getting ready for the new touring season, Gary said. He was trying to lose weight, as he tried every winter; he was doing his best to build up his stamina. He wasn't going to be a picture of youthfulness when the summer began—that, he knew, and we all knew—but he would be there, singing his songs. He always was. He was dependable.

There were no plans yet for a funeral or memorial service; it was all still too new. Gary and I hung up and a few minutes later I got a call from Jack Roth, sounding weak and shaken. He told me what the plans were for his course of treatment, and I said I would fly north and see him in Ohio.

At the Sarasota airport early that evening I was walking toward my gate and I passed a little bar in the concourse. I heard a familiar sound.

It was Jan and Dean, singing "Surf City" in concert. It was coming from a television set that was bolted to the wall in a corner of the barroom; one of the national network newscasts was on.

I remembered the night at the restaurant in Erie, Pennsylvania, when we were all eating ribs and Al Campanis's face from the old *Nightline* footage came onto one of the big TV screens and I knew he was dead. Knew it even with the sound turned down, because the only reason that Al Campanis was going to make a network newscast, all those years after he had been a newsmaker, was if his life had just ended.

So it was with Jan. I looked at the screen as the smattering of people at the bar drank their cocktails and read their newspapers and talked to their neighbors on the next stools.

I couldn't tell when the concert footage had been shot. Probably at least ten years earlier, maybe twenty.

I watched Jan and Dean sing:

. . . Two girls for every boy. . . .

Within seconds the network anchor was on to the next story and I walked the rest of the way to the gate.

He had managed to hold on to the last night of summer for so long.

That's what I kept thinking as I waited for my flight.

It was always such a bittersweet night for him anyway—the last warm evening, the last night of friendship and freedom, the last grab at fun.

He hated it so when summer had to end; that's what Dean had told us. He couldn't stand the thought of the empty months that lay ahead.

And somehow, by strength of will, he had made the last night of summer endure for almost thirty-eight years. Every time since 1966 that he had walked onto a stage, every time he had picked up his microphone, every time he had sung the first notes of the concert's first song and had been bathed in the cheers from the audience. . . .

He had set his fiercely private goal and he had reached it, again and again and again. Another chance at summer: that's all he asked for. That's all he wanted. Thirty-eight years since the accident, and he had refused to let the last night of summer end. I walked onto the plane so that I could go see my oldest friend, who, as it would turn out, would have only one more summer left in his own life.

Once someone very wise told me that we should regard the best moments in our lives as pebbles in a jar. The assumption should be that the pebbles are finite—even if we can't count them by looking into the jar, we should assume that one day they will run out. We should withdraw them with care, one by one, never doing it by rote or distractedly. If we withdraw them too rapidly, we are being greedy, and will hasten the day when they are gone; if we hoard them, if we are miserly in keeping them in the jar, then we will rob ourselves of the experiences the good things should give us.

So it is with summers. If all of life were summer, then our world would have no texture, no context. Summer would not taste the way it does if we thought it would last forever. There's no perfect way to remove the pebbles, no foolproof timetable. The closest we can come to perfection is to know just how precious those pebbles are, and to value each one.

I know that Jan did. More than anyone I think I have ever known, he never took a single one of those pebbles for granted. He withdrew each one of them from life's jar with gratitude, and with love.

The plane lifted off. Savor every day, every summer night.

TWENTY-FOUR

At a nightclub on the Sunset Strip some old friends of Jan's dating back to his earliest days in the music business—session men, record-label executives—held what amounted to a memorial service for him. The new season was already partially booked, and some of the promoters said that their preference was to have Dean and the band fulfill the contracts.

So as summer began they went out on the road and presented the show; they told the audiences that the performance was a tribute to Jan. Dean was fully realizing the impact of what he had long known to be the defining fact of his professional life: Jan and Dean were unlike most bands in an unalterable way.

If, say, the Coasters or the Ventures lost a member, they could still go out on the road as the Coasters or the Ventures. The names of those groups did not depend on the names of the individual members. After the deaths of Keith Moon and John Entwistle, no one said to Pete Townshend and Roger Daltrey: You are no longer the Who. Most bands were like professional sports teams: on even the best, the players came and the players went.

Jan and Dean—the act, not the men—presented a syntactical problem, and thus a logistical one. You could not very well proclaim that Jan and Dean were coming to town if one of them was permanently missing. When Elvis Presley died, an industry of imitators formed, but none of them said he was Elvis Presley. And Dean could not very well hire a new Jan.

So in those first unsettled months of the new season Dean and the band went out to honor the contracts in the cities where the promoters asked them to, but the bookings were slim and new ones were difficult, if not impossible, to come by.

Dean notwithstanding, the other men in the band faced a relatively pressing problem. They were not wealthy. They had to work. They did not have the luxury of being able to take even a single summer off.

Thus, when the offer from Disneyland came along, it at first sounded like just the solution they had been hoping for.

Disneyland had opened a new park known as California Adventure. One of the attractions it provided daily to guests was surf music—the Disney executives had come up with a generic name for a surf band: Wave Riders. A cart of sorts—a mini-float—had been constructed with the Wave Riders logo painted on it. The cart was a marvel of Disney engineering: as small as it was, if the musicians carefully aligned themselves on either side of it they could play their instruments and sing while being seen by customers on both sides of any Disney street.

That was the idea: the Wave Riders cart would be hauled around the theme park, stopping periodically, as the musicians played and sang live music while the cart was in motion. The vehicle towing the cart was made to resemble a vintage wood-paneled station wagon—a woodie— and was driven by a Disney employee.

Disney's plan was to hire several different configurations of Wave Riders—the cart was pulled through the park day and night, seven days a week, and no one band could be expected to work all those shifts—but the Jan and Dean band, who suddenly had no summer to speak of, were, because of their musical pedigree, offered the opportunity to work the most shifts.

They said yes. Each day they, without Dean, reported to the gates of Disneyland in Anaheim. Whenever we talked, they tried to put a good face on it. They got to sleep in their own beds every night, they said, and they didn't have to spend half their lives in airports. The pay was steady, and they could drive to work, often carpooling with one another. The Disney property was a clean, fastidiously organized place, and they seldom had to worry about details not being taken care of.

I could tell they didn't mean it. They sent me a photo of themselves posing on the Wave Riders cart, smiling for the camera; looking at the picture made me sad. These musicians were among the best in the world at what they did, and there was something demeaning—diminishing— about this new sustaining engagement of theirs. As they were tugged around the theme park they wore headsets with microphone mouth- pieces attached, like old-time telephone switchboard operators, or modern-time air-traffic controllers—Disney had provided the headsets because they were less space-consuming than microphone stands, and wouldn't fall down if the cart hit a bump or made a sudden turn. The men in the band were required to play five forty-five-minute sets per work shift; in between they were free to get a snack in the Disney com- missary. They were considered Disney cast members, in the same cate- gory as the people who portrayed Goofy and Minnie.

I didn't buy their feigned enthusiasm about being glad to sleep in their own beds, about being relieved to be freed from airport lounges. The hotel beds on the road, the never-ending string of flights across the country, were a big part of what they lived for; the joy they found in their work was in large measure because of where in America that work took them, the new places and faces they had always been able to count on seeing each day. They might not be rich men, but they had always, in their hearts, made up for that by not having to report to the same un- changing office front door every day, by always being able to count on fresh horizons.

Carpools? Company cafeterias? I was happy that they had found pay- checks in the months after Jan's death, but I knew that had he lived they would still be out bouncing around the country, bringing their show to people who were excited that it was coming to town for one night only. Gary's voice sounded weary when we would talk on the phone after his Disney shifts were over for the evening, and whenever he told me about the band being pulled day after day in that strictly circumscribed loop around the park grounds, seeing only artificial vistas, I tried not to let him hear how bad I felt for them. On the road for all those years the will- ful lostness of the Lost Boys had always felt romantic and vagabondish, something embraced by them, a lostness thoroughly worth longing for.

Second star to the right, and straight on till morning. Now the lostness seemed literal, and I didn't know what was going to become of them.

And then they came up with an idea.

They had been seeing something in the eyes of the people on the streets of the Disney park.

The men in the band might have felt stupid—or worse—being dragged through the California Adventure like a homecoming float. And they may have felt that they couldn't do justice to their musical talent having to play and sing while shoehorned onto the rolling cart.

But the music itself—the songs of surf and cars and girls—was affecting the people on the Disney sidewalks just as strongly as it had in all the stadiums and grandstands and ballparks over all the summers. The people heard the songs—"Little Deuce Coupe" and "Help Me, Rhonda" and "Surfer Girl" and "409" and all the rest—and they just lit up. It didn't matter that the people may have been on their way to some other ride or attraction on the property; it didn't matter if they had no idea that the men in the surf shirts being driven up and down the Disney streets were the real thing, not some amusement park stand-ins.

What mattered was that the magic of the music had faded not at all. The men in the band could see that, every day. And it dawned on them that, even with Jan gone, there might be a way to carry this music around the United States the way they always had, to let the songs be their ticket to going back out into the country again. A way to give themselves that which, with Jan's death, they thought they had lost.

None of them were businessmen—starting this on their own was going to be a challenge, one that they knew could conceivably fail.

But not to try?

And, by not trying, to allow those summers of meandering together through America to become merely a memory that recedes a little year after year?

Not trying was not an option.

Thus was born the Surf City Allstars.

Buoyed by hope.

"Five o'clock, lobby, soundcheck!"

David's voice—booming with the kind of glee he usually saved for an-nouncing a royal flush—came through the telephone receiver in my room at the Comfort Suites in Aurora, Illinois.

More than a year had passed. It was August of 2005. They had extri-cated themselves from their Disney commitments, and had fully re-claimed this life.

"Are we going to be coming back to the hotel before the show?" I asked.

"We can," David's voice said. "But bring stage clothes just in case we don't."

The hotel featured a sturdy winding wooden staircase, and when I walked down toward the lobby I could see, as I paused on a landing, Phil Bardowell looking at old-time railroad tickets. This Comfort Inn, the desk clerk had told me when I checked in, was on the site of the head-quarters of the original Burlington Railroad; there was a display near the front desk: tattered timetables, vintage tickets, photos of ancient locomo-tives.

"Hey!" Phil said, looking up.

He was back; he had decided to leave the Beach Boys and join this new enterprise. Dean was waiting in the lobby too. It had taken the Surf City Allstars a while to build momentum—the word had spread slowly to bookers and promoters from coast to coast—but by now business was picking up by the week. There would probably be no more National Foot-ball League stadiums or Major League Baseball parks—the band without Jan was going to have to find its paydays in smaller venues, was going to have to perform more often and travel more steadily—but it was a tradeoff they seemed fully inclined to make. And the truth was, the forty-thousand-seat dates had pretty much disappeared many years before.

Tonight was going to be the Downtown Alive! festival in Aurora, free to the public. Two women from the town committee appeared right on time in the hotel lobby; they drove us over to Stolp Avenue near the Fox River, where the stage had been set up.

We climbed onto it; the streets were still mostly empty. The show wouldn't begin for an hour or so. We looked at each other, and grinned, and this was the opposite of forlorn. There was going to be music in the middle of the country on an August night.

I plugged in my guitar. "Do you mind?" I said to David.

"You'll find the rules are kind of loose with the Surf City Allstars," he said.

I started playing "Twist and Shout," and the local guys working the sound board cranked it up full tilt, and the chords hit and then sprang back off the fronts of all the buildings in this part of Aurora, from Downer Place to Water Street to Galena Boulevard. The Vienna Opera House couldn't have felt any finer.

Matt Jardine's voice was so heartbreakingly pure, it would have fit right in with the Mormon Tabernacle Choir.

But he was singing "Wouldn't It Be Nice" in downtown Aurora. His father was Al Jardine of the Beach Boys; Matt, too, had sung for years with the Beach Boys, but after his dad and Mike Love had had a falling out that led to Al's departure, Matt had joined up with the Surf City Allstars.

He was a tall young man with a gentle manner about him and a nothing-rattles-me smile, and he seemed to fit right in with the others; he had spent the dreary Disney days with them, both in the carpools and on the theme-park cart, so by the time the band set out into the country, he, like they, felt as if he was busting out of prison. He made the group sound exponentially better—his voice was so beautiful, it stopped people in their tracks.

It was doing just that tonight, as pedestrians on the sidewalks near where we were performing tarried to listen to him. There were thousands of people in the audience—they filled downtown, spilling around corners and onto side streets where we couldn't see them—and at the end of the evening, our shirts sopped with perspiration, we left the stage hearing the applause bound off the buildings.

No one was tired, and across the parking lot from our hotel was an odd-looking structure that, it turned out, was the oldest existing limestone railroad roundhouse in the United States. Built in 1856, it had been used to house and repair locomotives; obsolete for many decades after the railroads had begun their decline, it had been on the verge of being torn down when developers had decided to convert it into a night-club complex.

We walked over. It was packed. There was a restaurant, and a comedy club, and a micro brewery, and a banquet hall, and a cognac bar, and an open-air concert area . . . it was like a limestone maze. Most of the customers were dressed for an evening out, but we were still in our sweaty stage clothes; we got separated from each other, and after about twenty minutes, as if in a house of mirrors, Dean emerged from the comedy club looking disoriented, and Matt emerged from the cognac bar, and Gary emerged from the micro brewery . . . and all we could do was look at each other and laugh. What were we doing here? What on earth were we doing, with midnight approaching, in a railroad roundhouse in Aurora, Illinois?

The answer, which didn't need to be enunciated, was that this was exactly where, still and always, we belonged on a summer night: someplace we'd never seen before, someplace to where the music had taken us.

That next winter they devoted themselves to fine-tuning the details of trying to make this work.

It wasn't the simplest of undertakings. In the shuffle of musicians that had brought Phil back to the band and that had resulted in the arrival of Matt Jardine, Randell Kirsch had been offered a job with the Beach Boys and had taken it. Another July came around, and we were in the Midwest again—this time in Bensenville, Illinois, for the town's annual Music in the Park series. After soundcheck we were escorted to an unusual dressing room: the village board chambers on the second floor of Bensenville's Village Hall.

This was where the business of Bensenville's government got done— where the mayor and the village trustees held their regular meetings. It was a starchily formal room redolent of zoning appeals and budget compromises. We took off the shirts and pants we had been wearing all day, laid them on the desks where the village officials customarily sat, and changed into our stage clothes.

In the midst of this, David's cell phone rang. When I'd started traveling with these men in 1992, none of us yet carried portable phones. If we weren't at home or in our hotel rooms, we weren't reachable.

Clutching his stage shirt in his free hand, David answered the phone, then said:

"Laughlin? Hold on a minute."

He said to the others:

"Can everyone go to Laughlin the second week in August?"

One by one, they pondered.

"I think I can go," Don said.

"Let me make a call and check," Gary said.

Dean, looking quite at home in the mayor's chair, turned to me. "Have you ever been to Laughlin in August?" he said. Laughlin, I knew, was an isolated town in southern Nevada.

"I've never been to Laughlin, period," I said.

"You take one step outside the hotel and the heat just about knocks you to the ground," he said. "You literally can't breathe. One step—seriously—and you feel like you're going to collapse."

"So everyone stays inside?" I said.

"No," Dean said. "That's the thing. Some of the people who go there are crazy. They're out in the heat, drinking beer all day—they *like* how it feels."

"Let me get back to you," David said into his phone. "It's a tentative 'yes.' I'll know for sure by tomorrow. Don't book anyone else yet."

Some of the Surf City Allstar engagements, as I was seeing, came in this way, through David. Dean still had his own booking agent from the Jan and Dean days—requests to that agency were arranged differently. For shows in which Dean's agent was not involved, David had pretty much taken over the business end of the band, but because he didn't have an office staff back in California, often it had to be done this way, on the fly, while he was on the road drumming. The Bensenville show was supposed to start within the hour.

"Excuse me?" a soft voice said.

It belonged to a shy young woman, standing in the doorway of the council chambers. She apparently had been there for a few minutes. She was wearing a uniform from a place called Sundaes Too.

"I'm from the ice cream shop across the street," she said. "We're providing dinner for you tonight. You have your choice of hot dogs or Italian beef sandwiches." The pre-show catering, we were finding out in these post-Jan days, was not invariably on the five-star level.

"I'm supposed to ask what you want, and then bring it back to you," the young woman said. She was very nervous.

"I think Italian beef is fine for everyone," David said to her. "Thank you for doing it."

"Hot peppers?" she said.

"Pardon me?" David said.

"Would you like hot peppers on your sandwiches?" she said.

"Why don't you just bring some on the side," Dean said to her.

She left, and the band members tried to figure out if they had other obligations for the Laughlin weekend, and within five minutes she was back, carrying a cardboard box.

"I brought you each a bag of potato chips to go with the sandwiches," she said. "I'm trying to get off work the rest of the night so I can see your show."

On the way to the stage we saw her ice cream shop—it was in the same building on Center Street as Bensenville's old downtown movie theater—and on the lawn behind the Village Hall it looked as if the whole town had turned out.

We started with "Do It Again," and those words we'd sung every night:

It's automatic when I talk with old friends. . . .

I turned toward the spot on the stage where Jan would always stand. Dean caught my glance, read my mind. He nodded.

By the time we were into "Shut Down" there was an unbroken line of people standing straight as a picket fence in front of and parallel to the stage, holding little metal objects aloft, the way fans at concerts used to hold lighters.

But these were cell phones. The people were taking pictures of the show with them. Another way the world had been altered.

Perhaps not really, though. Gary sang his lead, and the people pressed the buttons on their phones, and while the mechanics of preserving memories on a warm hometown night may change, the impulse to preserve those memories, it seems, stays ever the same. Toward the right side of the crowd I thought I could see the sandwich girl, dancing away.

"Anthony! *Anthony!* I *love* you, Anthony!"

The hardware used for communications and photography were not the only things to have changed during the span of time I'd spent with the band. We were on the southern tip of Rhode Island, on the edge of the Atlantic Ocean, getting ready to play a show at Misquamicut State Beach.

"Oh, *Anthony!*"

We were all, an hour or so before the concert began, standing on the performers' side of a fence near the stage. With us were Chad Stuart and Jeremy Clyde, the superlative British Invasion duo whose two big hits—"A Summer Song" and "Yesterday's Gone"—had all but defined the pain of summertime romance when the songs, and their listeners, were new. Chad and Jeremy were scheduled to sing just before us.

"*Anthony!*"

The girls doing the screaming were looking at us, but at the same time right past us. "Anthony!" "Anthony!" "*Anthony!*"

I turned around. A slight, blond-haired young man about ten feet behind us was waving self-effacingly at the girls. Every time he lifted his hands, they screamed some more.

"Who's that guy?" I said to Gary.

"An *American Idol* kid," Gary said. "He's opening the show."

He was Anthony Fedorov. Born in Yalta, Ukraine, he had moved to the United States with his parents when he was nine, and had learned to be a singer of ballads; he (this was news to most of us) finished in fourth place during the *American Idol* season in which Carrie Underwood was voted the eventual winner.

Apparently to come in fourth on *American Idol*, a television program that did not exist when I met Jan and Dean, was a high enough finish to provide for lingering cachet and sustaining public passion. "Oh, Anthony, I love you," came another cry, and a security guard standing with us said: "Can you imagine?"

Dean didn't answer. But he looked at Chad and Jeremy, who looked back at him, the three of them, I sensed, hearing echoes of other screams from long ago.

Atlantic Avenue, the main drag in Westerly, Rhode Island—the site of the Misquamicut State Beach show—seemed to be of two minds.

On the one hand, the town appeared desirous of making the nighttime concert a family-welcoming magnet for tourists and vacationers, a best-face-forward calling card for the area.

Yet there was something about Atlantic Avenue that felt disquieting, on edge—it was like what we had encountered on that trip to Bethlehem, Pennsylvania, but more pronounced. If you were filming a movie here, the scenes you chose to shoot would be setups for a story destined to end badly.

I got to town before the band. A fierce storm kicked up at sunset; the locally owned three-story hotel had a rickety, driftwood bandbox feel to it—in the parking lot by the front entrance there was a putrid old toilet bowl for the guests to use as an ashtray, and it was overflowing with dead cigarettes—and in a period of four hours the electricity in my room shut flat down seven times. There was no way to notify the front desk; the rooms were not provided with telephones (or clocks, for that matter), the result of an evident suspicion that the clientele might pilfer them on checkout day. Late at night, I could hear a local band across the street at a bar called Sandy's Lighthouse. They were playing a window-shaking rendition of a power-chord pile driver:

Life is a highway, I want to ride it,
all night long. . . .

Awakened by the sheer pounding volume of the music, I looked out to see two men fighting in Atlantic Avenue—just whomping each other, until one finally went down and lay motionless.

The next day, after the band arrived, things in town seemed more peaceable. We were having lunch at a seafood shack called Captain Zak's, and I said to Matt Jardine:

"Do you ever feel that your dad is looking over your shoulder?"

"Why?" he said.

I gestured at the wall behind him, where there was a poster from a concert the Beach Boys had performed in the area forty years before; the photo on the poster was the famous one of the group in their short-sleeved striped shirts: the young Brian, Carl and Dennis Wilson, Mike Love, Al Jardine. Matt turned around to be greeted by his father's cardboard eyes; he looked for a second and went back to his clam roll.

After we rehearsed and checked the sound system down by the beach, we were walking up Atlantic Avenue to our rooms and stopped at a place called Paddy's for a snack. As we approached the front door, a shirtless and sunburned young man with blood streaming down his face was being rushed out by a phalanx of bouncers. He kept trying to re-enter; shoulder-to-shoulder in a formation they looked as if they had practiced, the bouncers moved him toward the street. The men with whom he apparently had been fighting followed him, and he lunged toward them, and the punches started anew; young women in bikinis gathered near the sidewalk, ardently watching, calmly attentive as if the proceedings were a floor show. All of this was in broad daylight.

Two fistfights, then, that I had seen on this short stretch of street in less than twenty-four hours; there would be a third before we left (in an empty lot after our show). Somehow, traveling together as we did, this kind of thing didn't feel potentially threatening to us, even as strangers in town. Phil seemed to be having the same thought. Just loudly enough for us to hear and no one else, he half-spoke, half-sang those lyrics from "I Get Around" that had first been performed by Matt Jardine's dad and his bandmates:

"My buddies and me are gettin' real well known, yeah, the bad guys know us and they leave us alone. . . ."

The young man with the blood dripping thickly from his forehead continued to square off with his adversaries on Atlantic Avenue. We went into Paddy's and, on a deck out back, found a table in the sun.

By the side of the stage I stood and watched Chad and Jeremy's set.

The crowd appeared to stretch halfway from Rhode Island to the Bahamas, growing larger by the minute as the sun descended. "A Summer Song," when it was new, had carried a wistfulness that always made it seem different, more pensively felt, than its neighbors on the Top Forty charts, and tonight was no exception. The two men blended their voices and I heard the words once again:

> *They say that all good things must end some day,*
> *Autumn winds must blow. . . .*

By the time we were brought on to end the show, full darkness had arrived at the oceanside. The stage lights were turned up to maximum wattage, and in their superheated glare we felt as if we were all but marinating, but none of us was complaining; the audience was frenetic and full-throated and fervidly involved from the first song. For whatever reason, on this night the band was playing as if every one of the musicians was realizing anew why he had devoted his life to this craft in the first place. Phil's and Don's guitars meshed and intertwined with the energy and intuition of two roughhousing brothers ferociously tussling, Gary's keyboards were a teasing, towering counterpoint to every chorus, David's drums were like a jackhammer goosed by uncontainable electrical surges, Matt's vocals joined with Dean's to make songs that had been famous for four decades seem all of a sudden new and fueled by reckless impatience. . . .

On a night like this it was possible to remember when "409" had nothing to do with nostalgia, when it was a brand-new record just coming out of America's car radios for the first time in a nation that never for a second doubted a dominating Detroit's determination to keep the populace roaring open-throttle forever down a hundred thousand highways; when "Catch a Wave" could make you almost taste the salt spray from the surf off the California coast, even though you'd never been that far west and could not conceive that you'd ever get there; when "Shut Down" was a rude injection of adrenaline, a song to quicken the pulse, a dare, an unhesitating call to combat. . . .

On a night like this, with the band playing so boisterously and the people out in the dark shouting along with every single word, you wanted the set list to be never-ending, for the show to have no finale. But it did, as always, and for the encore Dean waved Chad and Jeremy and Anthony Fedorov back onto the stage to join us for "Barbara Ann." Fedorov appeared perhaps just the slightest bit intimidated now—*American Idol* aside, he was seeing for himself how a performance was paced and powered by men long experienced in understanding every nuance of reading an audience's appetite and feeding its hunger, he seemed to be watching Dean and making mental notes on how this was done—and then, for the final choruses, the governor of Rhode Island emerged from the wings.

Governor Don Carcieri had declared this to be Bay Day throughout the state, celebrating all of Rhode Island's beaches and parks, and because this festival at Misquamicut was the day's marquee event, he and his wife Suzanne had driven down from Providence. He was in a coat and tie, she in a blue pantsuit, and for a moment the two of them looked to be uncertain if they should be standing on the stage while the music was still being played.

But Dean motioned them to join him, and soon enough the governor and his wife were sharing Dean's microphone, harmonizing with the rest of us and with the vast crowd out in the darkness:

Ba-ba-ba, Ba-Barbara Ann . . .

And then it was over and, on cue, a fireworks display started to light the night sky. It was so resplendent that, even though the performance had ended and the klieg lamps had been doused, we did not leave, not any of us. It was shadowy on the surface of the stage now, and I could see in the dimness that Jeremy Clyde was to my left, and that Governor Carcieri was to my right, and that the men in the band were still behind their now-muted microphones. We all just stood there, looking up at the flaring colors as they exploded over the water.

"Yeah, the plane tickets were to Indianapolis, so I rented a car at the airport there," Gary said. "I'm on my way down to Cincinnati to see my dad."

He was calling from the rental car. We'd be playing in the small central Indiana town of Shelbyville two nights later.

"What do you know about Shelbyville?" I said. "I think I'm going to be getting there before anyone else."

"Let me take a look," Gary said. "I'm on I-74 right now, just approaching there. I'll pull off."

"You don't have to do that," I said.

"It's fine," he said. "I'll check it out for you."

A minute or so later:

"OK . . . here's the hotel where we're going to be staying. Lees Inn. Looks nice and clean."

Then:

"OK, I'm cruising through the Lees Inn parking lot. We have . . . an Applebee's, easy walk from the hotel. We have . . . a Ritter's Frozen Custard, right across the street. We have . . . what's this called? It's across this little grass lawn behind the hotel. Looks like it's called Halfpints Bistro. Like a tavern with food. Doesn't look bad."

"You're really doing this?" I said. "You're not kidding? You really pulled off the highway at Shelbyville?"

"Oh, yeah," he said. "I'm getting back on I-74 now. I'll see you day after tomorrow. If I were you, I'd go with Halfpints Bistro. You can eat at Applebee's anywhere."

I thanked him, but how do you thank someone enough for all of this? He was the one who had said: Come on out on the road. I think you might like it.

The Little League World Series was on the screen of the television set above the bar at Applebee's.

I'd already been to Halfpints Bistro, with Don, in the afternoon. Gary had been right—it was a good choice, particularly a house specialty hot sandwich made with corned beef, grilled onions and horseradish gravy—and Don and I had just sat at a corner table and talked for more than an hour while the rest of the world was working.

Now, though, we were about to go play the show, and we had taken Gary's dad to Applebee's for a beer. He was walking with a cane, which was a new development since the last time I had seen him; Gary's mother had died, and Mr. Griffin was living alone in Cincinnati, and he seemed very pleased that his son had picked him up to bring him to the concert.

"I'm really happy to see you guys again," Mr. Griffin said, and we said that we were happier to see him. He sat on a barstool, the Little League game flickering on the TV set, and of course there was no way for anyone at Applebee's to know. "LAUNCH PLANES," had read that cable sent by Admiral Halsey on the USS *Enterprise* to the crews on the *Hornet*. "TO COL. DOOLITTLE AND GALLANT COMMAND GOOD LUCK AND GOD BLESS YOU." I looked at Mr. Griffin. I hoped that, at least on some days, he thought that we who now live in the America he had helped to save were close to being worthy of what he and those men had done for us, before we were born.

We had to gulp the last of our beers because it was time to go sing. In front of the Lees Inn the mayor of Shelbyville, Scott Furgeson, was waiting for us; he had his car, and in front of that was a Shelbyville police cruiser with its dome light flashing. It seemed that we were going to be getting a motorcade.

"Could you hold on for just a second?" Gary said to Mayor Furgeson. "Let me get my rental car and pull behind you. I can take some people, too."

The police officer in the cruiser said: "I've got room for a few people."

So Phil and I walked over to the police car; I got in the front seat, Phil got in the back. A long-barreled gun—it appeared to be a shotgun—was fastened in a rack next to the driver's seat.

"Everybody ready?" the officer said, looking out his window and behind him, and the mayor signaled that everyone was in place. Almost as soon as we were out of the Lees Inn lot the police officer switched on his siren and stepped decisively on the accelerator; cars pulled over to let us pass.

"We'll get you there on time," the officer said.

I did my best to pretend that this kind of thing happened all the time—that we were long accustomed to motorcades with flashing lights and wailing sirens.

I turned around to look at Phil in the back seat. He, too, was doing his best not to grin, not to show how much this was making us feel like thrilled little boys.

The Bradley Hall Furniture Store looked exactly as it must have in 1951, when the citizens of Shelbyville did all their shopping in the streets around the town square, when the interstates that would eventually snake through the middle of Indiana were barely in their planning stages, when the center of a city truly was the center, the core, of that city's life.

Even though this was a steamy summer evening, I could half-close my eyes and imagine the Bradley Hall Furniture Store on a snowy December afternoon in the midst of some long-ago Christmas shopping season, with the sidewalks of Shelbyville crammed with people bundled up in scarves and overcoats, taking their time, looking into the display windows all around the square.

Nolley Insurance Services, Blue River Printing, C&C Custom Framing, Linne's Pastry Shop, the Shelby County Bank, Three Sisters Book Store, Sponsel Photography, Wetnight's Shelbyville Paint and Wallpaper . . .

This town square genuinely and geometrically was a town square—the public square was set down smack in the middle of downtown, and that is where our stage had been erected. One of the purposes of the Bears of Blue River Festival—named in honor of a novel written in 1901 by Shelbyville resident Charles Major—was, once a year, to remind the residents of the county that the public square was still here, that the merchants needed their business, that once in a while they might consider driving past the big-box stores out by the highway and spending a few hours here.

"You just want to take this place home with you, don't you?" Phil said quietly to me.

He was next to me on the stage; we had just finished "Little Deuce Coupe" and Dean was talking into the microphone, thanking the crowd for coming. Phil, taking in the sight of all the old buildings in the square, all the stores with local owners, said to me:

"After the show, let's walk around and take a look at all this."

"I was just going to suggest the same thing," I said.

Soon enough we were into "California Girls," and I looked over at the faces of the men on the stage—faces undeniably older now than when we had first met almost fifteen years before in that airport concourse in Chicago, en route to the Worlds of Fun amusement park in Kansas City for my first, and what I thought would be only, show—and I thought:

If what, more than anything else, the music had given these men was a lifetime of borrowed time, then maybe, as long as the music is still here, the loan never has to be called in. And I thought once more of Jan's Surf City. All of us, wherever we may live, deep into our own lives, still trying to get to that perfect place. Even, or so I was sure, those among us in the land who had never heard the song. The perfect place exists. It has to. We believed it when we were young, and somehow we believed it now.

We sang in the town square, and the people of Shelbyville, knowing the words by heart, sang with us.

By the time I woke up in the morning the band was gone. They'd had a crack-of-dawn flight back to California, and had left Shelbyville for Indianapolis before the sun was up.

So I checked out of the hotel by myself, and stepped out the front door toward the parking lot. There was a newspaper vending box, for the *Shelbyville News*.

Above the fold on the front page, in color, there we were. We were in midsong, all of us leaning into our microphones, the timeworn street lanterns and red-brick buildings of the town square visible beyond us.

There was infinitely more important news in the world that morning: warfare, and political infighting, and crimes and callousness and cruelty.

But last evening, the music had come to town.

I looked through the window of the vending box, saw us at the top of Page One, and remembered a song that, long ago, a nineteen-year-old Elvis Presley had sung on Sun Records:

Have you heard the news?
There's good rockin' tonight. . . .

The young man seemed to have been on to something. There is news, and then there is news.

The papers were fifty cents apiece, and I purchased one and then went back into the hotel to ask for change at the front desk. I wanted to buy some extra copies, and you should never cheat a newspaper honor box.

TWENTY-FIVE

Dean Torrence and I share a birthday.

On the tenth of March that I turned sixty and Dean turned sixty-seven, we had a show in Bradenton, Florida.

I came across a videotape of an old episode of the *Hollywood Palace* television variety show, originally broadcast nationwide on ABC in the first weeks of 1965.

The guest hosts that week were Roy Rogers and Dale Evans. One of the singing acts was Jan and Dean.

Roy Rogers's days as the television cowboy hero who, beginning in the early 1950s, had captivated America's children, were over by 1965; those children had become teenagers and young adults, and were smitten with different kinds of stars. Still, Roy and his wife enjoyed a lasting societal currency, even then, and they were the ideal kinds of hosts for a mainstream variety show like *Hollywood Palace*. It was quite a pairing that night—Roy Rogers, the King of the Cowboys, and Dale Evans, the Queen of the West, welcoming Jan and Dean.

Roy, on the show, was as amiable as could be—he always had that squinty-eyed man's-man look that viewers instinctively adored, he'd had it for years, well before Arnold Palmer came along with those same television-friendly squinty eyes (Rogers and Palmer even had similar speaking voices)—and Roy and Dale played up the jovial we're-the-old-fogeys-and-Jan-and-Dean-are-the-guys-the-kids-squeal-for act.

Jan and Dean sang a song, and when they finished Roy and Dale joined them on-camera for a little banter.

I don't know if the four of them were literally reading from cue cards, but from the looks of the telecast they very well may have been. In any event, it was obvious that the interchanges were scripted, and had been rehearsed before the show. (In one, Roy, squinting beneath the brim of his cowboy hat and referring to the screams coming from the girls in the audience, said to Jan and Dean: "You know, out at the ranch, when we have a critter bawling like that, why, we just have to rope him and brand him.")

As part of the Jan and Dean act in those years, Dean would bring a guitar case onstage with him, and at a certain point pick it up and then open it. Out of the case would fall a skateboard.

Dean would proceed to zoom around the stage, doing his best to keep his balance on the board. He'd done it this night, on the *Hollywood Palace* broadcast.

As I viewed the tape for the first time, there then came a moment I wasn't expecting.

Dale Evans, still on script, said to Jan: "Say, Jan, I hear you're going to medicine school. How come you're taking up medicine?"

And Jan, looking young and cocky and invincible, a man convinced that nothing in the world could ever slow down his plans, replied:

"Well, you know the way Dean works that little skateboard—sooner or later, he's going to need some medical assistance."

On Dean's sixty-seventh birthday I walked into the Bradenton Auditorium, where he and the Surf City Allstars were already running through soundcheck.

In the all-but-empty arena I climbed the stairs to the stage and greeted them.

"Happy birthday," Dean said.

"Happy birthday," I said.

We both just smiled and shook our heads. What more was there to say? On that Ohio day in 1963 when, backing out of Dave Frasch's driveway, I had first heard "Surf City," I was sixteen; Dean, out in California, was twenty-three.

The stage was a jumble of noise. Each man was testing the sound system in his own way, appearing all but oblivious to the others' presence. They played separately, working on different tunes, and while it may have looked haphazard now, they were like baseball infielders who, once the game began, would turn into a unit that knew each others' every move by heart.

I had seen all of this so many times. And still, standing once again in the midst of the seemingly formless preliminary hodgepodge, it made me exceedingly eager for the next few hours to pass and for the real thing to begin. Play ball.

"Who wants to go back to the hotel for a few minutes before the show?" David Logeman said.

He looked around the stage.

"We can do that," Gary said.

"I wouldn't mind cleaning up a little bit back there," Don said.

"I can't," Dean said. "Remember? I have to stay here for that meet-and-greet with the sponsors."

Dean was doing that more and more often: agreeing to have private social sessions with the host committees before the concerts. It was one more way to get the newly constituted band, without Jan, the bookings they needed.

"OK, we'll just go to the hotel for a little bit and see you back here," David said.

We went to the parking lot and got into a rented van. David was driving; that was another new fact of life: the Surf City Allstars couldn't always count on the promoters providing transportation. On many dates, they were their own drivers.

So all of us, minus Dean, were in the van, heading for the Hampton Inn in Ellenton. It wasn't that far away—fifteen or twenty minutes. And we wouldn't be staying there long; the show was scheduled to begin in about an hour and a half.

We were on a fairly deserted stretch of Highway 301 when the van began to go slower . . . and slower . . . and slower. . . .

David steered it to the side of the highway, where it glided to a stop in the grass.

"Guys, I'm sorry," he said.

We were out of gas.

And there was not a word of exasperation from anyone in the van.

Not a sigh.

Not a hint of annoyance.

Not a raised eyebrow, or a set of exchanged glances.

That's how close these men were to each other—that's how thoroughly these years and years on the road had drawn them together, and how completely they had embraced this life. Out of gas? On the side of an unfamiliar stretch of highway in the Florida countryside? With the unforgiving clock ticking toward the scheduled beginning of a concert?

Nothing to get irritated about. They were all here together, weren't they? This was the life they had chosen. One more unanticipated and open-ended episode.

"Anyone see a gas station?" David said.

We looked up and down the highway. Nothing.

"I can go look for one," Matt Jardine said. "There has to be one within walking distance."

There was an empty plastic cup in the van—about the size that would hold a large soft drink order from a fast-food outlet.

"Let me go see if I can find a service station, and if I can, I'll ask them to put some gas in the cup," Matt said. "I'll bring it back. It should be enough to pour in the tank and get us to the station."

He started to walk, and the rest of us got out of the van. The sun was going down; other cars on the highway had begun to turn on their headlights.

"What's that place?" Phil said.

There was a building near us—a ramshackle place with some sort of ceramic statue in front of it. The statue seemed to be in the form of a giant pig, but the head of the pig had fallen off, or had been knocked off.

Phil and I walked over to the pig. There was quite a bit of garbage that had been thrown into its open neck.

"The building's a restaurant," Phil called back to the others, who were standing by the van. The place was called the Hickory Hollow.

"Let's see if we can get a quick bite to eat while we're waiting for Matt," Phil called to them.

We trudged to the front door of the restaurant, only to be greeted by a handwritten sign in the window: IF YOU'RE IN A HURRY, YOU'RE IN THE WRONG PLACE.

"It's that kind of night, I guess," Gary said, and we returned to the van.

So we leaned against it, and watched the traffic stream past us. For just a second, standing in the muggy, darkening air in the grass next to Highway 301, I silently asked myself:

Is this any way for a man to spend his sixtieth birthday?

And the answer, I knew, was yes.

I couldn't think of a better way to be spending this night. Surrounded by friends, on the way, sooner or later, to sing the songs we loved, no one in a hurry, no one complaining, all of us just taking the evening exactly as it unfolded, and asking no more of it than that. . . .

These men were still out here, looking for that elusive place. Maybe the truth was that they never really were supposed to find it—maybe, in the end, that was the point: that they were destined never to get there. Maybe the searching for it—the nights like this—maybe that was the secret, the answer.

We looked in the direction of a little rise in the highway, to see if Matt was coming back, and maybe it was there, on the other side of the hill. Surf City. On an evening like this one, you could make yourself half-believe that if you looked hard enough, you could almost see its outskirts.

Just before midnight, we sat in a booth at a Ruby Tuesday next to the Ellenton Hampton Inn. We were the last customers in the place.

We'd made it to the Bradenton concert on time; we always seemed to, no matter what. And besides, as Don had said as we'd waited for gas by the side of the road: "The show's not going to start without us."

Now we were back here. Gary and I sat on one side of the table, Don on the other. Phil and Matt and David had said they were going to bed; the flight the next day was an early one.

"Don't lock the door," Gary called to the restaurant manager. "We still have one more coming."

"You already told me," the manager said.

The waiter brought our order: two platters of mini-cheeseburgers, one plate with American cheese, one with blue cheese.

From the window we could see Dean walking by himself across the parking lot from the hotel. He had changed from his stage clothes into a pair of jeans and a sweatshirt.

"So," he said as he entered the restaurant.

He looked at the plates of burgers.

"A birthday banquet," he said. He picked up the menu and studied it.

"What are onion straws?" he said.

"You know," Gary said. "Like onion rings. But they're straws."

Dean nodded. It seemed like a good piece of information to have. The music from the show still in our ears, the tables and booths in the restaurant unoccupied except for us, we sat and talked and at some point, without us noticing, the old day ended and a new one, as invisible and real as a promise, began.

Acknowledgments

There are some people whose help to me in the writing of this book made doing the work a particular pleasure, and I'd like to thank them here.

Phil Revzin, my editor at St. Martin's Press, is everything a reporter could ask for in a colleague: interested, intuitive, inventive, patient, imperturbable, and professional beyond words. His associate, Jenness Crawford, has been impeccable in her diligence and devotion to detail.

Eric Simonoff, as always, has been not just a source of advice and counsel, but a good and trusted friend. My gratitude to and affection for Mort Janklow have only grown stronger since the day we first met.

For their exceptional thoughtfulness toward me and kindness toward my work during the time I was writing this book, I'd like to express my heartfelt appreciation to David Shipley, Richard L. Harris, David Bohrman, Jon Alter, Emily Lazar, Cal Thomas, Isolde Motley and Ellen Silva.

To the men who are the subjects of this book, and are the reason for its existence, words are insufficient to express my gratitude. *When We Get to Surf City* is not a story that has come to an end; the band is still out in the country, bringing its music to towns large and small. If the songs in this book are still happily resounding in your head, and if you should find yourself running an event or celebration and desiring to hear those songs, and those singers, live, the way to get information about bringing them to your own town is to send inquiries to surfcityallstars@ sbcglobal.net. The best thing about Surf City, as you've undoubtedly surmised from reading the preceding pages, is that even if you can't get to it, it has a way of getting to you.

About the Author

Award-winning journalist Bob Greene is a CNN contributor and a *New York Times* bestselling author whose books include *And You Know You Should Be Glad: A True Story of Lifelong Friendship*; *Once Upon a Town: The Miracle of the North Platte Canteen*; *Duty: A Father, His Son, and the Man Who Won the War*; *Hang Time: Days and Dreams with Michael Jordan*; *Be True to Your School*; and, with his sister, D. G. Fulford, *To Our Children's Children: Preserving Family Histories for Generations to Come*.

As a magazine writer he has been lead columnist for *Life* and *Esquire*; as a broadcast journalist he has served as contributing correspondent for *ABC News Nightline*. For thirty-one years he wrote a syndicated newspaper column based in Chicago, first for the *Sun-Times* and later for the *Tribune*. His essays and reporting have been featured on National Public Radio's *All Things Considered* and on the Op-Ed page of the *New York Times*.

Readers may write to him in care of bobgreenebooks@aol.com.

Turn the page for a sneak preview of
Bob Greene's new book,

Late Edition:
A Love Story

Coming Summer 2009

"This next slide shows something even more alarming, which is the decline in readership. This is from a general social survey, and the question is, 'How often do you read a newspaper?' As to the percent who read every day, that's been declining an average of about one percentage point a year, and shows no sign of stopping. You extend that line with a straightedge, you find that the last daily newspaper reader disappears around 2040. In April."

—Philip Meyer, Knight Chair in Journalism,
University of North Carolina at Chapel Hill,
speaking at the Media Center at the American
Press Institute, March 9, 2005

"You and me, Tito, we've seen it all. . . ."

"Lots of changes, old Max, lots of changes."

"It's not the changes so much this time, Tito, it's that it all seems to be ending. . . . It feels like it's all slipping away."

—resort owner Max Kellerman and resort
bandleader Tito Suarez, at the end of the 1963
summer vacation season in the movie *Dirty Dancing*

ONE

I hadn't been expecting to see the place.

We were rolling through the country in a vehicle that was something out of an old-time science-fiction writer's most vivid futuristic dreams.

This was during the autumn in which Barack Obama was campaigning for president—the campaign which would culminate, that November, with his history-changing victory.

"We'll be at the hotel in a few minutes," Dale Fountain called back to me.

He was the driver of this vehicle—it was called the CNN Election Express, and from the outside it looked like a massive bus. Inside, though, it was a live television studio on wheels—control consoles, editing suite, satellite-uplink hardware, ten high-definition monitors. From the bus, even as it was speeding down a highway, we could transmit pictures and sound that would instantly be seen on television screens around the world. I was writing columns about the presidential campaign every day for CNN's political site on the Internet; we could stop in a town, report on a speech or a rally, interview some potential voters, snap their photographs. . . .

And then, even as the bus was on its way, I could write the column, send it and the pictures skyward, and within minutes, before we had reached the next stop, it would be available for reading by an audience in every corner of the globe.

We had been in many places during the course of the long campaign— in the days just before arriving in this town, we had reported from

Washington, D.C., from Maryland, from Pennsylvania, from West Virginia, from Mississippi, from Arkansas, from Kentucky. In a new-media age, the bus was an electronic marvel—it provided an almost incomprehensibly advanced digital delivery system for every kind of storytelling imaginable.

So I was writing away in the middle section of the bus—I was a sixty-one-year-old man enthralled by all the ways this three-million-dollar vehicle suddenly enabled a person to communicate his reporting to viewers and readers in the blink of an eye—and I looked up to see that the town into which we were heading was the capital city of Ohio. Columbus.

I stopped typing, and looked out the window.

On a downtown street—the address was 34 South Third Street—there was an old, stone-fronted building.

I had been there before, many times.

There once had been a certain room on the mezzanine.

Inside the bus, transmission-equipment lights blinked silently on and off.

I looked toward the building and tried to recall a sound from long ago.

TWO

The sound—the sound I can hear even now—was the sound of laughter.

Who would have thought that? The main sound in the room—a sound delicious enough that it was tasted as much as it was heard—was the sound of typewriters banging. A whole floorful of them, all being hit at once, a sound like a low-rent and off-tune concert, fingers pounding keys, keys striking rough sheets of paper curled around hard cylindrical rollers, palms swatting metal return levers, unseen mechanisms low inside the machines clicking like the teeth of steel combs as those worn rollers were hand-forced right to left so the men and women hunched over the typewriters could begin the next lines of their modest deadline compositions. . . .

That was the sound, you would think, that would remain most prominent—that was the sound that constantly filled the room. The symphony of those typewriters—long-gone instruments played upon by long-gone journeymen and journeywomen in the long-gone city room of a long-dead newspaper—was the sound you would think would endure.

And it does. I can close my eyes and listen to it.

But the laughter—the laughter coming every day and every night from the men and women in that room—the laughter is what overrides even all that other joyous noise.

Maybe it's because everything now seems so suddenly grim. Maybe it's because now, with all the dire predictions of a slow death spiral not just for any one newspaper, but for printed newspapers themselves, with all the dark worries and self-doubting and inner-directed recriminations in a trade once so happily cocky and seemingly free from care, a trade that welcomed misfits the way a family would welcome wayward brothers and sisters because most American city rooms were, in large and proud degree, indeed and in fact a brotherhood and sisterhood of misfits. . . .

Maybe, with everything on the business side of the newspaper world today turning gray and measured and fearful, it is the memory of the laughter in that room that stands out, precisely because the absence of laughter—the hollow sound when laughter is gone—can seem so hauntingly loud.

The laughter, at least to the young ears of an absolute beginner in the business, was what made it seem that it must be different from other businesses. You would hear it in that room every afternoon and every evening, as imperfect people put together an imperfect product chronicling the vagaries of an imperfect world, to be delivered by hand before dawn the next morning to doorsteps in one medium-sized and usually overlooked city in the landlocked and half-forgotten middle of the country. At which point the whole unlikely process would begin all over again.

The laughter may have been the laughter that comes with unconscious gratitude—with knowing reflexively, somewhere inside, how lucky you are to be allowed to work in a place like this. And with being blissfully unaware that, somewhere not so far down the line, it would all begin to fade into history.

The room in that city produced a newspaper you undoubtedly never read, and that you in all likelihood never heard of. But in your city, wherever you grew up, there almost certainly was a room just like it. Before the echoes of all that laughter drift away forever—before, one by one, in one big room after another across America, someone thins out the staff and then, eventually, switches off the lights for good—it may be worth the while to listen one last time.

THREE

Not to make too much of the paper hats, but they did have a way of setting the tone for everything.

How many businesses are there that offer, every day as you arrive at work, and every night as you leave, the sight of fellow workers wearing paper hats?

All right—maybe at certain fast-food restaurants, you see it. But those hats are mass-produced, part of a uniform. And you get the impression that, given the choice, the employees taking orders at the fast-food counters would just as soon not be wearing them.

The paper hats atop the heads of the men who worked around the giant Goss presses on the bottom level of the newspaper plant were made by hand each new day by the men who wore them. I still don't know how they did it—the hats, made from the previous day's editions, were neatly squared off, a wonder of on-the-fly engineering. When you stood and talked with the pressmen, you could read the headlines and stories on their hats. The paper hats were so much a part of their daily routine that the men didn't even seem to know they were there.

The hats served a function—the cavernous rooms that housed the presses were ink-laden, greasy places, and the hats did the job (sort of) of keeping the pressmen's hair relatively clean. But they also served as the signature of the spirit of the place. How could you not struggle to suppress a smile in an office building populated, in part, by men in hats made out of newspapers? By men who *made* their paper hats?

They still do it, I think, at newspapers around the country. The reason I say *I think* is that, more and more, the buildings where newspapers are printed are not the same buildings where reporters and editors and photographers put the newspapers together. The printing plants now tend to be in outlying areas, connected to the newsrooms by satellite links and fiberoptic lines. In many large cities, the people in the newsrooms never set eyes upon the people who operate the presses.

So the paper hats may still be there—but they are seen only by other people wearing paper hats.

A shame, really—a small shame, in the scheme of things, but a shame nonetheless. Coming to work every day, being greeted by the men in the paper hats—what a start to the shift. Made you feel glad to be getting up in the morning.

The story in these pages takes place over a circumscribed span of five years in the middle of the twentieth century, and the setting, in large part, is the mezzanine level of that building located at 34 South Third Street. Though the building is still there, the enterprise that occupied the men and women on the mezzanine is not.

That enterprise was known as the *Columbus Citizen-Journal*, and in the long run it never had a chance; by the end of 1985, it would be gone. The owner, proprietor, landlord and main tenant of that building on Third Street, the occupant of much more expansive news offices on the upper floors, was and is the *Columbus Dispatch*, the dominant newspaper in town, a considerably more prosperous and influential publication. On top of the building, in soaring, bright, electrified orangish-red Old English letters, was the name of the *Dispatch*, along with its slogan: "Ohio's Greatest Home Newspaper."

And then there was us, down on the mezzanine.

Yet we felt like we were in heaven. We got to put out our paper every day.

Maybe it was just because I was little more than a kid. I was still in high school when in the summer of 1964 I walked in the doorway of the *Citizen-Journal* for my first day on the job; when I walked out four years later to leave for a bigger town, I still had yet to complete college. Maybe, because I was seeing everything through eyes that young, it seemed more heavenly than it really was.

But I don't think that was it. The other eyes in that room may have been older, but it was behind those eyes that I first saw all that laughter.

Numbers are dry. But there is a statistical figure that, as much as any combination of words, explains the way that newspapers—newspapers printed on paper, newspapers that rolled off presses—mattered so much to Americans at one time.

That figure is 123 percent.

Other figures also tell the story of just how rapidly the importance of newspapers in American life has declined. Here's one: the peak year for newspapers sold in the United States was 1984, when 63.3 million copies per day were purchased. By 2007, even though the population of the United States had grown, that number was down to 50.7 million copies per day.

And: In 1964, 80.8 percent of adults read a newspaper every day. By 2007, only 48.4 percent read a newspaper every day. Of those newspaper readers in 2007, the most devoted were the ones with the shortest future potential as long-term customers: 63.7 percent of people 55 years old and older were daily newspaper readers, while only 33.7 percent of people between the ages of 25 and 34 were daily readers.

As sobering as those numbers are, though, it is the 123 percent figure that illustrates most nakedly how the country's newspaper habits have changed.

In 1950, the penetration of U.S. households by daily newspapers was 123 percent. By 2004 that number was 49 percent and falling.

"Penetration" refers to the percentage of households in which a daily newspaper is read.

How could a penetration rate be 123 percent—how could it be more than 100 percent?

It was 123 percent because many American homes chose to subscribe to more than one daily paper. Such a choice was quite common—for

American families, having a newspaper in the house was like having electricity or running water in the house: of course they were going to have a newspaper, often more than one. One paper to read at the breakfast table, one to read before sitting down to dinner. . . .

So as dizzyingly quickly as raw circulation has plummeted, that doesn't tell half the story. Newspaper circulation is dropping even as the population of the country is increasing—the numbers are even worse than they seem, because the potential audience for daily newspapers is getting bigger as the nation grows: more citizens are available to buy papers, yet even so, fewer do.

The social era in the United States when the penetration of households by newspapers was 123 percent—when the average household, as a matter of course and a matter of choice, purchased at least one and often more than one paper a day—made the texture of American life feel a certain way, and made certain things possible in the newspaper business.

One of those things was the existence of a paper like the *Citizen-Journal*—a second paper in a medium-sized town, a paper that families welcomed into their homes even though they already subscribed to another paper, a paper that gave people like those of us who toiled on the mezzanine a chance to do something with our lives.

The assumption throughout the country had always been that newspapers—frequently several in a single town—were necessary because Americans not only wanted them, which was important enough, but also needed them. Part of the assumption was that as older readers died off, they would be replaced by new ones—young people who would be just as eager to have papers in their homes as their parents had been, and their grandparents before them.

In Iowa, for example, as late as 1957 the *Des Moines Register* and *Tribune*, through an apparent arrangement with Charles M. Schulz, creator of the "Peanuts" comic strip, produced a comic book intended specifically to introduce boys and girls to the idea that the *Register* and the *Tribune* (separate papers produced in the same downtown Des Moines building) were going to be a part of their lives. In the comic book, Charlie Brown and Lucy (evidently drawn by a *Register* staff artist, with Schulz's permission) are given a tour of the newspaper office (while—in one frame of the comic—perched on the tour guide's shoulders). The comic treated the idea of becoming a newspaper subscriber as an inevitable rite of passage, like getting a driver's license: Boys and girls in Iowa were going to be subscribing to the *Register* and the *Tribune* some day, that was a given, so the comic book would get them ready.

Thus, on the way to the newsroom, the tour guide (in the comic book he is a man in a blue business suit and a red bow tie) shows the "Peanuts" characters "enlargements of nearly a century of the *Register* and *Tribune*'s front pages!" ("World-shaking events," Charlie Brown says as he looks at the front pages.) The guide takes Charlie and Lucy to every part of the building: "Here you are, kids," he says, "the big press room—filling the vast basement of the *Register* and *Tribune* building. When the presses are going full blast you can feel the vibration clear to the attic!" A cartoon version of a press operator, wearing a cartoon version of a paper hat, watches Charlie and Lucy as they watch the presses roll.

The message was clear: If you wanted to know what was going on in the world, this was the way you found out—on folded bundles of paper speeded to your home. The tour guide shows Charlie and Lucy the "fresh-off-the-press newspapers, down the chute from the mail room and into trucks waiting here in the loading dock . . . trucks that fan out from Des Moines in all directions. . . ." The children are informed: "Unrolled, the newsprint used by our papers in one year would cover a patch five feet wide and 290,000 miles long. The papers use $100,000 worth of ink a year."

As the comic book comes to an end, the tour guide asks a newspaper delivery boy—one of "our more than seven thousand carrier salesmen throughout Iowa"—to take Charlie and Lucy home: "Hey, Joe, can you drop off a couple of tired kids on your way 'round your route?"

"Sure thing!" says the delivery boy, and in the final frame, Lucy says:

"Well, Charlie Brown, what do you think of the newspaper business now that you've been fully exposed to it?"

And Charlie says: "It's here to stay."

I think we all believed that; wherever in the country we may have been working, I don't think we gave any thought at all to the possibility that newspaper offices—and newspapers themselves—might not feel pretty much like this forever.

When I opened the glass door to the city room of the *Citizen-Journal* for my first day of work in the summer of 1964, Walter Winchell was still writing his column in New York. I was seventeen, and the newspaper world still had one foot—sometimes it seemed like both feet—in the 1930s. Winchell's *New York Mirror* had folded the year before, but he had quickly found work elsewhere in town, and the stereotype of newspaper life continued to be the one that he had helped to popularize in the national mind. It was a life that was determinedly staccato, raffish, hurried, loud, short on reflection, long on hustle, lighted fluorescently, punctuated by indoor shouts, cluttered with balled-up wads of paper under the desks and the stubs of fat black pencils with soft black lead in the typewriter wells. . . . the Beatles had arrived in the United States earlier that year, and television had all but completed its conquest of the land, but newspapers everywhere, including in the middle of Ohio, were still living in the Winchell model. The nation may have been on the verge of breathtaking change, but it was as if newspapers hadn't gotten the memo.

Walking into that city room for the first time was like encountering some intoxicating sensory buffet. There were two levels of noise—all of those typewriters on all of those desks with reporters hammering away at them, but a separate, more muted, metal sound, too, the sound of the wallful of UPI teletype machines bringing the news of the outside world to the mezzanine. United Press International was the second-tier international wire service—the Associated Press was the big one, but the *Dispatch* had the local rights to the AP, we subscribed only to UPI—and inside those tall cast-iron machines, sitting side-by-side next to windows overlooking an alley, the machines' own sets of typewriter-style keys received signals from afar as they clacked all day and all night.

It looked like magic—those keys writing their stories, in all capital letters, with unseen typists in UPI offices hundreds of miles away making them move. The reason the sound was different from the sound of the staff typewriters in the room was that on each UPI machine the keys, as they struck the frayed purple/black ribbons and the rolls of cheap copy paper, were shielded from the city room by scratched, dirty, hard-plastic covers, intended to muffle the clatter. It worked, to a degree—the gunshot-cracks of those UPI keys were deadened at least a little by the plastic shields, but they were still clearly audible, even all the way across the room, and as they rapped out their stories, one letter of the alphabet at a time, that was the way—just that quickly, just that slowly—that accounts of events taking place around the planet arrived on South Third Street.

Everything was old; everything was new. That was what it felt like to just be getting started in the newspaper business in that short span of years when I was lucky enough to be one of the people on the mezzanine. The newness of the feeling: One evening I was sent out to cover a shooting in which the victim had been transported by ambulance to a hospital near downtown. I'd had no instructions about how to cover such violent occurrences; this was well before our current era in which every hospital has media-relations specialists hired to provide an official corporate layer between what goes on beneath the hospital's roof and what the public is told about those matters. I made my way to the hospital, walked around to the emergency room entrance, asked the nurses where I could find the person who had been shot, was pointed down a corridor, kept walking and looking into curtained-off examination cubicles . . . and eventually pushed open a set of swinging doors and found myself standing next to an operating table, which was surrounded by doctors and nurses in masks and gowns, and upon which lay the man about whom I had come to inquire, as the surgeons endeavored to remove the bullet from him. One of the physicians turned toward me—I couldn't see his mouth behind the mask, but I could see the surprised look in his eyes, and although he had no idea who I was or where I was from, those eyes told me he was not pleased to see me—and from behind the cloth he said: "Get out of here!" A nurse took my arm to lead me out of the room, and as we walked she said, "What are you *doing* in here?" I introduced myself, and—out of pure ignorance mixed with a certain innocence, because I truly had not known that this was not the way you were supposed to cover shootings—I said to her: "I'm on deadline." To which she replied: "*You're* on deadline?"

There were things to see and hear even when, ostensibly, there was nothing to see or hear. On evenings when I hadn't been assigned anything to do, I would slip out of the city room and walk up an interior stairwell to the composing room, just to watch the men make up the pages for the next morning's paper. They were metal workers and artisans at the same time, although they probably wouldn't have described themselves as either; the way the Linotype operators and their machines did their work is still one of the most mystifyingly intricate and impressive series of herky-jerky kinetics I have ever observed, with the forming of the hot-leaden-type letters and words being accompanied by a hypnotic high-pitched clicking sound that I'm tempted to compare to a forest rich with crickets on a windless night, but that probably was closer to a gymnasium floor full of stainless-steel dominoes stood on end in a snaking line, at the moment when someone tips the first steel domino and they all begin toppling to the hardwood floor. Not far from the Linotype machines were the men composing the front and inside pages of the *C-J*, laying the metal stories upside-down and backwards into the page forms, standing over them, pounding them level with wooden mallets, chefs in inky aprons getting something ready for breakfast tables all over town.

Sometimes on a story close to deadline, when I had been sent somewhere to find out what was happening and there was just no time to get back to the city room, I had been instructed in advance to hurry back to the press car I'd taken from the paper's parking lot, the Ford with the skinny wire antenna jutting from its roof. I'd slide across the bench front seat and unhook the big microphone from its moorings and, sitting there, I'd radio back to the city desk the basics of what I had found. It sounds like nothing, now, in the era of universal cellphones—but then, when there were no such things, when calling someone from a car felt like a scene from an outer-space movie, there was a sense of moment and of weight to the act of doing it, every single time: sitting on the edge of the

car seat, front door open, feet on the ground outside, broadcasting back
to the newsroom, taking it on faith that your voice would travel through
the night and be turned into words—words for the next edition—by the
person sitting at a typewriter on the other end.

And knowing that as soon as the rewrite man typed the story up, even
as you were putting the key into the ignition for the drive back to the office, his sheets of paper would be tossed one at a time into a wire basket
atop the night city editor's desk, from where that editor would grab them,
quickly read the story, send it sheet-by-sheet over to the copy desk, where
a copy editor would by hand write a headline, scratching short vertical
pencil lines above and below each letter in the headline to make sure it fit
the count. I can still do it now, even though there's no need, even though
computers measure the fit to complete accuracy. The little lines you'd
scrawl above the letters each signified a full count, the lines you'd scrawl
beneath the letters signified a half count. Each capital letter was worth a
count-and-a-half, except for M and W, which each took two counts, and
I, which took one; each lowercase letter was worth a single count, except
l and i, which were worth a half. Write the headline, hastily scratch the
lines above and below, add up the count, see if it exceeded the maximum
total number allowed for the width and font of the headline the copy chief
had ordered . . . it was like having to be a writer and a bookkeeping clerk,
all at the same time, it was as if someone had told each copy editor that he
had to be Charles Dickens—write the headline—and then turn into Bob
Cratchit—add it up and don't be wrong, and if the number doesn't work,
turn into Charles Dickens again and take another whack at writing it.

In the morning, boys on bikes would ride down every street in town,
reaching into their canvas bags, tossing rolled-up *C-Js* onto front stoop after front stoop. The most efficient way to get the news to the people who
were waiting for it: a boy on a bicycle. In all the houses, the alarm clocks
would be ringing, the clock radios would be snapping to life, and for
those of us with the great good fortune to have worked the night before to
put together the rolled-up paper that waited outside all the front doors,
there was that feeling—at least there was when all of this was new to us—
of opening our eyes and then realizing: "I get to go down to the paper
again today." Like when you fall in love for the first time, and you blink

to wakefulness in the throes of that new love and, even in your grogginess, you know without knowing why that this is going to be another good day. "I get to go down to the paper again today."

Not a cloud on the horizon. The paper came out every day. Like Charlie Brown said: "It's here to stay."

There was a series of television documentaries about baseball, consisting of old eight-millimeter and sixteen-millimeter home movies shot at ballparks by players and by fans, mostly before the television era. The documentaries were called "When It Was A Game."

What was striking about the old home-movie film, much of it in color, was the human scale with which it depicted big-league baseball. Gone was the stentorian mythology of Baseball as Grand Narrative Drama; in the soundless home movies there was a sense of playfulness, of boyishness, of laughter and shyness and fun. These were guys in the summer sun, in the summer of their lives, doing something they loved.

If, in fact, newspapers the way they used to be cease to endure as a ubiquitous part of American life, there will be a multitude of entirely logical, even irrefutable, reasons for it. The story in these pages is not about that.

Instead, it is about that one newspaper in its mezzanine newsroom in that building on South Third Street during the handful of years when, little more than a boy, I was allowed to be a part of it. I tell the story not because there was no other place like that newspaper office—but because there were so many places that were like it.

In some American cities, famous journalists writing for mighty and world-renowned papers changed the course of history with their reporting, and won national awards and high honors for their work. In most cities—including on the mezzanine on Third Street—we didn't. Hardly anyone outside town even knew we were there.

But there was noise and laughter in the night. When it was a game, that laughter—all that happy noise in that room—sounded like a promise. Sometimes, when I listen hard enough, I can still hear it.